D1347122

About the Author

Jan Bondeson is a respected true crime writer, and author of *The London Monster*, *Murder Houses of London*, *Rivals of the Ripper* and other books. He lives in Dunbar, Scotland.

Victorian Murders

Jan Bondeson

AMBERLEY

First published 2017

Amberley Publishing
The Hill, Stroud
Gloucestershire, GL5 4EP

www.amberley-books.com

Copyright © Jan Bondeson 2017

The right of Jan Bondeson to be identified as the Author
of this work has been asserted in accordance with the
Copyrights, Designs and Patents Act 1988.

British Library Cataloguing in Publication Data.
A catalogue record for this book is available from the British Library.

ISBN 978 1 4456 6630 3 (paperback)
ISBN 978 1 4456 6631 0 (ebook)

Typeset in 10pt on 12pt Sabon.
Typesetting and Origination by Amberley Publishing.
Printed in the UK.

Contents

Introduction

The *Illustrated Police News (IPN)* was inaugurated on 20 February 1864; it would remain in publication, as a weekly Saturday newspaper for no less than seventy-four years. Initially, it had four pages, the first of which was devoted to illustrations of recent crimes. It was not, as has often been proclaimed, a forerunner in its field of journalism; the concept of such 'illustrated police' weekly papers dates back as far as the 1830s. It is a matter of debate what event triggered the foundation of the *IPN*. The *Illustrated London News* was inaugurated in 1842 and still going strong in 1864, but it was priced at sixpence and aimed for a better class of reader with its elegant engravings. The year 1861 saw the foundation of the *Penny Illustrated Paper*, a downmarket version of the *Illustrated London News*, published weekly at the price of one penny; it boasted a variety of rather crude illustrations, occasionally concerning recent crimes. The early proprietors of the *IPN*, the publisher Henry Lea and the businessman Edwin Bulpin, may well have been impressed with the apparent success of the *Penny Illustrated Paper*; in spite of its lowly price of a penny, it sold enough newspapers to stay in business and prosper. The great interest in crime and criminals from the lower classes of society would imply that a weekly 'illustrated police' newspaper priced at just a penny would enjoy a wide circulation among working men all around Britain. A sanctimonious writer in the *London Review* of 1864 did not at all approve of the inauguration of the *IPN*, commenting that

> During the past month, the hoardings of the metropolis have been covered with large bills, announcing that the *Illustrated Police News* would shortly be published. Several numbers of this periodical have

now appeared, and we must say that we do not think the morality of the lower orders will be at all benefited by its publication. Wood engravings, very similar to the late Mr Catnach's Seven Dials pictures, illustrate the various murders and housebreakings that are narrated …

In July 1865, the *IPN* was taken over by a far more formidable figure in London's publishing world, George Purkess Jr. More business-minded than Lea and Bulpin, he offered readers subscriptions to the *IPN* for 8*s* 8*d* per annum; he did much to improve its circulation to newsagents and newspaper stalls all over Britain, and employed agents in Australia, Canada and South Africa to ensure the paper would be available to crime enthusiasts all over the world. From late November 1867 onwards, all text was banished from the first page, which would henceforth contain illustrations only. From his office in the Strand, George Purkess published a steady stream of books and pamphlets on crime, quackery and popular history. For many years, the mainstay of his firm would be the widely read *IPN*, which immediately established a firm *rapport* with the low-brow elements of the reading public. Its weekly circulation was 150,000 copies in 1872, and 300,000 copies in 1877. The *IPN* successfully protected its niche in Victorian publishing for many years. Murders at home and abroad, assaults and outrages, accidents and macabre events were described with gusto. Each weekly issue consisted of four pages, the first devoted to lurid illustrations that advertised the stories lurking within. These remarkable and dramatic illustrations have become part of the cult of Victoriana. Expertly executed by skilful draughtsmen, they make the most of the sanguinary and macabre subject matter. Brains are blown out, skulls crushed with blunt instruments, and limbs lopped off. In 'Singular Accident to a Parachutist', the end of the wretched aeronaut helplessly descending towards the ocean is precipitated by an enormous shark leaping up and seizing hold of his legs. In 'Outrage by a Mad Dog' a boy is bitten hard in the buttocks by the infuriated animal; the blood is spurting from the wound and the boy is yelling with pain. Women coming to grief in various ways were a favourite subject for the male-dominated readership of the *IPN*. A lady bicyclist is gored by a bull from behind and sent flying over the handlebars, her legs exposed for everyone to see. Each issue of the *IPN* had several columns of advertisements at the end, mostly dealing with 'rubber goods' for amorous gentlemen, as well as patent medicines aimed to make the hair regrow on balding pates, or to restore sexual potency.

More than once, clergymen wrote to the newspapers to complain about the *IPN*: its unashamed xenophobia, lurid illustrations, unfastidious contents and indecent advertisements. Reading such a newspaper surely must entice young people into an immoral and criminal life, they reasoned. In 1868, a young railwayman Thomas Wells murdered his superior, the Dover Priory stationmaster Edward Adolphus Walshe, and was duly arrested, tried and executed. There was newspaper speculation about the possible brutalising influence of a singular piece of reading matter found in Wells' pocket after he had been arrested – a copy of the *IPN*! In March 1870, a clergyman wrote to the *Times* to lament that in his country parish, the *IPN* had a very large circulation indeed. Recently, a murder had been committed by a man named Mobbs, who testified in court that he had read about a recent child murder in the *IPN* and paid close attention to the lurid illustrations. Surely there was an ominous connection here, and such a vicious newspaper should no longer be allowed to corrupt the minds of impressionable young people. The witty publisher Purkess replied that he had once known a murderer who had been influenced by another piece of criminal literature given to him by his grandfather, one that features the tale of Cain and Abel, among other sanguinary transactions! In November 1886, after a newspaper poll had voted the *IPN* 'the worst newspaper in England', a journalist from the *Pall Mall Gazette* went to interview George Purkess. The office of the *IPN*, in the Strand, could be detected from some distance, due to the small crowd gathered outside, in front of the pictorial placard advertising the current issue. Purkess, described as 'a stout, comfortable-looking man of middle age', received the news of the vote with the greatest composure, being thick-skinned with regard to such criticism. He jovially invited his fellow journalist into his private office. The *IPN* had most buyers and subscribers in the Manchester, Liverpool and Birmingham areas; its London circulation was just one-eighth of the total issue. The circulation abroad was fairly limited, although a friend had recently sent Purkess a copy of the *IPN*, which he had picked up in Hyderabad. Although the *IPN* was considered a working man's newspaper, Purkess claimed that a dowager marchioness was a permanent subscriber, and that an earl had once ordered his biography of Calcraft the Hangman; several clergymen had also been known to request copies.

George Purkess fell ill with tuberculosis of the larynx in the late 1880s, and in spite of an attempt at surgical treatment in 1892, he died not long after, leaving £10,399, a veritable fortune that owed much to his long and successful management of the *IPN*. That newspaper, the main asset left by George Purkess, was purchased by a syndicate of businessmen. They soon made detrimental changes to the newspaper:

new draughtsmen were employed, and the quality of the illustrations markedly declined. In December 1894, the number of pages increased from four to eight, with illustrations on the front page as well as on pages four and five. The focus on crime gradually weakened, with columns on racing, boxing and music hall actresses being introduced, as well as serialised novels and mildly indecent 'saucy songs'. In June 1897, the number of pages was further increased to twelve, and the adulteration of the newspaper's contents continued: the criminals were now in a minority, and the bruisers, racehorses and music hall performers were in danger of taking over the newspaper altogether. The *IPN* was still capable of reporting a good murder, but its quality, with regard to both journalistic prowess and the excellence of its illustrations, declined in the post-Purkess era.

This book owes its existence to a large ledger labelled 'Victorian Murders' and containing press cuttings from various newspapers, the *IPN* in particular, about a variety of murder cases from 1867 until 1900. From the 120 cases in the ledger, I have chosen to research 56 for inclusion in this book: some of the omitted cases were too obscure, involving botched abortions, insane women murdering their children, or husbands murdering their wives; some others had been 'done to death' in books and anthologies, like those of Thomas Neill Cream and Frederick Bailey Deeming. There is no overlap at all between this book and my recent *Rivals of the Ripper*, dealing with fourteen unsolved murders of London women, in order to avoid repetition. Some of the murders in this book are celebrated cases, like the Bravo Mystery of 1876, the Llangibby Massacre of 1878 and the Mrs Pearcey murders of 1890; others are little-known, like the Acton Atrocity of 1880, the Ramsgate Mystery of 1893 and the Grafton Street Murder of 1894. There will be nothing about Jack the Ripper – apart from the introduction of a new suspect, who was widely denounced as the Whitechapel Murderer in the Continental press in the early 1890s, but who has since become almost entirely forgotten.

1. The Murder Of Sweet Fanny Adams, 1867

In 1867, the bricklayer George Adams lived in a cottage at 141 Tanhouse Lane, Alton, with his wife Harriet and their six children. Fanny Adams, the fourth of these children, had been born in 1859. Described as a tall, comely and intelligent girl, she was known for her lively, cheerful disposition. On Saturday 24 August 1867, a fine and sunny day, Fanny

Adams, her younger sister Lizzie and their friend Minnie Warner wanted to go for a stroll to the Flood Meadows nearby. Mrs Adams had no objection to them going out since the small Hampshire town of Alton was considered a particularly safe and quiet place to live; in fact, there had been no serious crime there within living memory.

Frederick Baker approaches the children, from *Famous Crimes Past & Present*.

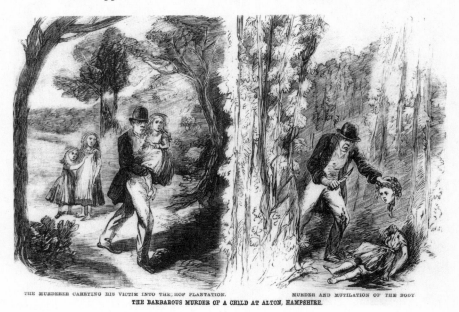

THE MURDERER CARRYING HIS VICTIM INTO THE HOP PLANTATION.   MURDER AND MUTILATION OF THE BODY

THE BARBAROUS MURDER OF A CHILD AT ALTON, HAMPSHIRE.

The murder of Fanny Adams, from the *IPN*, 31August 1867.

Baker on trial, from the *IPN*, 14 December 1867.

The execution of Baker, from the *IPN*, 28 December 1867.

As the three little girls were walking towards the Flood Meadows, they chanced to meet a neatly dressed young man, solicitor's clerk Frederick Baker. He was well known to be a friend of little children, and he often spoke to them, and gave them money to buy sweets. And indeed, the bonhomous Baker produced a penny and a half, which he gave to Minnie Warner and Lizzie Adams to buy sweets, and then he gave Fanny another halfpenny. The girls knew Baker, who stood quietly watching them as they played and ate berries. Then he suddenly and wordlessly picked up Fanny Adams and made off with her. The other two girls ran home, but were unable to tell an adult what had just happened. Instead, they carried on playing until the neighbour Mrs Gardener came and asked them where Fanny was. When she heard that Fanny had been carried off by a man, she and Mrs Adams made their way to the Flood Meadows, where they saw Frederick Baker skulking near a gate separating the meadows from the hop garden. When Minnie Warner, whom the two women had taken with them, saw him, she identified him as the man who had given her the money and taken off with Fanny. When they asked him what he had done with Fanny, he denied taking her, although he admitted giving the children some money to buy sweets. When the indignant Mrs Gardener exclaimed 'I have a great mind to give you in charge of the police!' he sullenly replied that she could do so if she liked.

Since both Mrs Gardener and Mrs Adams knew Frederick Baker was supposed to be a respectable man, they were reluctant to challenge him any further. Perhaps the other children were wrong, and perhaps Fanny had left them to go playing elsewhere, they hoped. The two women went home, but after Fanny had not returned home by 7 p.m., they alerted the neighbours, and a search was made. In the hop garden, one of the neighbours was aghast to find Fanny's head stuck on two hop poles. One of the ears had been cut off, both eyes had been gouged out, and the murderer had cut her from mouth to ear and across the temple. Shouting with horror and alarm, the Alton countrymen found parts of Fanny strewn all over the hop garden and nearby fields: her arms and legs had been cut off, and her abdomen and pelvis disembowelled. Various internal origins were scattered on the ground, although the heart, sternum and vagina were never found. When Harriet Adams heard what had happened to Fanny, she became frantic and rushed off to tell her husband, who was playing cricket in a field, but she collapsed on the way and was taken back home by the neighbours. When informed that his daughter had been murdered and dismembered, George Adams grabbed hold of a loaded shotgun and went into the hop garden to look for the creature Baker, but he returned home without having found him.

The local police were called and the very same evening, Superintendent Cheyney arrested the main suspect Frederick Baker in the solicitor's office. There was an uproar in Alton, news of the horrible murder spread like wildfire, and a hostile mob followed Baker all the way to the police station. He had been drinking in a pub nearby and had told the other pub visitors that he was going to leave town, for good. When his fellow clerk Maurice Biddle remarked that he might find it difficult to get another job, he answered, ironically considering what he had just accomplished, that he could always go as a butcher. Baker's shirt and trousers were stained with blood, and two small bloodstained knives were found on him. Then there was the matter of his office diary, containing the extraordinary note '24th August, Saturday – killed a young girl. It was fine and hot.'

Frederick Baker was a short, thin 29-year-old man of cadaverous appearance. His parents had been respectable, God-fearing people, who had provided him with a good education. Before he came to Alton he had worked in Guildford, where he had been a member of two literary societies, secretary to the Guildford Institute Debating Society, an active member of the Penny Savings Bank and a Sunday school teacher. He began to drink, however, and was ousted from his position at the debating society. He wanted to marry the lady's maid of a certain Mrs Haydon, but some mean-spirited person wrote a poison-pen letter to her, detailing all Baker's shortcomings, and the engagement was broken. After this, his drinking and dissipation grew worse. It was said that he had once been under suspicion for having lured a little girl into a disused chalk-pit for felonious purposes, but the matter had been hushed up by his family and friends, and the girl's family soon left town. After coming to Alton, Frederick Baker did his work at the solicitor's office in a relatively conscientious manner, although his hard drinking continued: he was a familiar sight at the local beerhouses. Some people thought him quite odd: he had a mania for various gluttonous exploits, like devouring large pork pies and drinking bottle after bottle of stout, or eating a number of uncooked pork sausages. Nevertheless, he had no police record prior to the murder of Fanny Adams.

The coroner's inquest on Fanny Adams was opened at the Duke's Head tavern in Alton on 27 August. Minnie Warner was old enough to be the first witness, and described the ill-fated outing to the Flood Meadows. A number of people described the ghoulish hunt for body parts in the hop garden, and Maurice Biddle recalled his sinister conversation with Frederick Baker the evening of the murder. Dr Louis Leslie thought that Fanny Adams had been struck down with a large stone, before being dismembered with a sharp knife. Professor Taylor, the London analyst, could verify that Baker's clothes and knives were stained with mammalian blood. The inquest returned a verdict of murder against Frederick Baker, and the local magistrates committed him to stand trial at the Winchester Assizes. A large mob had congregated outside the police station, and they booed and hooted at Baker. Several police constables were struck by objects thrown by this rowdy mob.

Frederick Baker stood trial for murder at the Winchester Assizes, in the Great Hall of the old castle, on 5 and 6 December 1867. The court was full of spectators, and a large mob waited outside. Since the horrible nature of the murder of innocent little Fanny Adams had caused widespread anger and revulsion, every newspaper in the country reported its outcome. Minnie Warner was given a large doll to keep her occupied during the long, dreary trial. Since the evidence against Frederick Baker seemed rock solid, the only thing the defence could try was to play the insanity card. His father testified that as a young man, Baker had suffered from nosebleeds and headaches and that he had always looked on him as being weak-minded. The father had himself had insane tendencies, a cousin had been in an asylum four times, and a sister had died from brain fever. The problem was that although several people in Guildford and Alton had disapproved of Baker's frequent drunkenness, few had found him obviously insane, and he had been fully capable of looking after his job. The jury was wholly unimpressed with the exhortations of the defence, and Frederick Baker was found guilty of murder and sentenced to death. He was hanged at the Winchester county gaol on 24 December, in front of a crowd of more than 6,000 people, none of whom seemed any worse for this singular Christmas entertainment.

Before the execution, Frederick Baker had written to Fanny's parents confessing his guilt: all of a sudden, he had got a strong impulse to steal away and murder the little girl. He had been enraged by her crying but had done her to death without any struggle. He vehemently denied having violated the child. A headstone for Fanny Adams was erected in the local cemetery in the Old Odiham Road, by public subscription. A tall, handsome stone shaped like a cross, it bears the inscription,

Sacred to the memory of Fanny Adams, aged eight years and four months, who was cruelly murdered on Saturday Aug 24 1867. Fear not them that kill the body but are not able to kill the soul but rather fear him which is able to destroy both body and soul in Hell.

The quote from Matthew, of course, makes a choice prediction concerning the fate of Baker in the Afterlife. There was a cabinet card photograph with the two girls Minnie Warner and Lizzie Adams standing by Fanny's gravestone; it is today quite a rarity, and much sought after by collectors of criminal memorabilia.

The murder of Fanny Adams caused considerable public concern: the contemporary newspaper reports concentrated on the youth and innocence of the victim, and the extreme brutality of the murderer. Everyone living in England at the time would have known the name of 'sweet' Fanny Adams. Two years after the murder, in 1869, tins of mutton were introduced into the rations of the Royal Navy. With grisly nautical humour, the sailors likened these unappetising lumps of meat and gristle to the butchered remains of poor Fanny. Indeed, 'Fanny Adams' became a naval slang word for mutton or mutton stew, and a naval mess tin or cooking pot is still referred to as a 'Fanny'. It was not until later that 'sweet Fanny Adams' came to mean 'nothing'. The term 'fuck all' has long been with us with that meaning, although how long is not clear as politeness caused it not to be recorded in print until the 20th century. The coincidence of Fanny Adams' initials caused F.A. or 'Fanny Adams' to be used as a euphemism for 'fuck all'. It is sad but true that this uncouth linguistic oddity is today all that the blameless young Alton murder victim is remembered by.

2. Mass Murder in Germany, 1868

As I pointed out initially, the *IPN* was a xenophobic newspaper, concentrating on the criminal goings-on in Merry Old England, and showing disregard even for Welsh and Scottish miscreants. Stories from

TIMM'S ATTEMPT TO CUT THE DOG'S THROAT   HORRIBLE TRAGEDY—THE MURDER OF A WHOLE FAMILY.   THE MURDER OF HIS MOTHER AND SISTER.
TIMM'S ATTACK ON HIS BROTHERS.

Timm Thode goes on a rampage at the farm, from *IPN*, 29 February 1868.

abroad were viewed with disdain, and for a Frenchman or American to make it into the pages of the *IPN*, they would have to commit murders of uncommon brutality. But what would it take for a German to qualify for the *IPN* – would he have to murder his entire family? Well – rather!

In 1866, the German countryman Johann Thode kept a farm in the village of Gross-Campen in Schleswig-Holstein. He and his wife Margaretha had five sons and a daughter, who all worked on the farm. The second son, Timm, 23, was a morose, discontented fellow, who quarrelled with his brothers and was on bad terms with his father as well. In early August 1866, there was a fire at the farm, and Timm Thode came running to the neighbours, shouting for help. The German peasants were appalled to find that the remainder of the Thode family had been brutally murdered: in the partially burnt barn were the mangled remains of the parents, the four brothers, the sister and the servant girl.

At first, it was believed that a gang of robbers had attacked the farm, but when experienced police detectives examined the premises, there was nothing to suggest that the farm had been broken into, or that anything had been stolen. In long, gruelling interrogations, pressure was put on Timm Thode, who was known to have been at loggerheads with his family and, in the end, he made a full confession. Early in 1866, he had made plans to murder his entire family, to put an end to the undignified squabbles with his siblings; he would then sell the farm he had inherited, and become a wealthy man. The problem was no firearms were kept on the farm, nor any other weapons he could make use of, meaning he would have to use stealth and cunning when he decimated his siblings and parents.

On 7 August 1866, when the parents went to pay a visit to some friends, Timm got ready to strike. He had got hold of a 5-foot handspike, which he used to beat his four brothers to death, one after another, after he had sneaked up on them while they were working on the land. When his parents had returned home, Timm told his father that the oxen had broken loose. Johann Thode dashed out to catch the animals, only to be waylaid and struck down by his son. Timm returned to the farm with his father's body in a cart. Two watchdogs guarded the courtyard of the farm and, adding canicide to his other crimes, Timm put a noose around the neck of one of them and hung the animal up. He then tried to cut the throat of the other dog, but the animal yelped and broke free. When the mother came to ask what the commotion was about, Timm struck her down with a hatchet, before finishing off his sister Anna and the servant girl Apollonia Dehn with the same weapon. After exclaiming, like the villain of a 'penny dreadful', 'Ha, I have them all dead!' he set fire to the barn and stacked up the bodies in there, hoping that they would be consumed by the fire.

The German detectives were appalled at the coolness and placidity with which Timm Thode told the story of his crimes. A photograph of him reveals an individual with almost simian features: a low forehead, a flat nose, large ears and a wide mouth. After a lengthy passage through the convoluted German legal system, he was found guilty of eightfold murder, sentenced to death, and executed on 13 May 1868. In spite of the extent of his murderous rampage, he is not the record holder when it comes to decimating one's family: already in 1694, Thomas Austin, of Cullompton in Devon, murdered his wife and two children, and his aunt and her five children; and in 1965, the Frenchman Roger Girerd murdered his wife, mother, brother, niece and six children, before committing suicide. In 1975, the American James Ruppert gunned down his mother, brother, sister-in-law and eight nephews and nieces; the shabby little house where this orgy of murder took place, in Hamilton, Ohio, still stands today, and is pictured in Steve Letho's book *American Murder Houses*.

3. The Winscombe Murder, 1868

John Wilkins was a lad of thirteen, living in Winscombe, a quiet North Somerset village 14 miles south west of Bristol. After leaving school,

THE FARMER'S BOY BEATEN SENSELESS WITH A BLUDGEON.   HORRIBLE MURDER OF A FARMER'S BOY AT WINSCOMBE, SOMERSETSHIRE.   DISCOVERY OF THE DEAD B
CUTTING THE THROAT OF THE VICTIM.

The murder of the Winscombe boy John Wilkins, from the *IPN*, 21 March 1868.

he worked at the farm of Mr Henry Hancock. On Friday 13 March 1869, John Wilkins was busy frightening birds away from Farmer Hancock's newly sown cornfield. All of a sudden, a tall young man in a rough blue coat came up to him and struck him down with a large hedge-stake. The intruder then produced a large pocket knife and nearly cut the unfortunate lad's head off.

The Winscombe murderer then made his way to the village of Banwell nearby, where he knocked at the door of the local police sergeant and said that he wanted to give himself up. The sergeant was out on duty, but Mrs Roynon, an old woman who kept house for him, invited the visitor in for tea. He introduced himself as Mr Alexander Holmes, the son of Colonel Holmes, late of the 12th Lancers. The colonel lived in Ireland, and since Alexander was not strong, and suffered from 'fits', he had been put into the care of the farmer and turf dealer Edwin Godfrey, who lived near Bridgwater. Alexander had escaped from there early on Friday morning and then tramped to Hanwell and Winscombe looking for some person to murder. He had been greatly tempted to attack several people in the road, and when he had seen the young lad in the field, he knew that he had found his victim.

Alexander Holmes wept and cried as he told Mrs Roynon all about his terrible crime. After battering the lad's head with the hedge stake, and nearly cutting his head off with the large knife, he had thrown both weapons into a stream, where he washed the blood off his hands. He felt amazed that he had not killed two or three more persons but for now, his blood-lust was sated. As the lunatic waited for the police sergeant, he ate and drank well, and kept up a conversation in a rather superior manner. The village constable came to take him into custody and, at the police station, Holmes willingly confessed to his crime and described where the body had been left. The mangled corpse of John Wilkins was found in the field, not far from the road, in a large pool of blood. On Saturday and Sunday, many country people came to see the spot of the murder, which had been marked with a long stake driven into the middle of the patch of discoloured soil; it was adorned with a couple of withey branches, and with one of the Dublin Tract Society's leaflets, entitled 'Come to Jesus!'

The inquest on John Wilkins was held on 16 March at the Woodborough Inn, before Mr S. Craddock, the Coroner for North Somerset, and a jury of respectable countrymen. Mrs Roynon and the police constable told how Alexander Holmes had confessed to his crime, and the local doctor told how he had examined the body of the murdered lad, and how he had spoken to Holmes at the police station; the lunatic had told him that two or three years ago, his father had spoken of putting him into an asylum, and he wished that this had happened as planned, since then he would have been prevented from causing any further mischief. It turned out that Lieutenant-Colonel Holmes had formerly inhabited the Manor House at Puriton near Bridgwater, and when he went to Ireland three years ago, he had left his lunatic son behind with the farmer Godfrey, who had taken care of him as well as he could. The coroner felt that Godfrey was to blame for the lunatic being set at large. The jury returned a verdict of wilful murder against Alexander Holmes.

The magisterial inquiry committed Alexander Holmes to stand trial at the Taunton Assizes on a charge of murder. Medical experts were called as witnesses, and he was acquitted on the ground of insanity but detained as a criminal lunatic. The farmer Godfrey was also prosecuted, on grounds of having taken charge of a dangerous lunatic without having a licence; Colonel Holmes paid his bail, but Godfrey was also committed to stand trial at the local assizes. As for the homicidal maniac Alexander Holmes, the Broadmoor asylum doors closed behind him, for good – he died there in January 1917, having been incarcerated for nearly 49 years.

4. The Murder Of A Stationmaster, 1868

In 1868, the stationmaster at the Dover Priory station was Mr Edward Adolphus Walshe. A grumpy character who did not suffer fools gladly, Mr Walshe prided himself on running a tight ship at the busy station. The clumsy young carriage cleaner Thomas Wells was more than once shouted at by the irate Mr Walshe for his sloth and general incompetence. The 18-year-old Wells returned his superior's dislike in full, once grumbling to a colleague that if Mr Walshe caused him to be discharged from the station, 'the old ____ should know about it!'

In May 1868, Mr Walshe had had enough of the slovenly, taciturn Thomas Wells. With the Superintendent of the London, Chatham and Dover Railway's stations in Dover, he summoned Wells to his office, where the two railway officials treated him to a severe tongue-lashing. Not only had his conduct been unsatisfactory, but Mr Walshe had once seen him firing off a pistol while on duty. The stubborn young railwayman answered them back, disputing that he was at fault until Mr Walshe sent him off to think over his conduct.

The two railway bosses were probably planning to sack Wells, on the spot, when the young railwayman unexpectedly burst into the office, brandishing a large, old-fashioned rifle. Without uttering a word, he shot

Thomas Wells shooting Mr Walshe, from the *IPN*, 9 May 1868.

Mr Walshe in the head and the Dover stationmaster was dead before his body hit the floor. Waving his rifle about, young Wells ran along the platform. He was seen to hide in an open carriage, and when a police sergeant arrived at the railway station, he was still there. He willingly handed over the rifle, and calmly walked to the police station.

When Thomas Wells was on trial for murder, at the Kent Summer Assizes, the defence emphasised that he had shot Mr Walshe in a burst of angry passion, and there had been no premeditation. The insanity defence was also used, since Wells had fallen off a train a few weeks prior to the murder and landed on his head. This had clearly unhinged his mind, his family alleged: he swore and shouted at the slightest provocation, and had once attacked his mother in the middle of the night, shoving her out of bed. But the judge and jury were unimpressed, since no other person had thought young Wells obviously deranged; nor had medical advice been sought about his condition. In spite of the questionable lack of premeditation, he was sentenced to death, and hanged at Maidstone Gaol on 13 August 1868.

There are three curious things about the murder. Firstly, he was the first person to be executed in private, inside a prison, after the old practice of public executions had finally been done away with. Secondly, a troop of journalists who had been admitted to witness the hanging could report that the execution had been badly botched: the drop was too short, and Wells had struggled for two minutes, being slowly suffocated to death. Thirdly, there was newspaper speculation about the possible brutalising influence of a singular piece of reading-matter found in Wells' pocket after he had been arrested – a copy of the *IPN*!

5. Murder in Artillery Passage, 1868

For the student of London architecture visiting the East End, a good place to go is the Artillery Passage conservation area, not far from Spitalfields Market. This relatively little-known part of London has an interesting history. The name Spitalfields originally came from the fields outside the Hospital of the Blessed Virgin Mary without Bishopsgate, established in the late 12th century. During the dissolution of the monasteries, the Priory of St Mary Spital was closed and, in 1537, part of the fields was designated as an artillery ground for members of the Guild of Artillery to practice with their longbows, crossbows and guns. In 1682, the old

Attempted Murder in Norton Folgate, a dramatic sketch of Alexander Arthur Mackay's assault on Mrs Grossmith, from the *IPN*, 16 May 1868.

Alexander Arthur Mackay murders Emma Grossmith, from *Famous Crimes Past & Present*.

artillery ground was purchased by four wealthy Londoners, who wanted to develop the area into housing. The street layout remains more or less unchanged from their plans, with Artillery Lane becoming the main thoroughfare from Bishopsgate, and Gun, Steward and Fort streets running off it to the north. Artillery Passage, a narrow alley even by the standards of the time, connects Artillery Lane with Sandys Row.

In 1868, the small eating house at 11 Artillery Passage was kept by Mr George Grossmith and his wife Emma, who had lived there at least since 1862. They had an 18-year-old servant named Alexander Arthur Mackay, who helped in the kitchen and waited at table. Their eldest son, Walter Grossmith, 11, ran errands and worked as a kitchen boy when he was not at school. Emma Grossmith, 45, was a fierce, angry woman, who had little patience with the clumsy, ignorant Alexander Arthur Mackay, who for some reason or other was nicknamed 'John'. She lost no opportunity to scold him for his sloth and general incompetence. When it was discovered that John had spoilt a dish of potatoes, then hidden it to conceal his 'crime', he was shouted at by both the Grossmiths. The nasty boy Walter also had some 'fun' at the hapless John's expense.

On the morning of 8 May 1868, Walter asked John to fetch him some water so he could wash his feet, but the truculent servant said he would be damned if he did. John got hold of a rolling-pin and made a threatening gesture towards the boy, but Mrs Grossmith came into the room and scolded him. After she had left, Walter could hear John mutter: 'If that damned bitch does not mind, she could get into the wrong box, and get something for her trouble!' Walter lingered in the house, thinking it would be very funny to watch yet another quarrel between his mother and John. But the servant, who was busy cleaning the shop windows, saw Walter lurking inside the restaurant, and called out 'The boy is not gone to school!' Mrs Grossmith ordered Walter to get going. The mischievous lad went away with great reluctance since he would have greatly liked to see a proper 'scrap' between his mother and John.

The next drama in Artillery Passage was that several neighbours heard loud screams emanating from No. 11. There was also the sound of repeated heavy blows. One neighbour heard Mrs Grossmith scream 'Oh, John, you will kill me!' and a hoarse voice replying 'Hold your row!' The widow Mrs Mary Sandiford, who lived at 13 Artillery Passage, went knocking at the door of the restaurant. When John opened it, she could see that he had a scratch on his cheek, and that his clothes were stained with blood. Going inside, she was shocked to see Mrs Grossmith lying motionless on the floor, covered in blood. 'Oh, John, you have done this!' she exclaimed. 'No, Ma'am, I have not', the servant replied, as cool as a cucumber. 'Where is Mr Grossmith?' asked Mrs Sandiford. 'Just round the corner. I will go and get him!' said John and made off. Several people saw the wild-eyed, bloodstained youth running through the streets, but John managed to make his escape.

When the local doctor arrived at No. 11, he found although Mrs Grossmith's head had been very badly beaten with a large rolling-pin, she was still alive. Her face was so swollen and distorted that Mr Grossmith could not recognize her. After a few days in hospital, she recovered enough to tell her husband what had happened the day she was assaulted. She had been making pastries, and the clumsy John had given her a very dirty and greasy cloth to wrap them in. When she had reproached him, he had gone for her with a large rolling-pin, beating her until she was well-nigh dead. The hue and cry was now up for Alexander Arthur Mackay, also known as John. A friend of his could report that a few days after Mrs Grossmith was assaulted, he had met John at Woolwich, near the Marine Barracks. When asked what he was doing in these parts, he had replied 'Oh, just looking for a job', with the greatest coolness.

Mrs Grossmith died a few days later, and the case was now one of murder. At the coroner's inquest on Emma Grossmith, her husband testified that Alexander Arthur Mackay was the son of an old friend of his, and that he had previously spent three years at Feltham Reformatory, for larceny. He had worked long hours at the restaurant, for a low salary. Once, when the mischievous Walter Grossmith had smeared some forks that John had just cleaned with some foul-smelling grease, the long-suffering servant had nearly had a fit from impotent rage. Another time, when Walter had told his father that John was in the habit of helping himself to some beer from the tap, John had told the boy that he had twice dreamt that he had murdered him. It was probably lucky for Walter that he had gone to school so promptly the day of the murder, since the frenzied John is unlikely to have spared him when he went on a rampage with the rolling-pin. Another time, Mr Grossmith had seen John strike a chopper into a large piece of meat. When asked what he was doing, the sinister servant had replied 'I am practising how to serve those that don't do as I like!'

The coroner's jury returned a verdict of wilful murder against Alexander Arthur Mackay. The problem was that no further clues were forthcoming about the Artillery Passage murderer's current whereabouts. But in July, a clever detective had a brilliant idea. It had happened before that wanted fugitives had been incarcerated in provincial prisons, under false names. A recent photograph of Mackay had been found in his bedroom at 11 Artillery Passage, and copies were circulated to all provincial police forces, and to all prisons. It did not take long for Maidstone Gaol to report that a young man matching the photograph was currently imprisoned for theft under the name George Jackson. He was promptly brought to London, where the Artillery Passage witnesses recognized him as the murderer Alexander Arthur Mackay. On trial at the Old Bailey on 17 August, the evidence against Mackay was rock solid, and he was found guilty and sentenced to death. This extraordinary 18-year-old murderer was executed at Newgate on 8 September 1868. The old eating-house at 11 Artillery Passage was still kept by the Grossmith family in 1881, but today it is a Chinese restaurant.

6. The Repentance of William Sheward, 1869

In June 1851, the Norwich newspapers reported a murder with dismemberment, of the most atrocious kind. All over town, in wasteland, ditches and sewers, small pieces of human flesh had been found. The police mobilised to make a search, and members of the public brought in

HIS DOG BROUGHT HIM A HUMAN FOOT.

A dog finds part of the Norwich murder victim, from *Famous Crimes Past & Present*.

bones, flesh and skin. The murderer must have acted with considerable coolness and determination, obviously spending a good deal of time cutting up his victim into tiny pieces. Soon, the police had a right hand, a right foot, parts of the sacrum and vertebrae, a pelvis sawn in half, arm and leg bones, a patella, and several specimens of skin, fat and intestines. These body parts were examined by three surgeons, who agreed that the dissection was crude, and definitely not the work of a medical professional. Due to the discovery of a female breast with a nipple, the murder victim was definitely a woman and, they speculated, around 5 feet tall and aged between 16 and 26 years. The finding of the dismembered body parts was widely advertised, but the problem was that no short young woman had gone missing in Norwich or vicinity, and the affair was gradually forgotten about. The body parts were given a decent burial in the cellar of the Norwich Guildhall.

William Sheward was a 39-year-old man who lived in Tabernacle Street, just off the Bishopgate in Norwich. He worked as an assistant in a pawnshop. In 1836, the 24-year-old Sheward had married the Martha Francis, 39, but the marriage was not a particularly happy one, and they had no children. Sheward was a short, insignificant-looking man; his wife was also short and of delicate build, with golden hair. In 1851, Martha Sheward disappeared. Her husband said that she had left him and moved

The execution of Sheward, from the *IPN*, 24 April 1869.

away, and no person seems to have doubted this story. Due to his gruff, taciturn personality, William Sheward did not have any close friends, and the only people who missed Martha were her aunt and sisters. Sheward told them that when Martha had left him, without telling where she was going; he had asked her 'If you won't write to me, will you write to some of your sisters?', only to receive the curt answer 'No, never!' And indeed, the sisters had not received any correspondence at all from Martha, who was normally an assiduous letter writer. They had their suspicions but did not report Sheward to the police. No person connected the disappearance of the 54-year-old Martha with the dismembered young Norwich murder victim of 1851.

After losing his wife, William Sheward went on with his life as well as he could. He sold the household effects, moved into a room above a pub, and opened a pawnshop of his own. He met a woman named Charlotte Buck and had five children with her, some of them born before their marriage in 1862. On their marriage certificate, Sheward described himself as a widower. Although not the most industrious of men, and fond of the bottle, Sheward had success with his pawnshop, which enjoyed very decent trade. In 1868, he sold it, and took over the lease of the Key & Castle public house in Oak Street, Norwich. Sheward now had a permanent roof over his head, a large family, and a steady income to support them. But becoming a pub landlord did not agree with him: he drank to excess, and suffered from insomnia, walking around in the dark rooms above the pub with a candle, well into the wee hours.

In late December 1868, William Sheward decided to go to London for a while. Drinking hard had not agreed with him; it had reduced him to a wreck of a man. On 1 January 1869, he came walking into the Walworth police station, saying he wanted to make a charge against himself, for murdering his first wife back in 1851. Since the inspector in duty thought he was delirious, he was given a bed in a cell to 'sleep it off'. The following day, Sheward repeated his admission: he had cut Martha's throat after an angry quarrel about some money Sheward had hidden away when going bankrupt in 1849. He had dismembered the body into tiny pieces, sawing bones and severing joints with gusto. He had then gone out walking with a large basket, scattering body parts in his wake. This simple stratagem had worked a treat, and Sheward had committed the perfect murder. He had then been able to get himself another more promising wife, and raise a large family; through purchasing the pub, he had achieved some degree of financial independence. His conscience had been gnawing away at him every day, however, particularly after he had started drinking hard to be able to sleep, and the reason he had gone to London was to revisit the Walworth street where he had first met Martha, intending to commit suicide there with a razor. But since he was squeamish about cutting his own throat, he had instead gone to the police, admitting his crime.

There was consternation among the Norwich police when the mystery of the dismembered body of 1851 was belatedly solved, and embarrassment among the surgeons who had confidently stated that the body of the 54-year-old Martha Sheward was that of a young woman. On trial for murder at the Norfolk Lent Assizes on 29 March 1869, Sheward was quite a pathetic sight: short, prematurely aged, and crippled by some kind of severe rheumatism of the ankles. His defence counsel had persuaded him to withdraw his confession but his previous detailed statements to the police had done the damage and he was found guilty and sentenced to death. In the infirmary of Norwich City Gaol, he wrote his final confession, a letter of thanks to his solicitor, and a heartfelt letter saying goodbye to his wife. Sheward was executed on 20 April, dying after a short struggle. The murder house in Tabernacle Street is long gone, but the Key & Castle pub stood until 1958.

7. The Pantin Tragedy, 1869

Jean-Baptiste Troppmann was a French crook, born in Alsace in 1848. As a youth, he had an ungovernable temper: he quarrelled with his brother, once knocked his father down, and was suspected of murdering a tramp, just for the fun of it, but never prosecuted. In 1869, when Troppmann was still a youth, he met the Paris brush manufacturer Jean Kinck, a credulous, foolish man who had been able to accumulate significant wealth. Kinck was completely taken in by Troppmann's scheme that they should earn much money by setting up a factory for counterfeit banknotes. In reality, the young crook planned to relieve Kinck of as much money as possible, by whatever means necessary. The two men went to a ruined country manor, to survey the basement for the proposed counterfeiting operation. Troppmann had poured some prussic acid into a bottle of wine, which he offered to Kinck. After having a swig, the luckless brush manufacturer dropped dead on the spot. Troppmann then stole his victim's money and valuables, dug a grave with a shovel, and buried Kinck in it.

The next part of his plan was to write to Mme Kinck, asking that she provided her husband with a sum of money. Being of a trusting temperament, she sent Kinck's eldest son Gustave with an envelope full of banknotes. Troppmann took care of the money, murdered Gustave as well, and got rid of the body. He then demanded that Mme Kinck should meet him at Pantin, a village just outside Paris, and bring some more money for her husband, who was very busy with his work, he claimed.

The body of Jean Kinck is discovered, from the *IPN*, 4 December 1869.

He took the money, murdered Mme Kinck and her five younger children, and buried them in a field. The octuple murderer then made haste to Le Havre, from where he planned to escape to the United States. The bodies buried at Pantin had been found, but the police suspected the husband Jean Kinck, whose remains had not yet been discovered. Huge crowds of

Sketches from Troppmann's extraordinary career, from the *IPN*, 8 January 1870.

Parisians came to see the 'field of horror' in Pantin, trampling the field so that it could not be ploughed for two years to come.

Troppmann went to see an old woman in Le Havre, knowing she was good at faking passports. Unfortunately for him, she dabbled in other criminal activities as well, and when he was inside her shop, the police came calling. When they demanded to see his identity documents, he tried running away, leaping into water from a bridge, but the French police constables captured him. He was carrying Jean Kinck's identity papers and it was soon clear to the police that he was deeply involved in the determined effort to exterminate the Kinck family. His exploits caused much uproar, in France as well as abroad, and he was the earliest French murderer to be prominently featured by the *IPN*. Troppmann tried to incriminate Jean Kinck and his son Gustave, saying he himself had only been an accomplice in their murderous crimes, but he was not believed. On trial for multiple murder in Paris, he was found guilty and sentenced to perish on the guillotine. He was executed at the Place de la Roquette on 19 January 1870, the *IPN* publishing a sketch of the event.

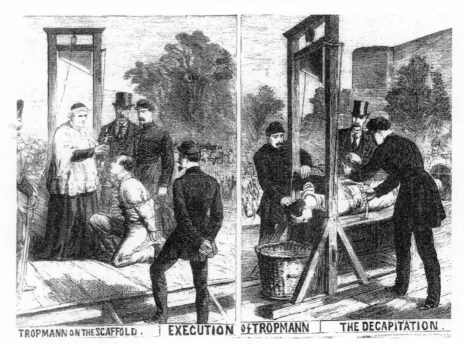

TROPMANN ON THE SCAFFOLD . | EXECUTION OF TROPMANN | THE DECAPITATION .

The execution of Troppmann, from the *IPN*, 22 January 1870.

8. The Chelsea Double Murder, 1870

The Rev. Elias Huelin was a French Protestant clergyman who became minister of the French Conformist Church in Soho, and assistant chaplain at Brompton Cemetery. Retiring early, he built up an impressive portfolio of fashionable Chelsea houses. In 1870, when the 84-year-old clergyman was living at 15 Paulton's Square, he also owned Nos. 24 and 32, as well as 24 Wellington Square, and various other houses. Letting all these valuable houses gave him a considerable income. He collected his rents in person, walking his little dog through the elegant Chelsea squares and streets, to call on his many tenants, the golden guineas jingling in his pockets as he went along.

In May 1870, Mr Huelin wanted to renovate his unlet property at 24 Wellington Square. Some workmen were recruited to do the plastering and papering, one of them was a 31-year-old Scot, Walter Miller. When Mr Huelin paid his workers, they saw the many golden guineas in his well-filled purse; the old clergyman seemed to like to show off his wealth. After work on the house was well under way, Mr Huelin told the workmen he wanted to go to Lincolnshire for a while, to spend some time at a farm property owned by a friend.

The body of Mr Huelin is found, from the *IPN*, 21 May 1870.

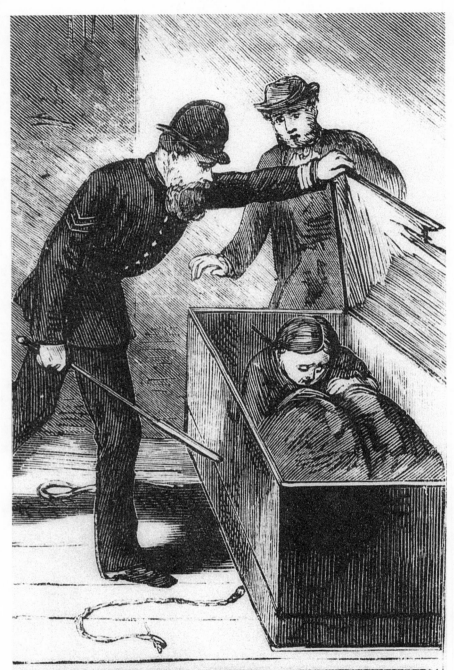

BREAKING OPEN THE BOX—
DISCOVERY OF MURDERED WOMAN

The finding of the body of Ann Boss, from the *IPN*, 21 May 1870.

Miller is taken into custody, from the *IPN*, 21 May 1870.

When nothing more was seen of Mr Huelin for several days, it was presumed he had left for the countryside. Then his French nephew appeared in London. A foppish, foreign-looking individual with a pince-nez and waxed moustaches, and an exaggerated accent, he took up residence at 15 Paulton's Square. He told people Mr Huelin's housekeeper Ann Boss had accompanied her master to Lincolnshire and hired a sluttish-looking woman as her replacement. The young Frenchman took charge of his uncle's affairs, collected his rents, ate his food and drank his wine, making merry with his female companion for several days.

One evening, young Mr Huelin sent for the removal man Henry Piper and ordered him to take a large trunk from the kitchen of 15 Paulton's Square to a small house in Fulham. But when Piper lifted the heavy trunk, he could see blood seeping from it. 'What does blood do here?' he asked, retreating. 'Go back, you *carman*, cord the box, and do your work!' the Frenchman commanded, but Piper steadfastly refused. 'Go back and cord that box!' the 'nephew' insisted, but this time in a broad Scottish accent rather than a French one. Sensing that something was very wrong, Piper sent his assistant for the police. Suddenly, the mystery 'Frenchman' bolted out of the house, with Piper in hot pursuit.

In a long, furious chase through the quiet Chelsea squares and streets, the agile Piper pursued the 'nephew' for half-a-mile, with a sturdy, panting police sergeant bringing up the rear. Finally, after the exhausted 'Frenchman' slipped and fell, he was collared by Piper and secured by some police constables. With the aptly named Sergeant Large, Piper returned to 15 Paulton's Square. When the box was prised open, it was found to contain the doubled-up body of Ann Boss. The harmless old domestic had been strangled with a rope that still dangled from her neck. The mysterious 'Frenchman' turned out to be the Scottish workman Walter Miller, who had donned an elaborate disguise and faked a French accent. It was remembered that when working at 24 Wellington Square, Miller had ordered a large hole to be dug in the garden and, sure enough, it was found to contain the body of Elias Huelin. The old clergyman had been knocked down from behind with a shovel, then strangled to death. An empty brandy bottle was also found in the pit, indicating that the Scotsman had required some Dutch courage before embarking on his murderous career.

The Chelsea Double Murder of 1870 caused widespread revulsion and alarm among Londoners. That some conniving menial could deliberately plan the destruction of two blameless, respectable people, and come quite close to getting away with it, was an alarming thought for many a well-to-do Londoner. Miller had always been a mean-spirited, jealous man, very envious of his betters. Although often thinking up various get-rich-quick schemes, the Scot had never before set any of them in motion and he did not have a criminal record. His plan appears to have been to murder Mr Huelin and Ann Boss, steal their money and valuables in the guise of the French nephew, then escape to America. The Scotsman's greed was his undoing: he sold the contents of 15 Paulton's Square, and dallied too long to collect the rental money. When the remains of Ann Boss became too 'high' to be kept indoors, he rented a little house in Fulham and planned to send the box there, but the seepage of blood and body fluids from it sealed his fate.

Sentenced at the Old Bailey on 14 July 1870 to death, Walter Miller was executed at Newgate on August 1. He died impenitent, in a manner corresponding to the brutality of his crimes. Tearing free from the keepers when he was to be pinioned he ran head-first into the unyielding stone wall of his cell, perhaps hoping to commit suicide by 'dashing his brains out'. But that kind of thing only works in French novels: the human skull is thicker and more solid than people think, and still conscious, the groaning, dazed Miller was pinioned and put on a chair on the scaffold. When the bolt was drawn, both convict and chair fell, but the hangman had got his calculations wrong: the drop was too short and Miller was strangled rather than executed cleanly.

For his heroism in tackling Miller, the removal man Piper was voted a reward of £50. He inquired if he could also be allowed to see the execution, a privilege that was granted him.

Elias Huelin's property, including the two murder houses, was inherited by his real nephew Edward. Ann Boss had been left a legacy in Mr Huelin's will; her, but the greedy nephew argued that since she had been killed before him, her descendants were not in a position to claim a penny. It took a year of legal wrangling to work out a compromise, largely in favour of Ann Boss's relatives. Walter Miller's young son Stocks Miller was sent to America, where he became postmaster in Moorcroft, Wyoming, before dying from pneumonia after working in an irrigation ditch. The two murder houses turned out to be hard to let: people did not like to live in houses where two respectable Chelsea citizens had recently been done to death in a horrible manner. It took decades for their lurid reputation to be forgotten. But when murder house devotee George R. Sims visited them in 1907, he found they were both inhabited by people who knew nothing about their gruesome past: 'in the room the murder was committed, the children romp and play'. The celebrated occultist Aleister Crowley, who lived at 31 Wellington Square in the 1920s, is said to have taken an interest in the neighbouring property at No. 24, expressing disappointment that it was not haunted. Both the Huelin murder houses still stand today.

9. The Denham Massacre, 1870

Mr Emmanuel Marshall was an honest, hard-working blacksmith in Denham, a village situated near Uxbridge, on the outskirts of modern London. In 1870, he was 36 years old and lived in a small cottage in Cheapside Lane, with his wife Charlotte and his four children. His mother, who had become widowed a few years earlier, also lived in the cottage, and his sister Mary, who was just about to get married, moved in with them in May 1870. This meant that Francis, his youngest boy, had to go and live with an aunt for a while, since there was simply not enough room for him. The Marshall cottage can be clearly seen on the Denham tithe map of 1843. The last house on the right-hand side on the horseshoe-shaped lane from the main London to Oxford road, it was relatively isolated, with the nearest houses being 150 or so yards away. Marshall's smithy was attached to the house itself.

Marshall's cottage and smithy, from the *IPN*, 4 June 1870.

The discovery of the murdered people, and a portrait of the murderer Owen, from the *IPN*, 4 June 1870.

Portraits of the leading lights of the case, from the *IPN*, 11 June 1870.

On Saturday 21 May 1870, the Marshall family went to the market in Uxbridge, where many people saw them. Later that day, the two young

The murderer Owen, before and after changing into the Sunday best of the murdered man, from the *IPN*, 11 June 1870.

daughters were seen playing outside the house, and Marshall was heard working inside the smithy. On Monday 23 May, a woman who was making a wedding-dress for Miss Mary Marshall, the sister who was getting married the very next day, came to the cottage. Since there was no response when she knocked on the door, she peeped through a window. She was horrified to find that a bloodbath had occurred: the floor of the cottage was drenched with gore, and strewn with children's corpses. Screaming, she ran to fetch the village constable.

Arriving from Slough with half a dozen men, Superintendent Thomas Dunham took charge of the murder investigation. The cottage contained six corpses: Marshall's wife, mother and sister, and the three children.

Superintendent Dunham arrests Owen, from the *IPN*, 11 June 1870.

The mob attempts to lynch the murderer, from the *IPN*, 11 June 1870.

They had all been beaten to death with a heavy, blunt instrument, presumably a sledgehammer. At first, it was thought that Marshall himself might have murdered his family, but a further search found his body in the smithy, bringing the tally to seven victims. His head had been beaten in with a series of powerful blows, just like those of the other victims, so it was impossible that he could have inflicted these injuries himself. The Superintendent instead presumed that Marshall had interrupted

THE "MURDER HOUSE" AT DENHAM.

The murder house in 1905, from *Famous Crimes Past & Present*.

a burglar trying to steal his tools and that after this brutal individual had dealt with the blacksmith, he had entered the cottage, driven its inhabitants before him, and murdered them one by one, before stealing all the valuables in the house. There were obvious signs that the murder cottage had been searched, and some of Marshall's clothes were missing.

It turned out that the Denham village constable had seen an evil-looking tramp lurking about in the neighbourhood. Early on Sunday morning, a woman had seen a respectably dressed man leaving the murder cottage; she had initially thought it was Marshall himself. The man had told her that the Marshall family had just gone for a holiday. The same individual had later been spotted having a drink at the Dog & Duck, carrying a canvas bag. The canny superintendent suspected this was the murderous tramp, who had donned Marshall's Sunday best after wiping out the family, and carried the stolen items in his canvas bag. The Denham atrocity had caused widespread revulsion, and the newspapers were full of it. In particular, the *IPN* sold like hot cakes since it had a number of high-quality drawings of the murder house and the Marshalls.

The hue and cry was up for the mysterious tramp sighted in Denham wearing Marshall's clothes. There was speculation that he must have held a grudge against the blacksmith for some reason or other. On Tuesday, a man named Coombes, a bricklayer who lived in a lodging-house in Uxbridge, informed the police about a rough-looking fellow lodger whom he only knew as 'Jack'. This individual had been very poor before the weekend, but flush with money on Monday. When shown some bloodstained clothes left behind in the murder cottage by the killer, Coombes identified them as the same clothes he had seen Jack wear. When he had met Jack on Monday morning, the lodger had told him that he was going to Reading on the 6.45 p.m. train.

The police found this information very valuable indeed, and Superintendent Dunham took Coombes with him to Reading to search for the absconded Jack. A Reading constable, who knew the ways of the local tramps, thought the suspect might have taken refuge in the Oxford Arms public house in Silver Street. When they entered a room known as the Tramp's Kitchen, Coombes called out, 'That's the man!' pointing at an ugly, dirty tramp with almost simian features. Although Superintendent Dunham knew that a loaded pistol had been stolen from Marshall's cottage, he went for the ruffian, seizing him by the throat with a hearty goodwill. To be sure, the tramp tried to draw the pistol, but it was torn out of his hand, and he was captured after a violent struggle. Not just the pistol, but several other items from the Marshall cottage were found on his person, as well as some pawn tickets for the items he had already pawned to get some spending money. When the suspect was taken to Slough Station, he would have been lynched by a furious mob, had Superintendent Dunham not been able to restore order.

The tramp turned out to be the former blacksmith John Owen, alias Jones, a desperate ruffian hailing from Wolverhampton. He had previously done time for larceny and sheep-rustling. Marshall had once employed him to mend some wheels, but since Owen had done the job so badly, he was not paid. The police speculated that this insult had stuck in the mind of this long-minded, work-shy tramp, and he decided to get even with Marshall by stealing his tools. As Owen had been about to be released from prison two days before the massacre, he had been heard speaking of a man in Denham who owed him money, adding that if he did not get it off him, he would murder him. Owen never admitted his crimes, nor did he provide any explanation why, after beating Marshall to death, he had run into the cottage and murdered the entire family. Hardly a criminal mastermind, he had left his own bloodstained clothes behind in the murder cottage, clothes that people could identify. Instead of swiftly absconding to some faraway place, he had remained in the area, and attracted notice by spending money freely after pawning some of Marshall's effects. When finally travelling to Reading, he had told a person he did not know, and could not trust, exactly where he was going.

The criminal prosecution of Owen was a straightforward matter, due to the stupidity and imprudence shown by the murderer. When the judge sentenced him to death, the tramp insolently replied, 'Thank'ee, sir!' His only regret was not shooting Superintendent Dunham as well. When his aged father and estranged wife came to see him in the condemned cell, he asked them what they had to snivel at. Owen denied the existence of God, the Devil, Heaven and Hell; when a kind Roman Catholic priest came to prepare him for death, he was driven away with blasphemous outbursts. Owen ate a hearty final supper, and asked to be allowed to sleep inside the coffin that had been made for him. On the scaffold at Aylesbury Gaol, he wanted to address the officials and newspaper reporters present, asserting his innocence, but he had forgotten the surname of the murdered man. Few were sorry when Calcraft the Hangman launched the septuple murderer into eternity.

In Buckinghamshire, the Denham Massacre was long spoken of with bated breath; fearful of murderous tramps, people invested in shotguns, watchdogs and powerful locks. The inhabitants of Slough made a collection and presented the hero of the day, Superintendent Dunham, with a fine gold pocket-watch, which is today at the Thames Valley Police Museum. A wax model of the murderer Owen, dressed in his own shabby and bloodstained clothes, was quite a hit at Madame Tussaud's. Young Francis Marshall, the sole survivor of the carnage since he was staying with his aunt at the time of the massacre, could have been adopted a hundred times over, but it is recorded that he died of tuberculosis while still a young man.

In 1905, the journalist Guy Logan went to do some murder house detection work in Denham, for his column in *Famous Crimes Past & Present*. Accompanied by the magazine's draughtsman, he took the electric tram from Shepherd's Bush to Uxbridge, then walked along the main road to Oxford [the A40 today] until he spotted a white signpost saying 'To Denham Village – half a mile'. Guy and his companion proceeded down this narrow, picturesque lane, passing the village church and the grave of the Marshalls, and entered the White Swan for some liquid refreshments. The landlady had an exciting tale for him. At 6 p.m. on the day of the murder, when she had been a little girl, her mother had sent her with some needlework for Mrs Marshall. Since no person answered the door, she had peered through the small window of the front room, before frantically running home and bursting into the White Swan exclaiming 'Mummy, they are lying dead on the floor at Marshall's!'

The readers of *Famous Crimes Past & Present* were not a squeamish lot, and the poetic Guy gave them a graphic account of what the village constable must have seen when he entered the silent house of death:

> Surely such a heart-rending spectacle as confronted him was never before presented to the awe-struck gaze of man. Marshall's wife and sister were lying in the front room with their nightdresses wantonly thrown up over their faces. The place swam in blood, and particles of bone and brain lay everywhere. Their heads had been battered into pulp. In the back room were found the bodies of the grandmother and the three children, with their skulls beaten in and mutilated in a still more horrible manner. Marshall himself lay dead in his workshop, with his smith's dress on, and his head battered to pieces. The whole place reeked of blood and resembled a shambles. A tribe of brutalised and ignorant savages could not have left a more terrifying picture of death and desolation.

The landlady gave Guy directions to the murder house, which she assured him was still standing. The murder house detective proceeded down Cheapside Lane, where he spotted the house on the right side; it was still the last house in the village, before the main road was reached. Guy had brought with him two 1870 drawings of the murder house, from the *Graphic* and the *Illustrated London News*, and although Marshall's smithy had been pulled down, and the house was now covered with ivy, it was clearly the same building. It was in a good state of repair, and obviously still used for human habitation. It no longer faced open fields, since the village school, and also a small inn called The Plough, had been erected on the other side of Cheapside Lane. As the *Famous Crimes* draughtsman executed a likeness of the murder house, Guy enjoyed an excellent meal, and some more liquid refreshments, at The Plough.

In the late 1920s, Guy Logan again went to see the Denham murder house. Although he was now 60 years old, he had just signed the contracts for his first full-length book, *Masters of Crime*, a study of multiple murders. Since murder is seldom more multiple than in the Denham atrocity of 1870, he wanted to include a chapter about it in his book. The cobbled village street, the ancient cottages, and the creeper-clad White Swan were all there – and so was the murder house! Ivy-clad and weather-beaten, it still appeared to be inhabited. Although Guy normally had no scruples about reproducing photos of murder houses, he ended up using a snapshot of the entrance to the village instead, with the church in the background.

The Denham murder house remained untroubled by murder house detectives for many years; nor did any other crime historian add to Guy Logan's account of the 1870 atrocity. In modern times, there have been two valuable retellings of the story, as well as some scattered articles and internet accounts. In one of the latter [now defunct] it was alleged that the murder house was demolished in the 1950s, to make way for modern housing as the village expanded along Cheapside Lane. Use of the ubiquitous Google-maps shows that no building resembling the murder house stands today. Nondescript modern houses occupy its former site opposite The Plough (today, The Fat Cow) and the village school.

When I went to Denham in November 2014, I chose a different route to that of Guy Logan. There is now a railway connection from Marylebone to the Denham railway station, situated to the north of the village. After a brisk walk, it was possible to have a good look at this quaint Buckinghamshire village, with its many curious old houses. In the churchyard, the gravestone of the murdered Marshalls was quite worn and overgrown with moss, but a small explanatory plaque has been erected beside it. For such a small village, Denham has no shortage of pubs: The Swan, The Green Man and The Falcon, to say nothing of The Fat Cow, formerly The Plough where Guy Logan had enjoyed a meal back in 1905. There is no trace of the murder house across the road, nor of any house that might have been built on its foundations; the houses in Cheapside Lane are all modern-looking, and the former abode of the Marshalls is clearly gone without a trace.

Peacetime massacres are unfortunately no rarity in modern society. Firstly there is the 'killing spree' form of atrocity, in which some deranged individual has had enough of life: in a final attempt at revenge against the remainder of humanity, he attempts to gun down as many people as possible before taking his own life. In Hungerford in 1987, 27-year-old unemployed labourer Michael Robert Ryan went on a rampage armed with two semi-automatic rifles and a handgun, killing 16 people including his mother, and wounding 15 others, before committing suicide. Another rampage killer, 52-year-old cab driver Derrick Bird, was at large in Cumbria in 2010. He started by shooting dead his twin brother, with whom he had disputed his father's will, and the family solicitor as well. He then settled the score with some other Whitehaven taxi drivers, with whom he had disagreed in the past, and shot dead a number of random people, before committing suicide; in all, Derrick Bird had 12 victims, and 11 more people were injured.

Then there is the 'family tragedy' type of massacre, in which a deranged parent decides to murder his or her spouse, and all the children as well, before committing suicide. Such tragedies were far from uncommon in Victorian times, with its large families, and the absence of firearms or noxious gas for the murderer to make use of sometimes led to the grossest scenes. In the 'Tooting Horror' of 1895, the unemployed plasterer Frank Taylor murdered his wife and six of his seven children in a bloodbath, before committing suicide. His eldest son was gravely injured by his razor-wielding maniac father, but he survived the ordeal; the murder house at what was then 12 Fountain Road, Tooting, still stands, although the houses have long since been renumbered. A writer in the *Pall Mall Gazette* pointed out that the Tooting Horror was the worst family tragedy in Britain since 1834, when the German Johann Nicholas Steinberg had murdered his common-law wife and four children in a bloodbath, at 17 Southampton Street [today Calshot Street; the house no longer stands]. Rather flippantly, the journalist commented that the German had fallen short of Taylor's record by two victims.

The Denham Massacre is an example of quite an uncommon type of mass murder: a tramp or robber enters a house and goes berserk, killing all its inhabitants. In the Llangibby Massacre of 1878, five members of the Watkins family were murdered at small Monmouthshire cottage: farm labourer William Watkins and his wife Elizabeth were lying outside, weltering in their gore, and their three youngest children were inside the burning cottage, brutally beaten to death. A foreign-looking vagabond had been seen skulking near the murder house, and he was suspected to be Joseph Garcia, a Spanish sailor turned burglar, who had just been released from Usk Prison. After his description had been circulated by the police, he was apprehended at Newport, with scratches on his face and a bloodstained shirt, and carrying a bundle of 'swag' from the murder cottage. Although objecting that he had found the bundle in a field, he was found guilty, sentenced to death, and executed at Usk Prison on 18 November. Although there have been some far-fetched conspiracy theories about the Llangibby Massacre, one of them that Garcia had fathered an illegitimate child with the eldest daughter of the Watkins family, there is nothing to suggest that the Spaniard had ever met the humble farm labourer and his family before the murderous attack. As for the murder cottage, it was severely damaged by the impetuous souvenir hunters, and later destroyed because nobody would live there.

The most sanguinary effort of any London mass murderer to match the Denham and Llangibby atrocities must surely be the Forest Gate massacre of 1919. Henry Perry, alias Beckett, belonged to a family of travelling hawkers, and had several convictions for theft. He served as a private soldier in the Great War, but was captured by the Turks. After the war, he briefly lodged with his step-aunt Mrs Alice Cornish and her family at 13 Stukeley Road, Forest Gate, but after misbehaving himself, he was shown the door. Poor as a church mouse, he was tramping around the West Ham area, when he got the idea to burgle the Cornish house. It turned out that Mrs Cornish was at home, and she was far from pleased to see him. In a furious rage, Perry knocked her down with a kitchen poker and dragged her to the garden shed, where he finished her off with a pickaxe and a carving fork. When the two Cornish daughters came home, Perry knocked them on the head with a hammer, and threw the bodies into the cellar. He then waited until Mr Cornish came home, hit him hard on the head with the axe, and chopped one of his fingers off. When Cornish died in hospital later the same day, Perry had succeeded in wiping out the entire family. The quadruple murderer was promptly captured and tried, and Lord Darling, in pronouncing sentence of death, said that he had never heard a case in which the circumstances of the crime were more horrible. After an appeal had been turned down, Perry was hanged at Pentonville Prison on 10 July 1919. The Stukeley Road murder house still stands, its former notoriety all but forgotten.

Thus the Denham murder house, home to one of the most horrendous massacres ever, stood for at least 80 years after the event, before being destroyed to make way for modern housing. Although it was far from an attractive house, its age and historical associations should have made people think twice before demolishing it. After all, it had inspired at least three picture postcards, probably more than any other Denham house apart from the church and the historic Swan public house. If Charles Dickens had resided in the Cheapside Lane cottage for a while, surely literary men would have been up in arms to object against such vandalism, but no person showed any inclination to save a house notorious in the annals of murder. In London, some historic Bloomsbury murder houses have suffered similar unlamented oblivion in comparably recent times: 12 Great Coram Street, site of the unsolved murder of Harriet Buswell in 1872, and 4 Euston Square, where Miss Matilda Hacker was found murdered in 1879, both stood for many decades after the crimes that made them notorious, but neither is in existence today. The two murder houses at No. 4 and No. 12 Burton Crescent [today Cartwright Gardens] are no more, victims of the expansion of the halls of residence of London University in the 1950s. When doing some murder house detection in Glasgow, I was, of course, keen to find Dr Pritchard's house at No. 131 [today 249] Sauchiehall Street, but although No. 241–243 in the street were original, the site of the Pritchard house was covered by a recently constructed kitchenware emporium! Again, it does not appear as if any person objected to the sole remaining memorial of a celebrated historical crime being bulldozed and carted off on a developer's lorry. Should famous murder houses perhaps have some kind of 'listed' status to preserve them?

10. A Very Strange West Bromwich Murder, 1871

At 5.30 a.m. on 25 June 1871, engine driver Isaac Blockridge saw smoke billowing out of the window of one of the pit hovels at the Hall End Pits in West Bromwich. Knowing that this hovel was the humble abode of a near-destitute banksman named Joseph Marshall, who possessed no

Black Jack stokes the fire around Lame Joe's lifeless body, from the *IPN*, 8 July 1871.

The Evil Eye

Black Jack - he was a simple man,
and wicked was Lame Joe,
The Evil Eye, he put on Jack,
soon caused a fatal blow.
The collier, from his cradle days,
detested cross-eyed folk,
bad luck, tiz known, they surely bring.
HOW COULD THE SPELL BE BROKE?

The Sedgley Wizard, Jack did see,
The Curse, he fain would hinder,
the only way to break the spell?
BURN LAME JOE TO A CINDER!
The Warlock lame, as all did know,
lived in the Hall End hovel,
at night Black Jack paid him a call,
and struck him with a shovel.

Next did he stoke the hovel fire,
'til it was glowing gleads,
then did he with that fiery mass,
consume Lame Joe's misdeeds,
the stench of flesh and awful screams,
did fill that tiny room,
as Black Jack sent the Warlock lame,
to meet his fiery doom!

Take heed, the moral of this tale,
and Simple Men - don't rile um,
for Black Jack lies with foaming mouth,
in Powick Mad Asylum,
yet his victim would prefer that place,
to where he now perspires,
a-hurling coal for evermore,
on Satan's scorching Fires!

A poem by Aristotle Tump, inspired by Lame Joe's dismal fate, from his *Tales of Terror*. Reproduced by permission of Bugle Publications.

house of his own, Blockridge went to investigate. He knew 'Lame Joe', as the old colliery worker was known, and called out to him, but there was no reply. When Blockridge entered the hovel, the stench of burning meat nearly made him vomit. He first thought Lame Joe had put a roast on the fire and forgotten about it, but when he looked round in the smoke-filled hovel, there were further horrors: in front of the fireplace was a human body terribly charred by fire. The trunk was liberally stoked with burning coal and embers, and 'seething' with smoke, as Blockridge expressed it. Only the head was intact; when Blockridge examined it, he recognized the features of Lame Joe.

Isaac Blockridge rapidly contacted the police, who made inquiries with commendable diligence. When Lame Joe's remains were examined, it was seen that his head had been hit three times with a blunt instrument, hard enough to break the skull. A heavy rake stained with blood was presumed to have been the murder weapon. The evening before, Lame Joe had been drinking with the collier John Higginson, known locally as 'Black Jack'. These two had been seen together quite frequently in recent weeks, although they had not always been on friendly terms. Several people had seen Lame Joe and Black Jack screaming abuse at each other, and even lashing out with their fists, as they lurched back to the pits after their drinking session at the Nag's Head tavern nearby.

Black Jack's landlady said that after the drunken collier had arrived home from the Nag's Head a little after 11 p.m., he had fallen asleep by the fireside. But at 3 a.m., he had woken up and gone out, saying that he wanted to pick some mushrooms, a very queer excuse for going out for a stroll in the wee hours. Jack was gone the best part of an hour, before returning looking quite distraught. When people reminded him of the mushrooms, he replied that he had not found any. Three witnesses had seen Black Jack walk toward the Hall End hovel; when he emerged from there after a quarter of an hour, one of them smelt something like rags burning. The morning after, there was an outcry that Lame Joe had been found burnt to a cinder. When Black Jack, who was lying in bed fully dressed, was urged to come along to have a look at the corpse, he replied that he did not like to see it. This was considered odd, since all the locals were thronging at the Hall End hovel, as if the circus had come to town, but Black Jack had always been a strange fellow, and very simple in his ways.

When the police arrested Black Jack, the big collier seemed very confused. At the inquest, he had nothing to say except that he was as innocent as a new-born babe. When on trial, he 'appeared to be utterly indifferent to the awful position in which he was placed'. The evidence against Black Jack appeared strong, but the barrister representing him did a good job. He emphasised the worthless, drunken life of Lame Joe, and suggested that the two had had another late-night quarrel, during which the simple-minded Jack had struck his opponent down, without the intention to kill him. The jury found Black Jack guilty of manslaughter only, although he was still sentenced to penal servitude for life.

But why had Black Jack and Lame Joe spent so much time together, when they had been on quite bad terms? And why had Jack gone to such extreme measures to burn Joe's remains? The solution might well be found in the second volume of Aristotle Tump's curious *Tales of Terror*. According to local tradition, Lame Joe had been a most unprepossessing character, very ugly and cross-eyed. He had a reputation for being cunning and mean-spirited, and perhaps even a warlock. Black Jack, a superstitious countryman, was very fearful of cross-eyed people, since according to tradition, they possessed magical powers. Thus, by threatening to put the Evil Eye on Jack, the crippled blackmailer made sure the collier kept his jug well filled with ale. Black Jack tried to evade him through changing his favourite watering-hole, but Joe's ugly, grinning features always kept turning up to share his drinking-money. After the blackmail had been going on for many weeks, Black Jack had had enough. He decided that the only way he could preserve his precious beer-money was to consult a local warlock of high repute, known as the Sedgley Wizard. He was told that the only way to avert the curse would be to kill Lame Joe, and reduce his body to a cinder. How Jack followed the Wizard's advice we already know. Whereas the locals had some degree of sympathy for the frenzied Black Jack, who may well have ended his life in an asylum, there was none for Lame Joe. To them, cheating somebody out of his beer-money was a more heinous crime than murder.

11. The Crime of Christiana Edmunds, 1871

Christiana Edmunds was born in 1828, the eldest daughter of the Margate architect William Edmunds and his wife Ann Christiana. William Edmunds constructed the Holy Trinity Church in Margate and the Trinity Church in Dover, as well as the lighthouse at the end of the pier in Margate. The Edmunds family, consisting of William and Ann Christiana, and their three daughters and two sons, lived at 16 Hawley Square [the house still stands] with their three servants. Christiana had a conventional education at a boarding school for girls. A plain, heavily

Christiana Edmunds attempts to poison Mrs Beard, from *Famous Crimes Past & Present*.

built young woman, she lacked a 'come hither' glance so did not attract any male admirers.

William Edmunds went insane in the 1840s, and the family had to have him removed to Peckham House Asylum, a private madhouse in South London. After he had died there in 1847, the family was in somewhat straitened circumstances: the house at Hawley Square was sold, and Ann Christiana Edmunds moved to Canterbury with her daughters. Her son William graduated as a doctor, married and emigrated to South Africa, but the youngest son Arthur died insane in an asylum. The daughter Louisa also married, but she died of gynaecological complications at an early age. Christiana showed no sign of marrying and settling down, however, and she seemed content with an idle and boring life with her mother and her unmarried sister Mary.

In 1867, Ann Christiana Edmunds and her two surviving daughters moved into lodgings at 15 Marlborough Place, Brighton. Christiana suffered from some kind of neuralgia and, in 1869, she went to consult the local practitioner Dr Charles Beard, who had his surgery in his home at 64 Grand Parade [the house does not stand]. He was not particularly attractive and was a 41-year-old married man with three children, but it did not take long for Christiana to discover him as the love of her life.

CHRISTINA EDMUND,
At the Bar of the Old Bailey, convicted of Poisoning at Brighton.

A portrait of Christiana Edmunds, and vignettes from her career, from the *IPN*, 9 September 1871.

She wrote him long, amorous letters, and seemed to have an ambition to marry him one day. Dr Beard seems to have been flattered by her attentions, and did not discourage her advances, although there were never any improprieties between them.

One evening in September 1870, when Dr Beard was away, Christiana Edmunds came calling at his house in Grand Parade. Mrs Emily Beard was pleased to see her, and invited her through to the drawing room, where they joined the Beard family's elderly lodger. Christiana said that she had bought some chocolate creams for the children, and gave one to Emily Beard. She was immediately disgusted with its unpleasant, metallic taste, and left the room to spit it out. Christiana simply made her excuses and left the house. In the evening, Mrs Beard suffered from excessive salivation and diarrhoea. She told her husband of this incident, and he immediately suspected foul play. He knew that Christiana was in love with him, and realized that he had underestimated what she was capable of. Dr Beard challenged Christiana with attempting to poison his wife, and broke off all contact with her. He did not report her to the police, probably because he felt embarrassed about previously having encouraged their friendship.

To the warped mind of Christiana Edmunds, all she needed to do to recover her friendship with her favourite doctor was to prove that the attempt to poison Mrs Beard was not her fault. She recruited small boys to purchase chocolate creams at the shop of the prominent confectioner J.G. Maynard of Nos. 39–41 West Street [the shop no longer exists], lacing them with strychnine purchased from the chemist Isaac Garrett of 10 Queens Road [the shop is today a tobacconist's] under the pretext of needing poison to destroy some marauding cats, and then returning the chocolates to the confectioner under the pretext that they were the wrong ones. Through these means, poisoned chocolate creams were randomly introduced into the confectioner's stock, and eaten by members of the public. Although Christiana had made an experiment with the strychnine by killing a dog, her dosage of the poison seems to have been quite random: some people merely complained of an unpleasant metallic taste in the chocolates, and others became sick but recovered without any ill effects. A man named Charles Miller bought some chocolate creams at Maynard's shop. He ate some himself, but found them quite noxious. He gave one to his four-year-old nephew Sidney Albert Barker, who immediately became ill with violent convulsions; the luckless lad expired the same day.

There was a coroner's inquest on Sidney Albert Barker and the question was, of course, whether he had been deliberately or accidentally poisoned. Analysis of his stomach contents showed he had been poisoned with strychnine. Christiana Edmunds herself appeared at the inquest as a witness, claiming she had fallen ill after eating some of Maynard's chocolate creams; she had given the remaining chocolates to an analyst to be tested for poison, but he had found none. Both Maynard himself and the chocolate wholesaler Mr Ware denied any wrongdoing, and the coroner believed they were telling the truth, returning a verdict of accidental death. Although disappointed that her attempt to incriminate Maynard had failed, Christiana wrote a passionate letter to Dr Beard, but he told her not to write to him again, adding that he had shown all her letters to his wife.

Christiana Edmunds wrote three anonymous letters to the father of Sidney Albert Barker, urging him to take legal action against Maynard, but he ignored them. Disappointed with the metallic taste of the strychnine, which had prevented her from claiming further victims, she got hold of a quantity of arsenic, which she used to adulterate a number of cakes and fruit, which she sent to various people, Mrs Beard included, through the mail. The dim-witted doctor's wife did not find anything wrong with cakes sent to her with an anonymous note, but she re-wrapped the parcel, intending its contents for a nice Saturday treat for herself and the children. There was another poisoning panic in Brighton, with several people falling ill after eating cakes and savouries sent anonymously through the mail, although no person suffered any permanent ill effects. After this second attempt on the life of his wife, Dr Beard went to the police and told them all about his suspicion of Christiana Edmunds. Although she protested that she had been poisoned herself, she was arrested and brought up before the Brighton Police Court.

Dr Beard and Mrs Beard told all about their experiences with Christiana Edmunds, and the chemists who had sold her strychnine and arsenic were tracked down, as were the boys she had sent to buy chocolate creams at Maynard's shop. The newspapers were full of the Brighton poisoning epidemic, and Christiana was burnt in effigy by an angry mob. Since she could hardly get a fair trial at the local assizes, due to the massive local prejudice against her, she was tried at the Old Bailey in January 1872. Serjeant Ballantine prosecuted, and the evidence against the prisoner was solid enough for the jury to find her guilty of murdering Sidney Albert Barker. Baron Martin donned the black cap and sentenced her to death. She claimed to be pregnant, but a jury of matrons examined her and found that she was telling untruths. There was some degree of sympathy for Christiana Edmunds, however, since she came from a middle-class background, and since her mother had told all about the strong family history of insanity. After being examined by Sir William Gull and Dr William Orange, she was reprieved of the death sentence, due to insanity, and incarcerated at Broadmoor.

In July 1872, Christiana Edmunds was transferred to Broadmoor. On admission, she wore a large wig and a set of false teeth, and was quite heavily made up. Dr Orange found her vain and untruthful, and she was often disposed to tease the other patients to make them hysterical with fury. Christiana Edmunds never appeared obviously insane, and had no psychotic tendencies whatsoever, but she never seemed to regret, or fully understand, the crime for which she had been sentenced to death. At Broadmoor, she lived on for many years, an old woman who was still inordinately vain about her fading looks. In 1900, she was bedridden with a cold for a while, but eventually recovered. By 1901, the eyesight in her right eye had failed, and by 1906, she was barely capable of locomotion. When she died from 'senile decay' in 1907, a churlish obituary in the *Daily Mail* ridiculed her passion for wearing primitive wigs made out of odd ends of rope, and estimated that her keep in Broadmoor for more than 35 years had cost the State in excess of £1,000. By this time, her mother, brother and sister were all dead. As for Dr Beard, he had himself gone insane and was incarcerated in a lunatic asylum.

In the paranoid world of today, not many people would feel disposed to eat chocolates or cakes sent through the mail wrapped in a parcel from some anonymous 'benefactor'. Clearly, as judged by the serial poisonings caused by Christiana Edmunds, the Brighton people of 1871 had a more lackadaisical approach to adulterated confectionery, something that could have cost them more dearly if she had been able to calculate the dosage of her poisons with more acuity. Her choice of strychnine as her poison of choice was an unwise one, since its unpleasant metallic taste alerted all but the most young and foolhardy to its noxious qualities. Her change to arsenic makes good sense, from a toxicological point of view, and since she was once more able to get hold of a large stockpile of poison without any questions being asked, only her haphazard dosing of the poison, and sheer luck, saved Mrs Beard and her other intended victims from certain death. With her mixture of insanity, amorality and cunning, Christiana Edmunds was a dangerous woman indeed.

12. A Victorian Scholar and Murderer, 1871

John Selby Watson was born in humble circumstances in 1804, to poor Scottish parents, but his grandfather took care of him and made sure he received a good education. In 1838, at the age of 34, he graduated BA at Trinity College, Dublin, as one of the gold medallists in classics. He was ordained deacon in 1839 by the Bishop of Ely, but his clerical career made little progress. Like many a half-starved curate at the time, he took up teaching, at the Stockwell grammar school. In 1844, he reached one of the few highs of his miserable life when he was elected headmaster. Finally, he had a reasonably paid permanent position, with a good deal of leisure time to make his name as a scholar and author. Decades before, when a Dublin undergraduate, he had admired a young lady named Anne Armstrong. He wrote to her detailing his new-found prosperity in Stockwell, and asking for her hand in marriage. She turned out to still be available and although the letters from the 41-year-old suitor were about as romantic as those from a farmer negotiating to purchase a pig, she willingly agreed to marry him.

THE STOCKWELL TRAGEDY

REV J.S.WATSON

A portrait of John Selby Watson, from the *IPN*, 28 October 1871.

Once married, the life of John Selby Watson became one of ceaseless industry. Being a profound Latin scholar, he prepared a series of translations from various classical writers, which were published in Bohn's Classical Library. He also wrote some dull but worthy biographical studies, but success eluded him. It was said that only one of his books made a profit, of a few shillings. I have one of Watson's

Watson's house in Stockwell, from the *IPN*, 21 October 1871.

The murder scene, from the *IPN*, 28 October 1871.

books, *The Reasoning Power in Animals* from 1870, which contains some curious early descriptions of 'learned' and performing dogs, some of them culled from the work by Edward Jesse. 'Strict observation of justice among themselves is maintained by the dogs of Constantinople,' the veteran author assures us, but without providing any source for this singular statement.

John Selby Watson's wife was an irascible woman, who often insulted her Doctor-Dry-as-Dust of a husband, and ridiculed his failed literary career. For every year that went by, Watson became increasingly grumpy and morose. A demanding teacher and a strict disciplinarian,

Watson concealing the body, from the *IPN*, 28 October 1871.

he declared his opinion of his pupils' doggy Latin in very forthright terms, and flogged them mercilessly for any misdeed or shortcoming. As a result, the number of pupils dwindled alarmingly, and the school governors decided to get rid of this veteran headmaster, whose methods of teaching they considered quite outdated. After an angry confrontation, Watson was sacked, on the spot, in September 1870. Since his performance in recent years had been so very poor, he was not awarded any pension.

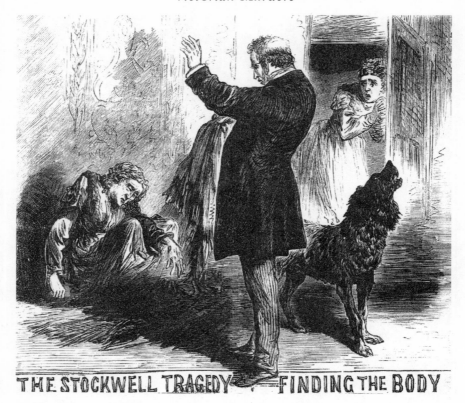

THE STOCKWELL TRAGEDY — FINDING THE BODY

Finding Mrs Watson's body, from the *IPN*, 21 October 1871.

John Selby Watson retired to the house he rented at 28 St Martin's Road in Stockwell, where he diligently beavered away at what he hoped would become his *magnum opus*, a multi-volume history of the Papacy until the Reformation. Poverty in old age was irksome to both the Watsons, and they had many angry quarrels. On 6 October 1871, after Mrs Watson had insulted her husband with some particularly bitter words, he angrily walked out of the room. He went to his library, where he kept a large old horse pistol. Bursting into the parlour, he struck Mrs Watson over the head with this implement, again and again, until she was dead. The room was liberally spattered with blood; a horrible sight for the frenzied old man as he recovered his senses and realized what he had just done. The impoverished old couple had only one servant, who was away at the time. After dragging the corpse to a small room next to the library, Watson pondered his future. Making plans to escape, he went out to order a large packing case, which he wanted to be air-tight and water-tight, for transportation of his wife's remains. But after brooding all night in the dark, empty house, he decided against becoming a trunk murderer. Instead, he wrote a long suicide note, admitting his crime. He gave instructions for the burial of his wife, and far more detailed instructions for the handling of his literary remains. He then took a dose of prussic acid, but the servant returned just in time to find him alive, since the dose had not been a fatal one.

At the trial of John Selby Watson, his counsel made use of the insanity defence, but various medical experts did not consider the old schoolmaster to be obviously deranged. Humanitarians, clergymen and Stockwell Old Boys wrote letters to save Watson from the gallows. In the end, he was found guilty of murder and was sentenced to death, but the sentence was commuted to penal servitude for life. There was much writing in the newspapers, and a long leading article in the *Journal of Mental Science*, about this singular case. Was it really right to sentence this old man, whose previous life had been exemplary, and who had been so 'outrageously provoked' by his termagant wife, to spend the remainder of his life in prison? What the 'provocation' amounted to was not detailed, but the couple were childless, and Watson probably impotent.

Twelve years later, on an early summer morning in 1884, John Selby Watson stirred to get out of bed, perhaps after a pleasant dream about getting to work early on his translation of Cornelius Nepos, but since he was a bookless inmate of Parkhurst Prison, he fell from his hammock, struck his head hard against the floor, and died.

13. The Park Lane Murder

In 1872, the French widow Marie Caroline Riel was living at the very desirable address of 13 Park Lane, London. As the long-term mistress of the Earl of Lucan, of Balaclava notoriety, she enjoyed independent means; the elderly peer liked to visit her from time to time, presumably for some hanky-panky. Since Madame Riel was a haughty, short-tempered woman, her servants had a hard time; they were sacked at regular intervals, and new recruits hired to replace them. In March 1872, Madame Riel was waited on by the dim-witted maid Eliza Watts and the sturdy, 29-year-old Belgian Marguerite Dixblanc, who doubled as cook and general servant. Marguerite was a lazy young woman of dubious honesty; she liked to drink beer and wine, and to listen at doors. After three months of service, Madame Riel decided that Marguerite must go. In an angry confrontation, Madame Riel and her daughter told Marguerite that she would receive just one week's wages, in the French tradition, since her performance had been so very poor. Marguerite, who had expected a month's wages, was very annoyed by this excessive thrift; exactly how annoyed, Madame Riel would soon find out to her detriment.

About ten days later, Madame Riel caught Marguerite idling in the kitchen. Since she suspected her of pilfering from the wine cellar, there was another angry scene, which ended with Marguerite punching her employer hard in the face, strangling her to death with a rope, and throwing the body into a large dustbin. She then dusted herself off and rejoined her fellow servant. The foolish Eliza did not find it odd that Madame Riel 'had gone away for a few days', as Marguerite described it, leaving her dog behind. Left to their own devices, the two jolly servants ate, drank and made merry, disposing of kegs of beer and choice bottles of wine from Lord Lucan's cellars. The devious Marguerite stole Madame Riel's keys, opened her safe, and purloined £80 in sovereigns and five-pound notes, before absconding to Paris.

The discovery of Madame Riel's body, from the *IPN*, 20 April 1872.

THE PARK-LANE MURDER: DISCOVERY OF THE BODY OF MADAME RIEL.

Another view of the discovery of the body, from the *Penny Illustrated Paper*, 20 April 1872.

Inspector Nathaniel Druscovitch, the Scotland Yard's international expert, went to Paris to join the hunt for Marguerite Dixblanc, the Park Lane murderess. She was soon traced to an address in the Rue St Denis, and taken into custody by the French police. Had Marguerite made a determined dash to the United States, as she had originally planned, she just might have got away, but she dawdled too long with friends in Paris. Some of the stolen money was found in her luggage. After some French obstructionism, Marguerite Dixblanc was extradited to face trial at the Old Bailey. Things were looking far from rosy for the Park Lane murderess. She did not deny doing away with Madame Riel, but asserted that her mistress had treated her to a severe tongue-lashing, saying that she would end up as a prostitute, and that there had been no premeditation. Marguerite was quite an ugly, brutal-looking woman, and many people suspected that she had intended to murder and rob Madame Riel all along.

Marguerite Dixblanc, the Park Lane murderess, and some features from her career, from the *IPN*, 27 April 1872.

During the trial, Lord Lucan had to suffer the indignity of being cross-examined about Madame Riel's various peculiarities. Displaying the same stubbornness and inertia he had once shown in the field of Balaclava, he grudgingly admitted that she had always been of a hasty and fierce temper. The question whether the crime of Marguerite Dixblanc was to be considered as premeditated depended very much on a letter found with her Paris friends. In this brief missive, Marguerite announced her intention to return to Paris, before going on to America. It was dated 6 April, the day *before* the murder, but postmarked April 8. Marguerite claimed to have misdated the letter, but the prosecution suspected that she had dated it correctly, although it had missed the last Saturday post. In spite of the massive prejudice against Marguerite Dixblanc, a disloyal servant who had murdered one of her betters, the jury gave her the benefit of doubt and recommended her to mercy. She ended up being sentenced to penal servitude for life.

At the time of the 1881 Census, Marguerite Dixblanc, aged 37, was a prisoner at the Female Convict Prison at Knaphall, near Woking. Her conduct and industry were very good, her bodily health good, and her mental health sound. The following year, in June 1882, she asked permission to see her aged parents, to atone for the sorrow she had caused them; this favour seems to have been allowed her, although a marginal note on her petition, kept in the Home Office file on her case, said 'She richly deserved to be hung.' In 1889, she petitioned for her release, claiming that she had respectable friends to receive her, but this petition was turned down. At the time of the 1891 Census, she was still at the Female Convict Prison, now aged 47. It was not until February 1893

Marguerite Dixblanc and the jailer, from the *IPN*, 11 May 1872.

that she was finally released, after nearly 21 years in prison. Nothing is known about her later activities, although it has been generally presumed that she returned to obscurity in her native land.

As for the murder house, 13 Park Lane, it was still there in 1906, when George R. Sims published his *Mysteries of Modern London*. Sims, a connoisseur of London's murder houses, could report that it had been restored and enlarged: 'A lady comes out with a lap-dog, from the premises where not long ago a woman lay strangled, and from which a murderess fled.' But since that time, No. 13 has become a casualty of the frenetic hotel-building along this famous London avenue. It is a pity it is no longer standing today, since some of the individuals now living in Park Lane could have been worthy recipients of a proper haunting, to make them mend their immoral and money-grubbing ways. What if, inside their luxury kitchen, two shadowy figures in Victorian dress would appear, struggling fiercely before the ghostly Marguerite put an end to her desperately screaming mistress …

14. The Whitechapel Road Murder, 1874

Henry Wainwright was a respectable and successful East End businessman, trading as a brush manufacturer, with one factory at 84 Whitechapel Road, and another at No. 215 across the road, not far from where the Whitechapel tube station is today. He lived at 40 Tredegar Square, Bow, [the house still stands], with his wife and four children. Well into his thirties, Henry was something of a ladies' man, seducing various actresses and domestic servants with gusto. A rather good-looking, bushy-bearded cove, he had vague thespian ambitions himself, and his sonorous recitations of Thomas Hood's *The Dream of Eugene Aram* attracted some notice in Whitechapel theatrical circles.

Henry Wainwright having some fun with the girls, from the pamphlet *Sensational Crimes and Trials*.

Henry Wainwright shoots Harriet Lane, from *Famous Crimes Past & Present*.

One of Henry Wainwright's many mistresses was the 19-year-old Harriet Lane. He had met her in 1871, and later set her up in various lodgings, allowing her £5 per week. In the coming years, Harriet gave

Henry Wainwright having murdered Harriet Lane, from the pamphlet *Sensational Crimes and Trials*.

birth to two children, both likely to have been fathered by Henry. But in spite of having a wife and family, and keeping a pretty young mistress as well, this bushy-bearded East End Lothario kept 'playing the field'. Harriet became increasingly annoyed by his pursuit of various women associated with the stage. Things went from bad to worse when she discovered that Henry kept another permanent mistress, the young ballet dancer Alice Day.

In the meantime, Henry Wainwright's financial position had markedly deteriorated. He had inherited the brush-making business from his father, and was not capable of running it successfully. His immoral and expensive private life, supporting two mistresses, cannot have helped either. The creditors were moving in, and Henry feared bankruptcy. He had to move his family from the elegant house in Tredegar Square to humble lodgings in Chingford. In September 1874, Henry realized that he needed to solve the problem of his mistress Harriet Lane. Not only was she expensive to keep, but he no longer had any use for her, preferring Alice Day. Furthermore, Harriet kept making angry scenes, particularly when drunk, infuriated by the caddish behaviour of her inconstant lover. On 10 September 1874, Henry invited Harriet to the brush factory at

Henry Wainwright tries to persuade the constable not to open the parcel containing Harriet's mangled remains, from *Famous Crimes Past & Present*.

215 Whitechapel Road. He shot her in the head, cut her throat, and buried her body in a shallow grave underneath the floorboards in the rearmost workshop of the long, narrow brush factory.

THE WHITECHAPEL TRAGEDY: SKETCHES BY OUR SPECIAL ARTIST.
(SEE "THE POLICE ON THE TRAIL." PAGE 196.)

The murder house, the Hen and Chickens, the workshop and som eof the major players in the case, from the *Penny Illustrated Paper*, 25 September 1874.

Not many people missed Harriet Lane, and Henry told them that she had gone off to continental Europe with a friend of his. But although he had secured the permanent silence of his former mistress, Henry's situation in life remained a far from pleasant one. In November 1874, the factory at 84 Whitechapel Road burnt down, but the insurers refused to pay out since they knew about Henry's straitened financial situation and suspected arson. In June 1875, when Henry finally went bankrupt, a solicitor named Behrend took over the lease of the house at 215 Whitechapel Road. Some tenants moved into the house, and in the hot summer months, they complained about a very foul smell that seemed to emanate from the rear paint shop. Henry blamed it on some rotting cabbages, but the tenants moved away, for good.

When Behrend advertised 215 Whitechapel Road for sale, Henry realized he had to act fast. The new owner of the house would not be as easily fobbed off regarding the foul smell emanating from the rear workshop. His brother Thomas, who had previously impersonated Harriet's new suitor, with whom she was supposed to have gone to Europe, was again ready to help. Like his brother, Thomas was a careless businessman, and an ironmonger's shop that he had kept in an old pub called the Hen & Chickens at 54 Borough High Street had just failed. Just as the cunning Henry had kept a key to 215 Whitechapel Road, Thomas had kept the keys to the Hen & Chickens. The old pub had deep cellars, very suitable for hiding unsavoury relics of past crimes.

On 10 September 1875, Henry Wainwright let himself into the empty house at 215 Whitechapel Road, lifted the floorboards in the rear workshop, and unearthed the remains of poor Harriet. They were surprisingly well preserved since the careless murderer had buried them in chloride of lime, which acts as a disinfectant and preservative, rather than in quicklime. It was tough work for Henry to dismember the body, using a large chopper, and pack the various body parts into two large canvas parcels. The following day, Henry went to a former workman of his named Alfred Stokes, and asked him 'Will you carry a parcel for me, Stokes?' 'Yes, with the greatest of pleasure!' the polite labourer replied. They entered No. 215 through the rear entrance, accessed through a covered alleyway called Vine Court, leading off Whitechapel Road. This took them straight into the workshop where Henry had unearthed and packaged Harriet's remains. He took the lighter of the two parcels and let Stokes carry the heavy one. But they had not got very far when Stokes complained that the parcel was very heavy, and that it stank terribly. Henry did what he should have done in the first place, namely to get a cab. But when he went off to the cab rank, Stokes could not resist having a look inside the parcel. To his horror, he saw a severed human hand and wrist, among other body parts. When Henry arrived with the cab, he loaded both parcels into it, thanked Stokes for his troubles, and went off.

Alfred Stokes was no fool, however, and he realized some terrible crime must have been committed. He ran after the cab, and at the crossing of Aldgate and Leadenhall Street, he tried to convince two policemen to spot it, but they thought him a madman. A few streets away, Stokes saw the cab stop; Henry had spotted Alice Day walking along the street, and he invited her for a ride! As they went along, Henry puffed hard at a large cigar to hide the nauseating stench emanating from the two large parcels. As cool as a cucumber, this extraordinary murderer kept up a light conversation with his mistress. The panting Stokes kept pursuing the cab as it crossed the Thames via London Bridge, and finally pulled up in Borough High Street, just outside the Hen & Chickens. But just as Henry unloaded his two parcels, Stokes found a police constable, and managed to get him interested in the cab and its gruesome load. In spite of Henry's protestations, the parcels were opened, and various pieces of Harriet Lane's dismembered body tumbled out onto the pavement of Borough High Street.

Nothing was found to incriminate Alice Day, who had enjoyed such a very sinister ride with her bushy-bearded lover and the remains of her predecessor in his affections, and she was released. Thomas Wainwright was sentenced to seven years in prison as an accessory after the fact. He was fortunate to have an alibi for the day when Harriet Lane disappeared since there was speculation that his help might have come in very handy for Henry, with regard to lifting the heavy floorboards. George R. Sims even speculated that Thomas Wainwright was the true author of the crime, and that Henry was an innocent man who took the blame for his brother. There was a third brother named William, another brush manufacturer, who committed suicide after a drinking spree in 1892.

But the evidence against Henry Wainwright was rock solid: the revolver bullet in what remained of Harriet's brain, the grave in the rear workshop of 215 Whitechapel Road, the spade and chopper found in there, and of course the mangled remains of poor Harriet herself. Found guilty of murder at the Old Bailey on 22 November 1875 and sentenced to death, he was taken to the condemned cell at Newgate. During his final night in there, he might well have been pondering some verses in Hood's *The Dream of Eugene Aram*, which he had once been so fond of reciting:

> My head was like an ardent coal,
>   My heart as solid ice
> My wretched, wretched soul, I knew,
>   Was at the Devil's price;
> A dozen times I groan'd: the dead
>   Had never groan'd but twice.

And now, from forth the frowning sky,
  From the Heaven's topmost height,
I heard a voice—the awful voice
  Of the blood-avenging sprite:
'Thou guilty man! take up thy dead
  And hide it from my sight!'

But still, it must be said that Henry Wainwright died like a man. On 21 December, the day set aside for his execution at Newgate, he calmly smoked one of his large cigars, before walking up to the scaffold. He glared at the people standing nearby, exclaiming, 'Come to see a man die, have you, you curs?', before the executioner, Marwood, pulled down the hood and launched the Whitechapel Road murderer into eternity.

Henry Wainwright was buried in the old Newgate burial ground, but when Newgate was being demolished in 1902, his remains were unearthed and taken to a cemetery in Ilford, with those of Amelia Dyer, Thomas Neill Cream, Mrs Pearcey, and other notorious criminals. The bullets inside Harriet Lane's skull, some skin and hair samples from her body, and the cigar Henry Wainwright had been smoking when he was arrested, were deposited in Scotland Yard's Black Museum, with the spade and chopper used to dismember the body. These interesting relics of the case are all said to have been lost or stolen over the years; for what was supposed to be a secure museum, accessed by professionals only, the Black Museum has certainly guarded its relics of criminal history with blameworthy carelessness. The contemporary press made much of Henry Wainwright and the Whitechapel Tragedy. The *IPN* published Henry's portrait and a drawing depicting the horrified policeman emptying the parcel full of Harriet's body parts into Borough High Street. Not to be outdone, the *Penny Illustrated Paper* published a drawing of the murder house, showing it as a three-storey building at 215 Whitechapel Road. To the east is a taller house, to the west a lower workshop marked 'Carr' and numbered 216 [and quite possibly also 217 on the other side of the sign]. The Whitechapel Road front of Henry Wainwright's murder house is no longer standing, but the workshop where he stored the mutilated remains of Harriet Lane still exists, and it can be seen from Vine Court nearby. Its position fits perfectly with the rear of the former No. 215, which became No. 132 after the renumbering of the houses. Although neither is inhabited, nor used for storage, the workshop is well looked after, presumably by some person who knows its terrible secret.

15. The Blackburn Sweeney Todd, 1876

On 28 March 1876, seven-year-old Emily Agnes Holland told her friends at St Alban's School in Blackburn that she had just met a nice man, for whom she would run some errands. She came home from school and went out to play, but then she was nowhere to be seen. After her father, the mechanic James Holland, of 110 Moss Street, had gone to the police, the relevant parts of Blackburn were thoroughly searched, but without anything interesting coming to light. On 30 March, Mrs Alice White, of 73 Bastwell Terrace, was alerted by a neighbour's child, who had found a strange parcel in a field, wrapped in newspaper. A dog was sniffing around nearby, as if interested in its contents. Mrs White was horrified when she opened the parcel and found the trunk of a small girl, the head, arms and legs having all been severed by the murderer.

An extensive search was made, in the hope of finding the remaining body parts, but without any success. However, a man named Richard Fairclough had seen a man behaving suspiciously in a lane at Lower Cunliffe; he later found a parcel containing two severed legs, perfectly matching the trunk discovered earlier. Dr William Maitland, the local police surgeon, examined the body parts. He found evidence that the little girl had been violated before she was murdered. A strong, sharp knife had been used for the mutilation. The trunk and the legs had been wrapped in old copies of the *Preston Herald*, and it interested Dr Maitland that

A portrait of the barber Fish, from *Famous Crimes Past & Present*.

Morgan and the Clumber spaniel rush upstairs, from *Famous Crimes Past & Present*.

the newspapers were covered with hair. He was curious to find that it was most likely human hair, of different lengths, colours and textures, all mingled together. Now who would have access to the hair of many different people? Was the murderer a barber?

The inquest on the remains of the child was opened on 31 March, before the coroner Mr Hargreaves, at the Blackburn Town Hall. Since the murder and mutilation of a blameless little girl had outraged the Blackburn locals, a large and excited crowd gathered outside. James and Elizabeth Holland, the parents of Emily, identified the body as hers, from a mark on the back, although the head was still missing. Alice White and Richard Fairclough described how they had found the body parts. Mary Ellen Eccles, a little girl attending the same school as Emily Holland, had heard her say she was going for half-an-ounce of tobacco for a man she had met in the street. This individual had worn a billycock hat, a mixture cloth coat, a yellow waistcoat, dirty fustian trousers, and wooden clogs. Mr Potts, the Chief Constable, said that in his opinion, the murderer

Morgan sniffs at the fireplace, from *Famous Crimes Past & Present*.

was most probably a tramp, but the coroner objected that tramps do not often carry newspapers around with them. Three tramps had already been arrested on suspicion of involvement, and later discharged. The inquest was adjourned for a week.

The police had two witnesses who had seen the murderer: two little girls aged eight and nine, who vaguely described him as a scruffy-looking tramp. A man named Charles Taylor, a vagabond who had been begging in the Moss Street area of Blackburn, roughly matched their description, so he was arrested, and the police could proudly announce that they had a suspect in custody. Due to the suspicions of Dr Maitland, the police also took an interest in the local barbers. It was noted that one of them, William Fish, of 3 Moss Street, had a pile of old *Preston Heralds* in a corner. Fish was a man of low repute, who had been in a workhouse as an adolescent, and who had two previous convictions for larceny; he

A portrait of Fish, and other scenes from the Blackburn Murder, from the *IPN*, May 6 1876.

was 25 years old, and married with two children. Although Fish was not charged with murder, the local residents had strong suspicions about him. Fish's business boomed as a result since many people came to see him as a curiosity. As the singing barber warbled 'Tomorrow will be Friday, and we've caught no fish today …', a chorus of street guttersnipes outside sang back 'Yah boo! Barber, barber, who killed the girl?' and 'Emily, Emily, who murdered little Emily?' When a woman entered his shop, to stand staring at him, the startled barber asked what she had come for. 'To see a murderer!' she responded. In the end, Fish had to ask for police protection against the angry locals who kept harassing him.

When the coroner's inquest was resumed on 7 April, the tramp Charles Taylor had just been discharged due to the lack of evidence against him. Several schoolgirls had seen the man who lured Emily away, but none of them could describe him properly. The tobacconist Frederick Cox testified that he had sold a little girl, matching the description of Emily Holland, half-an-ounce of tobacco on the day she disappeared. The inquest was once more adjourned. The police kept looking for tramps, and another number of local vagabonds were arrested, although nothing could be found to incriminate them. After several weeks had gone by, the newspapers began to express critical sentiments: were the police entirely baffled, and would the murderer escape scot-free? But the Blackburn police found an unexpected ally: a man named Peter Taylor, of 72 Nelson Street, Preston, who was the handler of two dogs: the half-bred bloodhound Morgan, and also a clumber spaniel. These two animals were employed to search the area where the trunk and legs had been found, in the hope of finding the arms and head, but without the desired result.

Some bright individual suggested that the dogs should also be employed to search the two barber's shops in Moss Street. In the first shop, nothing incriminating was found, so the animals were taken to Fish's shop at No. 3. Morgan led the way into the back shop, where he stood scenting by the door to the stairs. When the door was opened, both dogs galloped upstairs. Morgan first sniffed at some clothes in the back room, but he then ran into the front room with a howl, sniffing at the fireplace and thrusting his head up it. 'There is something here!' cried Mr Taylor, and after the dog had been pulled away, Emily Holland's burnt skull and arms were found thrust up the chimney, wrapped in her remaining clothes. This was the earliest instance in Britain in which a dog was instrumental in solving a murder.

Fish initially denied all involvement in the murder, but he eventually made a full confession. After abducting and raping Emily Holland in the room above the barber's shop, he had cut her throat with a razor, and dismembered the body. He had burnt the head and arms in the downstairs fireplace, and tried to dispose of them up the chimney in the upstairs room. Witnesses among the locals had seen a particularly large fire in the empty barber's shop, as the murderer tried to destroy the remains of poor little Emily; it was also remarked, with horror and disapproval, that the Blackburn miscreant had later shaved several people with the very same razor he had used to cut Emily's throat. No motive for the murder ever emerged, apart from perverted lust; Fish denied premeditation, but he was probably lying, since a certain degree of planning had definitely gone into the plans for the disposal of the body.

As Fish was languishing in prison, rumours were buzzing about his parentage, since the good burghers of Blackburn thought that such a dastardly murderer and child-ravisher must surely be of foreign birth. Some thought his real name was Fiesch or Fieschi, and speculated that he might be related to Giuseppe Marco Fieschi, who had tried to assassinate King Louis Philippe of France. The chapbook *Betrayed by Bloodhounds* contained an even spicier version of the antecedents of 'the monster known as William Fish, the fiendish violator and diabolical murderer of the poor child, Emily Holland'. It was confidently stated that his maternal grandfather was one Jacopo Fiesch, a Corsican who was exiled after taking part in a Bonapartist plot, and went to live in London. His widow remarried a wicked Jew named Matamoros, and they took care of the little daughter Marguerite Fiesch, alias Margaret Fish. Matamoros forced Margaret to marry the Italian anarchist Felice Orsini, who was later guillotined for attempting to blow up Napoleon III and his Empress in their carriage. William Fish, their only son, born at Derwen in 1850, had been forced to enter the workhouse after his mother had died from a broken heart. Unamused by these fantasies gaining credence among the locals, Mrs Elizabeth Fish spoke out to a representative of the *Blackburn Times*: her husband was as English as they came, and the son of the block printer William Fish, born at Brinscall near Chorley and dead since ten years ago. The murderer William Fish Jr was born at Derwen on 1 April 1851 and christened by the old vicar Robert Cross, known as the 'Derwen Bishop'. Far from being an only child, he had two brothers and two sisters alive, and his father's twin brother was also still living, at the age of 75.

William Fish, the Demon Barber of Blackburn, was charged with murder and committed to stand trial at the Lancaster Assizes; he was found guilty and was hanged at Kirkdale Prison, Liverpool, on 14 August 1876. There was as little pity or sympathy for a creature of his description back in 1876 as there would have been today, and there was jubilation in Blackburn as the detested child murderer died. Fish's final words was a public-spirited appeal to other would-be murderers:

> I wish to tell you, while you have a chance, to lead a new life. You can see my bad end through breaking off Sunday school, and through bad companions. Those were happy days when I attended Sunday school.

After I neglected it I went from bad to worse, and so I have been brought to this sad end. If I had my time over again I would lead a different life. It is not too late for you to mend. Avoid those bad cheap journals on which I wasted so much spare time. May we meet in heaven, through God's mercy!

As for the half-bloodhound Morgan, he was the hero of the day. After the police had been entirely baffled, he had brought Fish to justice. Although the dog had been handled by Mr Taylor during its crime-fighting exploits, and although it lived with a beerhouse-keeper named Thomas Bailey, its rightful owner was Mr James Parkinson, a lamp and oil merchant in Church Street, Preston. And indeed, in a swift dawn raid, Mr Parkinson came to call at Bailey's beerhouse, with a troop of assistants, and secured the ownership of Morgan. He explained to the newspaper journalists that the dog was his: it had been brought up with the greatest of care, and when Parkinson got dressed, he could employ Morgan as his butler, since the dog could fetch his clothes and boots from the wardrobe. Morgan had always been a highly-strung dog and, in his younger years, he had been disposed to attack and bite tramps and other scruffily dressed people. After Morgan had bitten a certain Mr Lamb, Parkinson gave the dog to a man named Spencer, a resident of Bolton, for the animal to be re-educated to abolish his vicious tendencies. Spencer had illicitly sold the dog to a druggist named Smith for 10s, however, and Morgan had then been handed over to a farmer, and to the beerhouse-keeper Bailey, who had been taking care of the dog for seven months.

Mr Parkinson was offered £200 for Morgan, but he turned this offer down, instead taking £6 per evening from a Blackburn theatre, where the dog was exhibited before the curious. Morgan was petted by the people of Blackburn and Preston, and many stories were told about his wonderful sagacity. Mr Parkinson could employ his dog to fetch various objects from his warehouse to his house, he boasted, and if he had dropped a glove in the market-place, he could send Morgan to retrieve it. A letter to the *Dundee Courier* praised the public-spirited Mr Parkinson and his sagacious dog: 'I also hope that some photographer will give us a picture portrait of Morgan and that he (Morgan) will get a silver collar with an inscription thereon giving day and date when he, with unwonted display of sagacity, handed over that bloodthirsty Fish to justice.' When the beerhouse-keeper Bailey became aware of Morgan's extensive fame, and the dog's value to the showmen, he took Mr Parkinson to court at the Manchester Assizes, but Parkinson emerged as the undisputed owner of the famous dog.

After exhibiting Morgan for several months, and milking the valuable animal for all he was worth, Mr Parkinson gave the dog into the care of Mr Spencer, who appears to have been an expert dog-handler. In 1881, when the embalmed body of the Earl of Crawford and Balcarres had been stolen from the family mausoleum in Dunecht near Aberdeen, Mr Spencer and Morgan were called in to help search for it. Mr Spencer told a newspaper reporter that apart from his heroism in Blackburn, bringing the murderer Fish to justice, Morgan had once tracked a pair of poachers for a distance of 17 miles, being instrumental in capturing them. He was optimistic with regard to finding the Earl's kidnapped body: if it was not too deeply buried, the sagacious hound would find it. The Earl's body was recovered by more conventional means, however, and a local poacher was imprisoned for stealing it.

In June 1884, the body of eight-year-old Mary Cooper was found in shrubbery in Albert Park, Middlesbrough. She had been sexually assaulted, and her throat had been cut. Inspector Swanson, of Scotland Yard, who was put in charge of the case, suggested the celebrated Morgan should again be called in as an auxiliary crime-fighter. This time, Mr Parkinson's son-in-law handled the dog, which was transported from Preston to Middlesbrough on the railway. When led to the shrubbery where the body had been found, Morgan gave a howl, before sniffing around with interest, and seemingly following several tracks. Nothing valuable came of this experiment, however, and the murderer of Mary Cooper was never found. In 1888, when the newspapers discussed the employment of bloodhounds in the hunt for the elusive Jack the Ripper, Morgan's great feat back in 1876 was mentioned more, but by this time, the celebrated Preston half-bloodhound had himself long since expired.

16. The Great Bravo Mystery, 1876

In a search for London's greatest murder mystery, the case of the young barrister Charles Bravo, who was poisoned in 1876, has much in its favour. It concerns wealthy and socially prominent people living in a grand Balham country house, there is a multitude of potential suspects, and the moral standards of the people involved leave much to be desired. Such a spicy tale of love, sex and murder in Victorian London has attracted the attention of many authors, whose analysis of the mystery has been wildly divergent.

As a young girl, Florence Campbell seemed to have everything going for her. Good-looking and vivacious, she was born into a rich Scots landowning family. In 1864, she married a handsome young officer, Captain Alexander Ricardo, whose family was also very wealthy. The problem was that Ricardo was an alcoholic, who drank like the proverbial fish, particularly after he had left the army. Florence left him after he had beaten her up in a drunken rage, and returned to her parents. Although she said she would not return to her cad of a husband under any circumstances, they persuaded her to become an inpatient at the Malvern hydrotherapeutic establishment of Dr James Manby Gully.

James Gully was a fashionable society doctor, known for his excellent bedside manner rather than his diagnostic skill or prominence as a medical scientist. He was a proponent of the 'water cure' for various

Father Joseph
"He was not at all a man likely to commit suicide"

Mrs Campbell
"I thought she entertained an extraordindiry infatuation for Dr Gully"

Mrs Cox
"He said Mrs Cox I have taken poison for Dr Gully dont tell Florence"

Dr Gully
"I thought he was the greatest hydropathic doctor in the world" *Mrs Cox*

Mrs Bravo

Mr C. Bravo

All the major players in the Bravo drama, from the *Penny Illustrated Paper*, August 5 1876.

Two contemporary sketches of Charles and Florence Bravo.

diseases. In the Malvern hydro, the patients could look forward to lengthy baths, and plenty of water to drink. Present-day medical science would suggest that the benefit of the 'water cure' was largely that the florid, hard-drinking patients were fed a light and easily digestible diet, and not allowed any alcohol. Dr Gully gave the impression of being a solid, reliable family man, and a good father to his brood of children. There was a Mrs Gully, but she was much older than him, and he had put her in a home in Brighton.

When Dr Gully met Florence Ricardo, he was in his mid-sixties, thus old enough to be her grandfather. A short, sturdy, bald man, he was nothing much to look at but, nevertheless, it did not take long for this extraordinary practitioner to seduce his beautiful young patient. He arranged to become her legal guardian, and she lived openly as his mistress. When Alexander Ricardo dropped dead from vomiting blood, Florence inherited £40,000, an enormous fortune in those days. She made use of this money to purchase the lease of a fine mansion in Balham, known as The Priory. The besotted Dr Gully bought another property nearby, so that he could continue to keep an eye on his favourite patient. Florence employed a full staff of servants at The Priory, and also got herself a lady companion, a rather furtive-looking widow named Jane Cox, who served her with commendable loyalty. When Florence got pregnant after some anti-contraceptive mishap, Dr Gully performed an abortion in her bedroom at The Priory, with Mrs Cox acting as nurse.

Mrs Cox gives evidence before the coroner's jury.

In the meantime, Florence's respectable parents were becoming seriously worried about their daughter's immoral conduct. Her affair with Gully was widely known, and her reputation in society suffered as a result. And indeed, Florence was beginning to tire of her elderly lover, particularly as she had met a more promising swain, the young barrister Charles Bravo. An intelligent, cultured gentleman who was the same age as Florence, he was a vast improvement with regard to looks and general vigour, compared with the aging doctor. It did not take Florence long to

Florence Bravo,
from the *IPN*,
September 28 1878.

marry Charlie Bravo, and leave her favourite practitioner high and dry.
Gully was very displeased about losing his dear Florence, but there was
nothing he could do. Since their affair was quite well-known in society,
Florence confessed to Charlie, who took the news quite well. Indeed, he
promised to give up his own long-time mistress if Florence never saw
Gully again.

But Charlie Bravo gradually showed a more unpleasant side of his
personality. A male chauvinist even by the standards of the time, he
wanted to be master in his own house, The Priory, although Florence
had actually purchased the property. He had a strong sexual appetite
and insisted on Florence being 'available' at all times, even after she had
suffered a miscarriage. Charlie was remarkably mean and avaricious,
and Florence must have suspected that he had married her for the money.
He made himself obnoxious by insisting on domestic economy, and
dismissing some of the servants. One of them, the coachman George
Griffiths, who very much disliked being sacked from his comfortable
job, was overheard cursing Mr Bravo, and predicting that he would not
live for very long. Florence was becoming fearful that Charlie's threat to
dismiss also her loyal friend Mrs Cox was not an empty one.

On 18 April 1876, Charlie Bravo wanted to take a ride around the
grounds of The Priory, but the horse bolted with him, and he returned
home very shaken and exhausted. He ordered the maid Mary Ann

Bedford Hotel, Balham.
The Royal Standard Series

A postcard posted in 1904, showing the Bedford Hotel, where the coroner's inquest on Charles Bravo was held.

Keeber to prepare a hot bath for him to recover from his ride, and it is an illustration of both his parsimony and his defective sense of hygiene that he told her to leave the dirty water in the tub, for use the following morning. By dinnertime, Charlie had recovered enough to eat a three-course meal, and drink four glasses of Burgundy from the decanter. He was still in a truculent mood, after having received an obnoxious letter from his stepfather, about his unsuccessful gambling on the Stock Exchange. Conversation was minimal, and Florence and Mrs Cox sat gloomily watching Charlie puffing hard on his pipe. Although she had drunk champagne with her luncheon, and although she and Mrs Cox had polished off two bottles of sherry between them at dinner, Florence ordered a glass of sweet white wine. When going to bed, she wanted another tumbler of white wine and water, and Charlie complained about her incessant tippling. All grew quiet at The Priory, until Charlie Bravo came lurching out from his bedroom, screaming 'Florence! Hot water!' in a terrible voice.

The maid Mary Ann Keeber clearly heard Charlie Bravo cry out. Too timid to dare to enter her master's bedroom, she knocked at Florence's bedroom instead. Surprised that no one answered the knock, she opened the door herself, to find Florence asleep in bed, and Mrs Cox sitting knitting by the fire. When Mary Ann explained that Mr Bravo had been taken ill, Mrs Cox accompanied her into his bedroom. They found him standing by the open window, vomiting spasmodically. He then turned and fell, but Mrs Cox managed to break his fall. Seeing that he was clearly very ill, she ordered Mary Ann to fetch mustard and hot water, and to make sure that the coachman was sent to fetch a doctor. Mary Ann herself took the initiative to wake up Mrs Bravo, who she had seen in bed, seemingly comatose. As soon as the drunken Florence understood that Charlie was ill, she leapt out of bed and insisted that another doctor, who lived closer to Balham, should also be fetched. The medical team was later reinforced by Mr Royes Bell, a surgeon who was a friend of Charlie Bravo's, and the distinguished physician Dr George Johnson, who took charge of the case. The volatile Florence made various far-fetched diagnostic suggestions: the ride on the bolting horse might have upset Charlie's constitution, he might have suffered a fainting fit, or he might have eaten something that disagreed with him. But it was clear to the experienced doctors that this was a case of poisoning. Either Charlie Bravo had taken poison himself, or some person had made a determined attempt to murder him.

The question was which poison had been used, and here the doctors were in a quandary. Mrs Cox told one of them that she thought Charlie might have drunk chloroform, but the doctors did not believe her, since there were signs that a strong irritant poison had been used. Mrs Cox did not tell the doctors that a sample of the patient's vomit was available outside the window, and she made sure that his bloodstained nightshirt was thrown away and exchanged for a new one. When poor Charlie passed some bloodstained stools, she ascribed the effect to him drinking red wine with his dinner!

When Charlie Bravo regained consciousness, helped by the various ministrations from the doctors, he denied taking any poison. Although he had rubbed his gums with some laudanum for toothache, he had not swallowed any. Even when harshly spoken to and reminded that if he denied attempting suicide, suspicion might fall on some person accused of murdering him, the dying man still denied having swallowed any poison. Mrs Cox then told Royes Bell that before the doctors had arrived, Charlie had confided in her that he had taken poison! The angry surgeon shouted at her for not telling any person about this vital fact earlier, but when confronted with her statement, Charlie again stoutly denied having attempted to destroy himself. In spite of the celebrated physician Sir William Gull being called in as a last resort, Charlie Bravo died after two-and-a-half days of agony.

The autopsy and forensic analysis showed that Charlie Bravo had been poisoned by tartrate of antimony. This corrosive substance had literally eaten his intestines away, and it is a testimony to his strong constitution that he had been able to linger for more than two days. At first it was suspected that the poison had been administered through the Burgundy that Charlie had drunk with his dinner, but since antimony makes wine go cloudy, and since its effect sets in within 15 minutes, this could not be the case. Although Charlie had drunk four glasses of wine, his health had appeared fine until he reached his bedroom. Since it was his habit to drink thirstily from a large carafe of water before going to bed, and since no other suitable receptacle for the poison was detected, the doctors suspected that the antimony had been mixed with the water in this carafe. The only drawback to this theory was that one of the doctors had himself swigged from this very decanter, without any ill effect! Clearly some person, probably the poisoner, must have emptied, rinsed, and then re-filled it?

The police investigation of the mysterious murder of Charlie Bravo, led by Detective Chief Inspector Clarke, made disappointingly little headway. Mrs Cox gave nothing away, and the police did not think that Florence Bravo appeared to be a guilty woman. There was a coroner's inquest on Charles Bravo, held privately in the dining room at The Priory, which returned an open verdict. This suited many of the people involved in the case but the problem was that the active and scandal-mongering press had found out about some of the most sensational issues, such as Florence's affair with Dr Gully, and the role played by Mrs Cox. As a result, a second inquest was held, in public this time, at the Bedford Hotel, Balham [it still stands]. In this 'Trial by Crowner's Quest', Florence and Mrs Cox had their backs against the wall. While undergoing a hostile examination, Mrs Cox changed her story once more, claiming that Charlie had told her that he 'had taken poison for Gully. Don't tell Florence.' This statement let the cat out of the bag, and offered Florence up for some searching questioning, as Mrs Cox had probably intended. Florence wept bitterly and pleaded for mercy, as she was forced to tell all about her relations with Gully. The good doctor himself faced an equally hostile questioning, and both he and Florence were professionally and socially ruined, for good. Gully was hounded out of his clubs, and the newspapers were full of the merry goings-on at The Priory. At the inquest, both Florence and Mrs Cox made much of Charlie Bravo's cruelty and mean-spiritedness, and they tried their best to allege that he was near-suicidal from his jealousy of Dr Gully. But Charlie's letters made no mention of suicide, or any serious pangs of jealousy for that matter, and his loyal friends stoutly denied that this money-loving young barrister had ever entertained any suicidal notions. The jury eventually returned a verdict of murder against some person or persons unknown.

The verdict from the coroner's jury came as a disappointment to the Bravo family, and was another hard blow for Florence and Mrs Cox. The newspapers did their best to emphasise the infamy of Dr Gully, the immorality of Florence Bravo, and the sneaky behaviour of Mrs Cox, although the laws of libel prevented them from making any open accusations. There was also an illustrated magazine about the case, in seven penny issues, entitled *The Balham Mystery*, with some ribald images from the coroner's inquest. It is sad but true that Florence Bravo drank herself to death in September 1879, expiring at the house where she had sought refuge, 19 Eastern Parade, Southend [it still stands]. Dr Gully died in obscurity in 1883, giving instructions that his remains should be disposed of in an unmarked grave. In contrast, that extraordinary Mrs Cox lived happily ever after. Having cashed in a considerable inheritance, she could live in comfort and have her sons educated in some style; she did not expire until 1917, at the age of 90.

Over the years, there has been much speculation about who really murdered Charlie Bravo. Agatha Christie, who liked speculating about true crime mysteries, opted for Dr Gully as the guilty man, although she did not explain how the obese, unfit doctor could have acquired Spiderman-like superpowers, enabling him to enter The Priory, put the poison into Charlie's water-jug, and then leave the premises undetected. As for the coachman Griffiths, he had a solid alibi, being at work in Kent at the evening of the murder. The remaining domestics at The Priory lacked a motive to murder Mr Bravo, although I would have been interested to know more about the maid Mary Ann Keeber, and her relations with her master. Amazingly, Sir William Gull, who was known for his stubbornness, stood up at the coroner's inquest to testify that in his opinion, Charlie Bravo had most likely committed suicide. But why would an educated man, who had some knowledge of toxicology due to his legal training, use such a painful and protracted way to kill himself, instead of making use of a handgun or a bottle of morphine? The veteran crime writer Yseult Bridges, who liked to think up 'solutions' for celebrated murder mysteries, proposed the unlikely version that Charlie wanted to poison Florence, but drank the poison himself by mistake! Professor Mary Hartmann, an American academic who took an interest in feminist aspects of crime, suggested that Florence had wanted to put some antimony tartrate in Charlie's water jug to make him feel nauseous, to prevent him from pestering her for sex, but that in her drunken condition, she made a mistake with the dose. But there is no independent corroboration that Victorian wives made use of this dangerous poison to control the sexual appetites of their husbands, and anyway, the dose Charlie had swallowed had been enough to kill him several times over.

The more cerebral commentators on the Bravo Mystery have concentrated on the two main suspects: Florence and Mrs Cox. The novelist Elizabeth Jenkins and the crime writer John Williams both thought Florence was guilty. A story has been going around that when her first husband Captain Ricardo's body was exhumed, antimony was detected in his remains, but this story was invented by the mischievous alienist Dr Forbes Winslow, who sometimes tried to falsify 'solutions' for historical crimes. That great Edinburgh chronicler of crime, William Roughead, thought Mrs Cox had poisoned the obnoxious Charlie Bravo, in order to keep her comfortable job at The Priory, and the crime writers Bernard Taylor and Kate Clarke agreed. Mrs Cox must surely have heard Charlie cry out, but she did nothing until she had been summoned by the maid. She told a number of untruths at the inquest, and gave the impression of being quite a conniving, wicked woman. But in the most recent book on the Great Bravo Mystery, journalist James Ruddick effectively disposed of the theory that Mrs Cox was keen to keep her job for financial reasons: she had a quite considerable inheritance coming her way, something she was well aware of. Ruddick thought Florence the guilty woman, with Mrs Cox as an accessory after the fact.

James Ruddick's hypothesis is a good one, and it deftly explains some of the mysterious matters about the murder: the volatile Florence was able to keep her cool since her loyal friend was supporting her, and the two women had had good time to co-ordinate their stories and accuse Charlie of being suicidal at the inquest. Sensing the hostility against her, and aware of the various untruths she had already told, Mrs Cox then cleverly made use of 'Plan B', telling another pack of lies about Charlie taking poison for Gully, to make sure attention was shifted away from her onto Florence and her immoral shenanigans. The 'blurb' for Ruddick's book, and the exhortations of a number of over-enthusiastic London journalists, pronounced the Great Bravo Mystery 'solved', but this is far from being the case. Although Ruddick has shed much new light on the case, the mystery remains.

If one thing is clear about the Bravo mystery, it is that Mrs Cox knew the identity of his murderer, and that she tried her utmost to protect this person from being detected. I would also suggest that the murderess was either Mrs Cox herself or Florence Bravo, or most likely the pair of them acting together. Mrs Cox is likely to have been the dominant partner in such a murder conspiracy, being clever and possessing admirable coolness of mind, whereas Florence was impulsive and volatile. There is also the matter of a pension which, according to a confidential letter to William Roughead, was paid to Mrs Cox by one of Florence's brothers: was this for 'services rendered'? As for the source of the poison, and the toxicological expertise affecting its choice, we must contemplate that witnesses saw Mrs Cox and Dr Gully together several times in the months leading up to the murder. Hell hath no fury like a doctor scorned, and Gully's defective grasp of medical ethics may well have extended to providing some friendly advice to Mrs Cox about how to get rid of his impudent younger rival, for good.

As for the murder house, it is reported to have been haunted by Charles Bravo's restless spirit for many years. The father of Mr James Clark, a chronicler of London ghosts, knew The Priory as a haunted house in the 1940s. The Bedford Hotel, where the inquest had taken place, was also haunted. Although The Priory has been subdivided into flats, the haunting has continued. According to the abovementioned James Ruddick, Charles Bravo haunted his former bedroom with such frequency that one of the residents called in a priest to perform a ceremony of exorcism. This ceremony is said to have had the desired effect. The Priory still stands today, but its grounds have been severely decimated.

17. The Pimlico Murder, 1876

In 1876, 99 Stanley [now Alderney] Street, Pimlico, was home to the wealthy 58-year-old builder, John Collins. He was known for his financial astuteness, his considerable property portfolio, and his reluctance to spend sixpence if he could avoid it. Although his terraced Pimlico townhouse was quite large, the only live-in servant was an elderly cook, and there were several lodgers. Mrs Collins had to perform quite a few of the household chores herself. Since Mr Collins did not trust banks, he kept his entire fortune locked away at No. 99.

On 14 December 1876, Mr and Mrs Collins were visited by a young man named Frederick Treadaway, to whom they had been introduced by some relations. The following morning, Treadaway unexpectedly returned to 99 Stanley Street, without an invitation. Mr Collins was out at the time, but his wife showed Treadaway downstairs to the dining room. Since he complained of feeling tired, since he had been 'walking about all night', she suggested he should take a nap, and kindly put some pillows on the back of one of the chairs. When John Collins returned home for luncheon, he was surprised to see Treadaway sleeping on one of his dining room chairs. He woke the young man up and Mrs Collins could hear them having a conversation. As luncheon approached, Mr Collins said 'What do you say to broth?' and Treadaway replied 'I'll have some.'

Mrs Collins went into the kitchen to help the cook serve at table. All of a sudden, she heard the report of a firearm. Running back to the dining room, she was confronted by the wild-eyed Frederick Treadaway, who was brandishing a shiny revolver. He took a shot at her but missed. Seeing that her husband sat slumped in his chair, with blood pouring from his head, she bravely seized Treadaway by the collar to prevent his escape. He then thrust his thumb into her mouth and tore her cheek, before knocking her down and making his escape from No. 99. In spite of the punishment she had taken, Mrs Collins pursued him out into the street, shouting 'Stop thief!' A young man pursued the gunman as far as Eccleston Square, but lost him in the crowd.

When the local constable came to 99 Stanley Street, he found John Collins dying from a revolver shot to the head. Mrs Collins was alive and conscious, and she provided the name and description of the fugitive gunman. Inspector Bishop, who took charge of the case at the College Road police station, made sure that Treadaway's description was widely circulated to police forces throughout London and the Home Counties. It was presumed that the gunman had planned to murder both Mr and Mrs Collins, and possibly the old cook as well, in order to be able to search the house with impunity, and steal the money the capitalist builder had hoarded on the premises. Frederick Treadaway's parents, who were both respectable people, faced some searching questioning as to where their son might be hiding.

In the hunt for the Stanley Street murderer, railway stations and omnibus terminals were kept under police surveillance, as were the homes of known friends of the Treadaway family. It turned out that Frederick had been staying with a lady friend, Mrs Milton, at her house in Castle Street, for two days before the murder. He returned there after the murder, cut off his whiskers, and replaced his deerstalker with a tall hat. The police kept watch at the Isleworth cottage owned by a close friend of Frederick Treadaway's. And indeed, a whiskerless cove in a tall hat was observed to come up to this very cottage. As Treadaway was leaving, he was arrested.

It turned out that after he had murdered John Collins, Frederick Treadaway had been tramping aimlessly around London for 24 hours. He was entirely penniless, and the motive of his visiting the Isleworth friend had been to borrow £1. Young Treadaway had once been working as a hosier's assistant, but his lack of industry and punctuality had earnt him the sack. He was fond of drinking and partying, was a talented singer and pianist, and very popular among his fun-loving friends. He was just 22 years old and looked even younger; the journalists marvelled that this unmanly-looking, neatly dressed youngster stood accused of a callous murder. The police were much praised for having apprehended the fugitive within 24 hours. The murder house at 99 Stanley Street, where the body of Mr Collins had been laid out in one room, and his widow was recovering from her injuries in another, was daily visited by a thousand curious people.

On trial at the Old Bailey for the wilful murder of John Collins, things were not looking good for Frederick Treadaway. There was no doubt that he had shot Mr Collins, with a pistol purchased beforehand. The only tactic open for the defence to try was to play the 'insanity card'. Treadaway's father testified that several of his relatives were quite insane, including the prisoner's sister. Young Treadaway had once fallen down, foaming at the mouth, and he often suffered from headaches. His mother had once heard

Portraits in connection with the Pimlico murder, from the *IPN*, 30 December 1876.

Frederick Treadaway and other features of the Stanley Street Murder, from the *Penny Illustrated Paper*, 30 December 1876.

him speak of committing suicide. Both the defence and the prosecution called medical witnesses, but their opinions diverged wildly. The defence argued that Treadaway suffered from 'epileptic vertigo'. He had purchased the pistol to commit suicide. Inside the Collins house, he had one of his epileptic fits, and murdered the Pimlico miser in an unconscious state. During the first day of the trial, one of the witnesses had made a derogative remark to young Treadaway, who immediately began shaking uncontrollably.

The prosecution pooh-poohed all these concerns: there was no convincing family history of insanity, no doctor had diagnosed Treadaway with epilepsy before the murder, and they suspected that there was a good deal of hysteria mixed up with the theatrical fainting fit inside the courtroom. In his summing-up, Mr Justice Lush was scrupulously fair: he said that if the jury believed that the prisoner had not been aware of committing a crime, they should acquit him on grounds of insanity. But after deliberating for half-an-hour, the jury returned a verdict of Guilty. Mr Justice Lush accordingly sentenced Frederick Treadaway to death.

There was a good deal of debate in the medical journals about the Treadaway case. Some doctors argued that the Stanley Street murderer had really suffered from epilepsy, and that a great miscarriage of justice had been committed. Others claimed that at most, he suffered from 'vertigo' or 'hysteria'. Treadaway was to be executed at Newgate on 26 February 1877. All preparations had been made to carry out the death sentence, and the executioner Marwood was in readiness. But two days before the planned execution, the Governor of Newgate received a message from the Home Secretary, saying that after a careful medical inquiry, Treadaway had been reprieved from the capital sentence. The prisoner 'was very much affected, and appeared deeply sensible of the mercy that had been extended to him.' The last we hear of Frederick Treadaway is that the 1881 Census lists him as a prisoner in HM Convict Prison, Chatham, and that at the time of the 1891 Census, he was still a convict, at Portsea. There has been internet speculation that he was identical to a George Frederick James Treadaway who married in 1894, was listed in the 1911 Census, and died in 1939.

The medical debate concerning Treadaway has continued into the present time. Dr J.P. Eigen has argued that Treadaway was justly absolved, since he suffered from epilepsy, and committed the murder in a state of automatism, snapping out of his dazed state after having assaulted Mrs Collins. But Eigen's account contains some obvious errors: Collins was no friend of Treadaway, just an acquaintance, and Treadaway was not arrested at the crime scene, but disguised himself and fled London.

He may well have suffered from some variant of epilepsy, but this is irrelevant, since there is evidence of premeditation [the purchase of the pistol beforehand], motive [Treadaway was poor as a church mouse, and Collins known to be a wealthy miser], and planning of the crime [disguise and flight]. Frederick Treadaway was a lucky man to escape the hangman's noose. In 1878 or 1879, Stanley Street was renamed Alderney Street, quite possibly because of the murder. According to the relevant Post Office directories, the houses were not renumbered. The murder house at 99 Alderney Street still stands, and looks virtually unchanged since the time of the murder.

18. The Macclesfield Murder, 1877

Harry Leigh was a young man who lived in the village of Sutton near Macclesfield, with his wife. He had worked as a weaver, but lost his job due to his general incompetence and unsuitability. A short, thin man, and very shabby and unkempt, he was fond of drinking beer at various public houses. He did not dare to tell his wife about losing his job, and soon

Harry Leigh murdering Mary Ann Halton, from *Famous Crimes Past & Present*.

The finding of the body, from the *IPN*, April 14 1877.

The Macclesfield murderer and his victim, from the *IPN*, August 4 1877

found it very difficult to provide victuals for the family. His parents, who were both alive and well, handed him a shilling or two, but this did not prevent him becoming desperately poor.

Next door to Harry Leigh's parents lived a widow named Mrs Halton and her eight-year-old daughter Mary Ann. Mrs Halton worked as a weaver, and on 23 March 1877, Harry overheard her telling his father that the following day, she would send her daughter to pick up her wages from Bamford's factory. The impoverished Harry Leigh thought of a cunning plan. He went to the factory, where he met some boys lounging about. He persuaded two of them to go and see the factory manager, with a note saying 'Please pay the bearer my wages as my daughter is sick and cannot come. Wrap it up with paper and a piece of string, so he won't lose it, and oblige, yours, E. Halton, 60 Fence Street.' The boys, who had been promised a couple of pennies for themselves, duly went to see the manager, but he did not want to give away 12s 6d to some unknown urchins. When the boys returned to Harry Leigh, he cursed angrily at having been thwarted in his scheme to lay his hands on the money.

But Harry did not go home, but remained skulking outside the factory until Mary Ann Halton appeared. When she started walking home with the money, he came up to her and started a conversation. Since she knew him as the neighbour's son, she was not alarmed, although it took some persuasion to make her take a longer route home, by the canal. All of a sudden, when the two were alone, Harry cut away the pocket in Mary Ann's dress and stole the purse with 12s 6d. The girl, who was strong and vigorous for her age, gave a yell and started struggling fiercely. Harry tried to hold her mouth, and to choke her, but she fought back angrily. In the end, he lifted her up and threw her into the canal with great force. The coward then stood and watched her drown, since the canal was deep and she could not swim.

Harry Leigh then walked to the Old Ship public house, where he had three pints of beer, before returning home and giving his wife three half-crowns and sixpence for the household expenditure. But when Mrs Halton realized that her daughter was missing, she went to the police, and since several witnesses had seen Mary Ann with Harry outside the factory, the local constables came calling at Leigh's cottage. The coward Harry ran to the outhouse and locked himself in, but the constables broke open the door and took him into custody. As Harry sat in his cell at the Macclesfield police station, a number of witnesses came forward to further incriminate him: the boys he had tried to bribe to get the wages, several witnesses who had seen him with Mary Ann, and a girl who had seen him outside the factory carrying a basket answering the description of one found where the murder had been committed. Mary Ann Halton's body had been retrieved from the canal, and it showed clear injuries from the assault that had preceded her murder.

On 26 March, Harry Leigh was charged with the murder of Mary Ann Halton. A large, hostile crowd of locals stood outside the Macclesfield courtroom, and they would have lynched him had he not been protected by the police. The *Liverpool Mercury* unflatteringly described him as a 'dwarfish, dark-complexioned, puny man, and of somewhat irregular habits.' He was committed to stand trial for murder at the Chester Assizes, before Baron Bramwell. His defence counsel could not deny the formidable evidence inculpating his client, but he tried to persuade the jury that Mary Ann had become frightened after the money had been stolen, and fallen into the canal. But the jury was impressed with the callousness of the crime, and the youth of the victim, and they refused to accept the manslaughter theory. Harry Leigh was found guilty of murder and sentenced to death; since his crime had been a dastardly one, there was no hope of a reprieve. In the condemned cell at Chester Castle, he was visited by his parents, wife and cousin. He wrote a full confession, detailing his premeditated and cowardly murder of a little girl, to obtain the sum of 12s 6d. He was hanged at the county gaol in Chester on 13 August 1877; the executioner was Marwood, who made use of the long drop due to the murderer's diminutive stature, with good success.

19. The Wymondham Double Murder, 1877

Henry March was a 59-year-old blacksmith, who lived in a cottage in Pople Street, in Wymondham, not far from Norwich, and worked in a small smithy owned by the retired veterinary surgeon Thomas Mayes. Marsh was a married man, with a son in the army; his wife and teenage daughter ran a small shop from the cottage where they lived. In 1877, when Mr Mayes was 76 years old, he decided to close down the smithy; he warned the two blacksmiths March and Bidewell that they would have to look for employment elsewhere. Henry March, who was an angry, mean-spirited man, did not like this at all, since he feared unemployment in his old age, and suspected that Mayes was thinking of giving the smithy to Bidewell, who was his longest serving employee.

On the evening of Friday 19 October 1877, the two blacksmiths Henry March and Henry Bidewell went out to drink beer at the Three Feathers public house in Wymondham. Although they had both drunk thirstily, they seemed to get along just fine, and they reported for work early on

The Wymondham double murder, from the *IPN*, 3 November 1877.

Saturday just as normal. March went to Kimberley Hall to examine some of the Earl of Kimberley's horses; in spite of the early hour, he was given some beer, and when he returned, he seemed in quite jocular. In the afternoon, he worked away in the smithy with Bidewell. All of a sudden, Mr Mayes' servant girl Sarah Bailey heard an outcry of 'If you don't hold your tongue, I'll knock you down!' coming from the smithy. She had a look through a window to see what was going on, and was horrified to see March approach Bidewell, who was tending the fire in the smithy with his bellows, brandishing a large iron bar. Shouting 'I may as well finish you; I can only be hung!' he brought down the iron bar onto Bidewell's unprotected head, time after time. Sarah Bailey gave a scream and called for Mr Mayes, who had lingered in bed that day since he had been feeling unwell. Sarah told him that March had just struck Bidewell, and Mr Mayes, who may well have thought there had been a minor tussle between the two rival blacksmiths, put on his hat and went out to the smithy. When he saw Bidewell's body on the floor, Mayes exclaimed 'Oh! March, what have you done?' 'Nothing' the truculent blacksmith muttered, and during a hiatus of a few seconds, Mayes would have had a chance to escape. But the elderly former veterinarian's instinct of self-preservation was not in good working order, and instead of running off, he bent down to tend to the stricken Bidewell. This gave the murderer an excellent opportunity to seize his iron bar and belabour the defenceless old man until he lay motionless on the floor of the smithy.

After the horrible paroxysm of violence inside the smithy, Henry March was left alone with his two victims. Their skulls terribly battered, they were still breathing, but it was clear they would not live for very long. The servant girl Sarah Bailey had alerted her parents, but they were of course reluctant to go into the smithy where two men had just been struck down, fearing that the murderer might still be lurking inside to further extend his tally. But Henry March calmly closed down the smithy and walked home, where he took off his blood-spattered blacksmith's apron and walked over to the Three Feathers to have a pint of beer, the *penultimus* in the long drinking career of this bibulous blacksmith, as it would turn out. March then walked back home but, by this time, many people in Wymondham knew about the murders. Two young shed builders named Flint and Plunkett, who were known to March, were brave enough to enter the house with him, to ask 'Harry, what have you been after?' 'I have not been after anything!' the truculent March replied angrily. 'This is a rum job!' Plunkett exclaimed, since he had heard all about the murders inside the smithy. 'Well, what would you do if you had to fight for your life? You stoop down and I'll show you how we went to work!' 'No, I won't stoop down!' replied Plunkett warily. March then ordered some beer, and emptied his ultimate pint with relish, with Flint and Plunkett also swigging away thirstily.

Wymondham was very short of policing at the time of the double murder in Pople Street, since the police inspector had taken an ailing constable to Norwich for some medical attention, and since the remaining constable for some blameworthy reason kept a very low profile that dismal day. Instead it was an experienced Norwich policeman, Sergeant John Scott, who happened to be in town in an off-duty capacity, who was alerted by the crowd in front of Mayes' house, and received directions where March lived. The tough police sergeant took him into custody without any drama, except that March shouted 'This is a rum half-day's work!' to the crowd of spectators outside his house. At the police station, he told a yarn about acting in self-defence after Bidewell had attacked him with an iron bar, and then dispatching Mr Mayes, after the old man had tackled him as well. Since March had no injuries whatsoever, this story was not believed. The coroner's inquest returned a verdict of wilful murder against him, and he was committed to stand trial at the Ipswich Winter Assizes, before Mr Justice Hawkins.

Henry March was defended by the local solicitor Mr Linay and by the barrister Mr Blofeld. The latter did his best for his client, suggesting that Sarah Bailey had been frightened and confused, and that both Bidewell and Mayes had tried to attack March with iron bars before they were killed. Surely, this was a case of manslaughter only, he pleaded. Mr Justice Hawkins, a 'Hanging Judge' of unremitting severity, then delivered a hostile summing-up. Declaring that Sarah Bailey was an alert, truthful witness, and that there was nothing to suggest that either Bidewell or Mayes had seized up any iron bars. The jury was out for just a quarter-of-an-hour before returning a verdict of Guilty, and Mr Justice Hawkins sentenced Henry March to death.

The solicitor Mr Linay appealed to the Home Secretary, arguing that March had been temporarily insane while committing the murders, but since this had been a both brutal and dastardly crime, and since medical experts found March fully same, the petition was turned down. Alcohol certainly played its part in the murders, and if March had not been at the beer already before luncheon, he might well have been less cantankerous and irritable. Before his execution, Henry March admitted the justice of his sentence, and confessed that the murder had been premeditated: he had always resented Bidewell due to their rivalry about taking over the smithy, and he had never forgotten that his master Mr Mayes had once spoken harshly to him about a field of rotten potatoes. Henry March was executed for the Wymondham Double Murder at Norwich Castle on 20 November 1877.

20. The Halesowen Triple Murder, 1878

In early 1878, all was not well in the household of James Jones, a labouring man living in a small cottage in Halesowen in the Black Country. Living with him were his wife Phoebe, his son Adam, his daughter Amelia, her husband Joseph Harris and their two daughters Alice and Eve. James Jones was labouring away at the Coombes Wood Brickworks, his wife used the back scullery to make nails, and the son Adam was also hard at work. The problem was that Joseph Harris, who worked as a miner at the Black Wagon Pit in Old Hill, was often

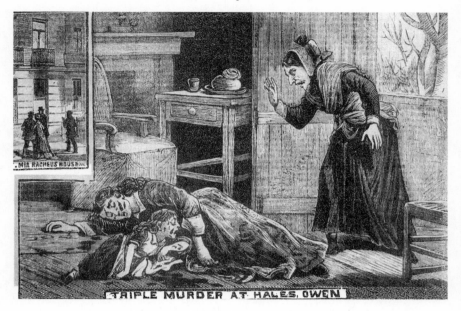

Phoebe Jones finds two of the murdered people, from the *IPN*, 2 March 1878.

not at all disposed to go to work. He had a long history of psychiatric disease, and had recently been an inpatient at Powick Asylum, from where he had been discharged in what was supposed to be an improved state of mind. But in spite of the optimistic prognosis from the Powick psychiatrists, Joseph Harris was as morose and paranoid as ever. He developed the fixed idea that his wife Amelia had been unfaithful to him while he had been incarcerated in the asylum, and they quarrelled bitterly. Once, Amelia threatened to stab him with a hot nailing rod. James Jones and his son made fun of Joseph for his reluctance to go to work, something that he resented very much.

On 5 February 1878, James Jones and Adam went to work early in the morning, but Joseph Harris preferred his warm bed, saying he felt unfit to do any work. It had been snowing heavily in the Black Country that day but, nevertheless, Phoebe Jones cooked breakfast for her husband and took it to him at the brickworks at 8.30 am. Amelia urged her to make haste back, since she was frightened of what Joseph might be up to. The previous evening, they had quarrelled hard until midnight, and she was apprehensive what her deranged husband was capable of in one of his bad moods. Phoebe Jones was away for an hour, but when she returned, she was surprised to see the house door open, although it was very cold. She was then aghast to see bloody red footprints on the snow, leading away from the cottage.

When the frightened Phoebe Jones went indoors to investigate, she found Amelia's battered body in the blood-spattered kitchen; she had been brutally beaten to death with an axe, as had the four-year-old Eve, who was lying next to her. Their heard were battered in and the brains protruding. Upstairs was seven-year-old Alice, still alive in spite of her horrific injuries from the axe. A doctor and a police constable were called in, but young Alice died a few hours later. The constable and two neighbours spotted the blood-spattered Joseph Harris skulking in a field nearby, and they arrested and handcuffed him. The coroner's inquest on the murdered family was opened on 12 February. Joseph Harris, who had been brought from the Worcester county gaol, maintained the greatest indifference and unconcern, even when the injuries to his three victims were graphically described. When asked to explain himself, he said that his wife and mother-in-law had vexed him by saying that they would send him back to the asylum in Powick. The jury returned a verdict of wilful murder against him, and he was committed to stand trial at the Worcester Assizes on 15 March. Insanity was set up as a defence, and after deliberating for two hours, the jury found Joseph Harris Not Guilty of murder. He was ordered to be detained at Broadmoor at Her Majesty's pleasure, and died there in January 1889.

21. Horrible Tragedy In Paris, 1878

In April 1878, the landlady of the Hôtel Jeanson, situated in the Rue Poliveau not far from the Jardin des Plantes in Paris, noticed a disagreeable smell in the staircase. She pinned it down to a room that had been taken by two young men, who had paid for their lodgings in advance a fortnight ago, but never returned. When the door was broken open, a wrapped-up parcel was found in one of the cupboards, containing a pair of severed arms and a pair of severed legs. The head and trunk were nowhere to be found. Upon inspection of the hotel ledger, it was observed that one of the two young men had signed it 'Emile Gérard'. The hands of the murder victim, presumably a woman, were gnarled and horny, as if she did manual labour for a living. The left arm was marked with an old wound. The police found out that the milkwoman Madame Gillet, of Rue Paradis-Poissonière, had disappeared around a fortnight earlier; she was known to have a cauterised wound on the left arm.

Having made a provisional identification of the murder victim, the police went on to look for the elusive 'Emile Gérard', making several arrests of various suspicious characters, who were all able to clear

The murder of Madame Gillet, and other features from the careers of the murderers Barré and Lebiez, from the *IPN*, 17 August 1878

themselves. Madame Gillet had been seen with a young man named Aimé Barré, who had a small office as a stockbroker. His own speculations had been unfortunate, and he was in the process of becoming a bankrupt. When tracked down, Barré denied all knowledge of Madame Gillet, but the police found an old soldier turned commissionaire who could testify that these two had met more than once, and that she had consulted him about her finances. Madame Gillet had always been a very prudent, hard-working woman, and she had 12,000 francs invested in Government securities. The commissionaire Démol also volunteered that after the murder, Barré had been in possession of a good deal of money, and he had managed to pay off quite a few of his creditors. Démol had once helped Barré to carry a black wooden portmanteau he had just bought, allegedly for the transportation of some clothes; this very portmanteau was found at the railway station warehouse in Le Mans, containing the trunk and head of Madame Gillet, badly putrefied but still identifiable by her friends. Barré was arrested, and the landlady at the Hôtel Jeanson picked him out as the mysterious 'Emile Gérard' who had once taken a room at the hotel.

Aimé Barré was the son of honest country folk, who wanted him to make a career as a business man in Paris, but he had got into debt and tried his luck as a petty swindler. He had a mistress, a slovenly woman named Leontine Lepin, who lived apart from her husband. In police custody, the coward Barré admitted his guilt, and he denounced a friend of his, the medical student Paul Lebiez, as his accomplice. Lebiez was known for his radical views: he was a communist and an atheist, but he also kept an expensive mistress, and had racked up considerable debts. Barré had tried to swindle Madame Gillet by suggesting that he should look after her finances, but the canny old woman had not trusted him. Barré then swore Lebiez into a murder conspiracy, and they lay in wait for the old woman as she came to deliver the milk; Barré knocked her on the head with a hammer, and Lebiez finished her off with a knife, before making use of his anatomy skills to dismember the body. Barré took Madame Gillet's keys and stole all her valuables from her flat.

On trial for murder, Aimé Barré was described as a short young man, just 25 years old, with regular features, brown hair, moustaches and a beard. Lebiez was a handsome man, just 24 years old, with an intelligent countenance. Leontine Lepin, who was also on trial as an accessory, was described as a stupid, vulgar-looking young woman. Barré and Lebiez did their best to blame each other for the planning and execution of the murder, but it was clear to the jury that they both were guilty men: they were both sentenced to perish on the guillotine for their cowardly crime, whereas Leontine Lepin got three years in prison as an accessory after the fact. The two murderers were executed together on 7 September 1878, at a scaffold in the Place de la Roquette. There was a scarcity of criminal sensations in Britain at the time, and the murderous activities of the two Parisian ruffians were covered by the London papers; they also got their likenesses into the *IPN*, which was something of an achievement for these two French crooks.

22. The Llangibby Massacre, 1878

In 1878, Llangibby was a sleepy little village in South Wales, situated on the main road from Newport to Usk, and remarkable only for its 14th century church of St Cybi, and the 16th century White Hart inn. A farmer, William Watkins, occupied a small cottage in Llangibby, situated just by the turnpike road, with his wife Elizabeth and their three youngest children. There were four older children, all of them out in service. William Watkins was a native of Herefordshire, but he had moved to South Wales at an early age, to work as a farm labourer. In 1860, when in service with Mr Crump at Estavarney, he became acquainted with local girl Elizabeth Ann Jaspar, and they got married at Caerleon. William Watkins continued to work as a farm labourer, although he was able to settle as a smallholder in Llangibby, moving to his cottage after a few years.

The finding of the murdered family, and the arrest of Garcia in Newport, from the *IPN*, 27 July 1878.

A portrait of Garcia, from the *IPN*, 3 August 1878.

Yusaf Garcia was a young Spanish sailor, who was stranded in Cardiff after the company of a Spanish ship had been paid off. Although he could hardly speak a word of English, he decided to stay in South Wales for a while, ending up in Newport. Soon, he had spent all his money in the seedy bars and pubs in the Pill area. On 25 September 1877, Garcia tried to burgle a cottage in St Bride outside Newport, but he was

Vignettes from the Llangibby Massacre, from the IPN, 3 August 1878.

Garcia murders Mrs Watkins, from *Famous Crimes Past & Present*.

overpowered and caught by some sturdy locals, and handed over to the police. Although a slow-witted fellow with near negligible linguistic skills, and illiterate at that, he was considered *compos mentis* and fit to stand trial for his crime, and sentenced to nine months in prison, with hard labour. After he had served his time in Usk Prison, the intention was to put Garcia on a train with a single ticket to Newport, to get rid of him, but the Spaniard managed to evade the prison warders, and strayed out into the unfamiliar countryside. He had not been given the discharge money doled out to every prisoner on their release, so his

PORTRAIT of GARCIA THE LLANGIBBY MURDERER.

Garcia awaiting execution, from the *IPN*, 9 November 1878.

pockets contained only seven pence and a halfpenny, apart from some foreign coins.

Yusaf Garcia was quite a young man, born in 1857 in Puebla in the province of Valencia; presumably there were schools in that part of Spain, but the masters had been quite unable to teach young Garcia how to read or write. It would appear that he joined the army as a young man, and fought on the republican side in the civil war against the troops of Don Carlos, the pretender to the Spanish throne. He then became a merchant seaman, before being stranded in Cardiff. Garcia was a short, thin man, just 5 feet 5 inches tall, with a swarthy complexion, coarse black hair and beard, and an unprepossessing countenance. After leaving Usk Prison, he went on the tramp, and a woman saw him sleeping in a field. Mrs Ann Gwatkin, of Llangibby, was quite startled when a villainous-looking foreign tramp came knocking at the door of her cottage at 7p.m., asking, in very broken English, for some water and directions for Newport. She gave him some water, and described how he should proceed southwards to reach his destination; she later described her relief when this evil-looking individual walked off, on a route that would take him past the cottage of the Watkins family, not far away.

On the following morning, 17 July 1878, the 11-year-old lad Frank James left his home and walked half-a-mile to the Watkins cottage, where the plan was that he would join William Watkins and go to a farm to do some work. But when he opened the front gate, he saw Elizabeth Watkins lying on the garden path, in a large pool of congealed blood. The terrified lad ran home to alert his mother. Not long after, a young man, John Evans, came riding past the Watkins cottage. Being on horseback, he could see both William and Elizabeth Watkins lying dead on their backs in the front garden; they had clearly been murdered, and some person, presumably the murderer, had taken the trouble to sprinkle some Sweet William flowers over the face of the murdered man. Evans made haste to alert the farmer John Morgan, who lived nearby, and they returned to examine the cottage, only to find that it was on fire: thick smoke bellowed out when the front door was opened, and it took further assistance to put out the flames. The floorboards of the children's bedroom were burnt through, and the men could see through to the lounge below. All three children were found dead, having been murdered by repeated stab wounds by a frenzied intruder, who had then set the house on fire.

The police sergeants in Usk and Caerleon were soon communicated with, and they both came to inspect the Llangibby murder house. In the meantime, the Usk prison authorities had an idea. They could well remember the convicted burglar Yusaf Garcia, and for some unspecified reason, they thought him a prime suspect for the Llangibby Massacre. It may well be that Garcia had impressed the prison warders as a man capable of any atrocity; his villainous looks cannot have helped; then there was the powerful factor of xenophobia, since in rural Wales at that time, foreigners were viewed with much suspicion. At any rate, the description of Garcia was circulated to the Newport and Cardiff police forces, which both put their constables on high alert. And indeed, late in the evening, a scruffy-looking foreign tramp made his way into Newport. In very broken English, he asked for directions to the railway station, but there he was informed that the next train to Cardiff was not due until 2.30 am. He was spotted by a local police constable named Tooze, who alerted Sergeant McGrath who had seen Garcia when he was arrested for the burglary back in 1877. McGrath immediately recognized the fugitive, and Garcia was promptly handcuffed and locked up in the Newport police cell.

Already on 18 July, both the Cardiff *Western Mail* and the London newspapers had been alerted that a family of five had been murdered at Llangibby, and that the sailor Joseph (as he was called in the press) Garcia had been taken into custody in Newport. A Press Association telegramme said that Garcia's face and arms were found to be much scratched, as if he had been involved in a prolonged struggle. His shirtsleeves had been washed, but the remainder of the shirt was stained with blood. He was wearing two pairs of trousers, one outside the other. The bundle he had been carrying at the time of his arrest was found to contain a large clasp-knife, several items of female clothing, the mechanism for a clock, and a loaf of bread. Garcia had been wearing canvas shoes when leaving the prison, but now he wore a pair of heavy boots, similar to those worn by the murdered William Watkins. On 19 July, the *Western Mail* had a further article on the Llangibby outrage, and the newspaper leader pointed out that since mass murder was wholly alien to the Welsh mind, a foreigner must obviously be the guilty man. When Garcia was taken to Caerleon to be charged with murder before the magistrate, he was hissed at and booed by an angry mob.

The coroner's inquest on the murdered Watkins family opened at the White Hart, Llangibby, on 19 July, before the coroner Mr W. H. Brewer. The twelve jurors made their way to the murder cottage to see the mangled bodies, which had been left lying in their original positions after the post-mortem examination. When the shaken jurors returned from their grisly duty, the local doctor was ready to give details of the injuries: the throats of William Watkins and his wife had been cut with a formidable knife, and the same instrument had then been used to massacre the three children in a murderous frenzy. A clasp-knife had been found in Garcia's bundle when he had been searched by the police, but it seemed to small and blunt to be the murder weapon; instead, it was speculated that after stunning William Watkins, the murderer had seized one of the kitchen knives to decimate the family. The inquest returned a verdict of wilful murder against Joseph Garcia, and he was committed to stand trial; due to the massive local prejudice against him, the trial would not be held in Monmouthshire, but at the Gloucester Assizes in late October. In the meantime, Garcia was incarcerated in Usk Prison.

There was great public interest in the grisly Llangibby Massacre, and much enthusiasm all over South Wales to come and see the murder house. As a local newspaper expressed it,

On Saturday a great number of persons visited Llangibby, but the great concourse of persons took place on Sunday, when some thousands thronged to the village during the day in vehicles of every description, whilst it is stated that many pedestrians from the Hills commenced their journey at break of day to pay a visit at the spot. Stalls for the sale of ginger beer, fruit, buns, &c, were erected on the road sides; the two inns of the village were filled during the whole day. Towards nightfall some drunken brawls ensued, and amidst vociferous exclamations, vile language and oaths resounded through the hitherto quiet and well-ordered village. At the cottage any portion of the gate, door, stone, or piece of wood, which bore any trace of blood, was eagerly seized by the sensation and mystery-mongers as souvenirs, and it is proverbial that, whilst men flock to the spot from curiosity to see the locality, the women have a hankering desire to see the slaughtered remains of the ill-fated family, and some have expressed themselves that they did 'not care a pin to go there if they could not see the bodies.' It is rumoured that it is the intention of Mr G. W. Nicholl, to whom the cottage belongs, to raze it to the ground, and throw the site and the garden into an adjoining field.

This disgraceful 'murder tourism' continued for some weeks to come: well-laden vehicles descended on Llangibby, from all parts of South Wales, and the public houses were full to capacity.

The trial of Joseph Garcia began on 30 October 1878, at the Gloucester Assizes. Baron Bramwell presided, Mr Bosanquet and Mr Lawrence prosecuted, and Garcia was defended by Mr Gough and Mr Maddy. The case for the prosecution was expertly put forward: Garcia was a known burglar, he had been spotted near the murder cottage, his face was scratched and his shirt stained with blood, and he had worn the boots and trousers of William Watkins and carried a bag of objects stolen from the household. Garcia had carried a knife when arrested, but this was unlikely to be the murder weapon. On 11 October, a dog had found a bloodstained butcher's knife in a hedge near Llangibby. There was newspaper optimism that it matched a leather sheath found at the crime scene, but nothing was made of this discovery in court. The defence had to think of an explanation as to why so many of the Watkins household items had ended up in the bundle carried by Garcia, and Mr Gough suggested that the family had been murdered by tramps, and that the Spaniard had discovered the murdered people, and decided to steal some property from the house.

He may well have got his clothes stained with blood in the process, it was optimistically added. Much was made of Garcia's lack of motive, and his tardiness in tramping from Llangibby to Newport. In his summing-up, Baron Bramwell declared that there was no doubt that the murderer of the Watkins family was the same person who had stolen effects from the house. The jury never left the box, but arrived at a verdict of Guilty after just a few minutes of discussion. Baron Bramwell put on the black cap and sentenced Garcia to death. He was executed at Usk Prison on 18 November 1878, amid much public uproar: the executioner Marwood was toasted by the mob at the Crown Inn and the Three Salmons, and three rousing cheers were given as his train steamed out of Usk Station.

Over the years, doubts have remained concerning Garcia's guilt. There is no doubt that there was immense prejudice against him, and Thomas Ensor, the solicitor employed by the Spanish Consul to conduct Garcia's defence, was not at all impressed by Mr Gough's feeble efforts in court. There was no eyewitness testimony, and Garcia had no motive to commit murder. A mystification was added in May 1994, when a certain William Watkins spoke up in a newspaper interview, claiming that Garcia had been the boyfriend of Mary Ann Watkins, the eldest daughter of the murdered family, and that they had an illegitimate child, his grandfather. Garcia had come to the cottage to meet Mary Ann, but he had murdered every person on the premises after William Watkins had attempted to throw him out. Mary Ann was just 15 years old at the time, however, and the ugly, monoglot Garcia was hardly the kind of person a young girl was likely to fall in love with. The manuscript diary of a certain Henry Jones mentions a sailor arrested in Newport on suspicion of being the Llangibby murderer, but this is likely to represent one of the men briefly taken into custody before Garcia was caught, and has little significance with regard to the question of his guilt. The *Western Mail* reproduced some anonymous letters, to the effect that Garcia was innocent; one of them was supposed to be from the real murderers, some French sailors, and had the wording 'me and mi mates killed the ole foks at Langley … We throed the close and clok away, we lay in the dich an see Gracia find them, the we shipped two days afterward an now get back an see you have hung por Gracia, you can's kitch us now so long after – for we ship again – but you british be dam fools. 'The newspaper classified this badly spelt missive as an impudent hoax, however.

As for the hypothesis that the Watkinses were murdered by tramps, it has little to recommend itself, since the Welsh tramps of those days were hardly capable of a wholesale massacre, for no profit at all. The Watkinses do not appear to have had any enemies, and violent crime was practically unknown in Llangibby and its vicinity. Personally, I remain convinced that Garcia was the guilty man, but was justice the ultimate result of the flawed process of trying him? A rather difficult question to answer is whether Garcia was really sane and fit to plead. As we know, he was illiterate and incapable of learning proper English, and his crime was that of a lunatic, butchering a family for hardly any gain at all. His utterances, at various stages of his criminal career, were entirely stupid and confused, even when a Spanish interpreter was present. There is nothing to suggest that he was ever seen by a competent psychiatrist, with an interpreter present, so the unpleasant possibility remains that a halfwit was hanged at Usk Prison, for the Llangibby Massacre of 1878.

When I went to the Usk Rural Life Museum back in 2001, an old photograph of the Llangibby murder house was on display, with a brief account of the crime. Another vintage photograph of the murder cottage was made into a picture postcard in Edwardian times, and a copy is reproduced in this book. The Llangibby murder house was razed to the ground a year or two after the massacre, since no person would live there, but the knowledgeable locals are aware of where it once stood. Of the four surviving Watkins children, at least two had issue, and there may well be descendants alive today. In 2005, former Detective Chief Superintendent Gerald Thoms discussed the Llangibby Massacre in the 'Crime Solver' show on BBC Wales, arriving at the conclusion that Garcia was guilty. The 80-year old Mr Keith Watkins, a former merchant seaman whose grandfather was the brother of the murdered man, and who had taken care to study the case, agreed in a newspaper interview.

23. The Bradford Murder, 1878

Anthony Owston was born in Calverley, Yorkshire, in 1841. He was apprenticed to a Bradford cabinetmaker, and made good progress in his chosen trade. By the time of the 1861 Census, he was living at 147 Belgrave Place, Bradford, with his two elder sisters and his brother-in-law. In 1862, he married Jane Binns, and they soon had four children: two sons and two daughters. Anthony Owston set up shop at 58 Westgrove Street in Bradford, next-door to a public house run by a certain John Smith. Jane Owston, who liked to have a drink or two, soon became a regular customer at the beerhouse at No. 56 next-door, and this

Anthony Owston goes on a rampage in Bradford, from the *IPN*, 12 October 1878.

worried the long-suffering Anthony Owston, who began to suspect that she was having an affair with the landlord Smith.

On Saturday 28 September 1878, Jane and Anthony Owston had been quarrelling bitterly about her fondness for the beer-shop and its owner. All of a sudden, in the presence of all four children, he seized hold of her and cut her throat from ear to ear. Through an upstairs window, Owston saw John Smith in the yard below, and he threw a heavy chair at him. Smith managed to dodge this missile, and he ran into the beer-shop, with his servant girl who had just been getting some water from the pump.

Having armed himself with another knife, Owston ran out into the street. He jumped headlong into Smith's beerhouse, through the front window, shattering two large panes of glass. Smith was behind the counter, and could not make his escape. The infuriated Owston knocked him down, jumped on him, and stabbed him hard in the face. He then seized Smith, and would have cut his throat, had not a sturdy coachman named Sidney Hindle just come to have a pint of beer. Seeing Owston leap headlong through the front window, he ran into the shop and saw Smith being attacked; he managed to throw Owston on his back and release Smith. The landlord gave a scream and ran out of the shop, and Owston would have pursued him if Hindle had not seized hold of him. The coachman tried to secure the knife, but Owston made use of it to cut his own throat, bleeding profusely all over the beer-shop.

Out in the street, John Smith managed to alert a police sergeant, who came back to the beerhouse with him. Owston was still bleeding badly, but it looked like he would survive; nor was Smith's own injury in any way life-threatening. Jane Owston was lying dead in the kitchen of No. 58, however, and after his throat had been stitched up by the local doctor, her husband was taken to the Bradford Infirmary under police guard. He was unable to speak after his attempt at self-destruction, but he wrote on a sheet of paper that he was happy that his wife was dead, and that he would have murdered Smith as well had Hindle not come to his assistance. He was the guilty man, and he was willing to meet his Maker; he hoped that without their parents to look after them, his four children would become good boys and girls.

The coroner's inquest returned a verdict of wilful murder against Jane Owston's husband. Her remains were interred at Undercliffe Cemetery on Wednesday 2 October, with a long and impressive procession attending, as well as the brother, aunts and children of the deceased. Owston himself made slow but steady progress at the hospital with regard to the wound in his throat, but his mental condition deteriorated and he had to be transferred to the lunatic ward at Bradford Workhouse, in a state of deep despondency. In mid-November he was charged in the Bradford Borough Court with murdering his wife. Mrs Binns, the mother of the murdered woman, made quite a scene in court, but Owston took little notice of the proceedings. His defence counsel argued that his mental state was unsound, and that he was not in a fit state to plead. When he stood trial for murder at the Leeds Assizes in late January 1879, he was found Not Guilty on the grounds of insanity, and was committed to Broadmoor at Her Majesty's pleasure.

There was some degree of sympathy for Anthony Owston in Bradford, since it was common knowledge that his wife had cuckolded him with Smith. When Smith bought a new shop in March 1879, his application for a licence to sell beer was firmly refused, and there were newspaper comments about his involvement in the Owston tragedy. In September 1889, when Owston had been in Broadmoor for more than a decade, some of his friends in Bradford petitioned for his release: Owston had been a respectable man, who had killed his drunken and dissolute wife in a fit of temporary insanity. His mental state had improved during his time at Broadmoor, and he was able to work as a joiner. It was argued that he had fully expiated his crime after nearly eleven years of confinement, and that his friends in Bradford would look after him when he had been released. Broadmoor records agree that by this time, he was in good physical health, and also rational, tranquil and industrious. The Home Secretary turned a deaf ear to this petition, however, and Owston remained incarcerated in Broadmoor, where he suffered from several attacks of what was called acute mania with melancholia. His son John Charles Owston visited him more than once, and sent him many letters. After Anthony Owston's death, from exhaustion following mania, in October 1905, the son sent wreaths for his father's grave at Broadmoor for several years running.

24. The Woodnesborough Murder, 1878

Captain William Gillow was a wealthy Kent country squire and magistrate, residing at a large farm in Woodnesborough, a small village a few miles outside Sandwich. Captain Gillow and his wife Sarah had a large family of seven sons and two daughters. The good Captain had a liking for modern agricultural machinery and, in late 1878, he bought a steam traction engine to speed up the ploughing and threshing work on the farm and, as a result of this machine being made use of, he was able

The murder of Arthur Gillow, from the *IPN*, 21 December, 1878.

Gambrill's cottage, Captain Gillow's house, and the Sandwich lock-up, from the *IPN*, 21 December, 1878.

to lay off several of his farm labourers. One of the remaining labourers, a truculent fellow named Stephen Gambrill, seemed to greatly resent the introduction of the engine. A few days later, Captain Gillow was dismayed to find that some miscreant had done damage to his steam engine: both the pressure gauge and the water gauge had been smashed. He alerted the police, and issued a reward for the capture of the vandal; his two sons Richard and Arthur offered to stand guard by the valuable machine, hoping to be able to teach the culprit a hard lesson, should he return.

On the morning of 5 December 1878, the 23-year-old Arthur Gillow was found dead not far from the steam engine. His head had been battered in with a heavy stick or bludgeon. The previous evening, he had declared his intention to stand guard by the engine, to try to catch the vandal who had broken it. The weather had been wet, and the police could clearly see the footprints of a man wearing heavy hobnailed boots walking away from the murdered man. Richard Gillow thought the footprints matched the boots of the labourer Gambrill, a mean-spirited and pugnacious man, who had been among the suspects for the previous vandalism at the farm. When the police spoke to Gambrill, who was ploughing in the fields, he said that he had spent the previous evening with his father, and denied any involvement in the murder. Another workman thought Gambrill looked 'queer', as if he had something to hide. In the evening, Gambrill went to the Green Posts public house to have a few drinks. The murder of Arthur Gillow was, of course, the main subject of conversation and Gambrill declared that he was very sorry about what had happened, for young Mr Gillow had been the best master he had ever had. But as the beer was taking effect on the rather sluggish machinery of his brain, Gambrill began talking confusedly about having been drunk the evening before, and doing something wrong. He was worried about the police making inquiries about him, and told the landlord William Bagg that if they came asking for information about the stick he used to carry, the landlord should say that he had broken it while cleaning his boots, and thrown it in a field. The landlord thought Gambrill's behaviour very suspicious, and after he had informed Superintendent William Stokes, who had taken charge of the murder investigation, Gambrill was taken into police custody.

The coroner's inquest was held the day after the murder, when Gambrill had just been arrested. The motive for the murder had not been robbery, since Gillow still had his silver watch, and some coins as well. The murderer had beaten his victim down with a stick, and then cut his throat to make sure he was dead. A verdict of murder against some person or persons unknown was returned. The police had made plaster-of-Paris casts of the footprints in the mud, and they matched Gambrill's boots perfectly. His clothes were found to be liberally sprinkled with blood, and the trousers were soiled with mud, suggesting that he had been down on his knees, and struggled to get up. His chest was very bruised, like if he had been in a fight. The stick he used to carry was nowhere to be found. While in police custody, Gambrill belatedly showed some concerns for his wife and his two children. He shared a cell with two other suspected felons, and confided in them that he was all right, for the man he had beaten and kicked was dead, and could not testify against him. After killing him, he had gone home and enjoyed a hearty meal and a good night's sleep. If he was to be hanged, he hoped to meet the celebrated executioner William Marwood, and he would not mind being dead, if it had not been for his family, he declared. On Christmas Eve, Gambrill was brought from St Augustine's Prison to the court house in Canterbury, where he was charged to stand trial at the Maidstone Assizes, for the murder of Arthur Gillow.

On 14 January 1879, the 28-year-old Stephen Gambrill stood trial at the Maidstone Assizes, before Lord Justice Cotton. The eloquent Mr Serjeant Ballantine led for the prosecution, and a long row of witnesses gave evidence against Gambrill: Richard Gillow, the shoemaker who had made the distinctive boots, the pub landlord Bagg, and a variety of police officers and medical experts. Twice, at the pub and in the police cell, Gambrill had made remarks indicating that he was the guilty man. Mr Deane, for the defence, suggested that Arthur Gillow had attacked Gambrill by the steam engine, and that Gambrill had knocked him down. Some other enemy of young Gillow had then appeared on the scene, and cut his throat. Serjeant Ballantine effectively closed this loophole by pointing out that there had been only two sets of footprints in the mud: those of the murdered man and those left behind by Gambrill's distinctive boots. The jury was not out for long before delivering a verdict of Guilty, and Lord Justice Cotton sentenced Gambrill to death.

Awaiting execution, Gambrill confessed to the prison chaplain that after Arthur Gillow had collared him near the steam engine, he had knocked him down after a furious fight. He had then cut Gillow's throat to make sure he did not give evidence concerning the identity of his assailant. The Sheriff of Kent is said to have received letters from landed proprietors all over the country, offering to be the executioner of Gambrill, but since a professional hangman was already at hand, they were all turned down. On 4 February 1878, Gambrill's ambition to meet the executioner Marwood was fulfilled at the scaffold erected at Maidstone Prison: he was given an 8 foot drop, and died without a struggle.

25. A Richmond Horror Story, 1879

In 1879, two semi-detached small cottages in Park Road, Richmond, were owned by a certain Mrs Ives. This old lady herself lived at No. 1 Vine Cottages, as she called it, and rented the other cottage to Mrs Julia Thomas, a 60-year-old former schoolteacher who had been twice widowed. After the death of her second husband in 1873, this rather eccentric and pernickety old lady had moved into No. 2 Vine Cottages, a two-storey semi-detached villa built in grey stone with gardens at the front and back. The difficulties of the Victorian postman, with all these 'Rows', 'Terraces' and 'Cottages' in every road, was further aggravated by the fact that before Mrs Ives had moved in, the two houses had been known as No. 1 and No. 2 Mayfield Cottages, and the names were used interchangeably. The area around Park Road was not heavily populated at the time, although Vine Cottages were close to a public house called The Hole in the Wall.

Mrs Thomas' short temper and high demands of cleanliness meant that her servants usually did not remain at No. 2 Vine Cottages for very long. In late January 1879, she employed yet another general servant, the 30-year-old Irishwoman Kate Webster, This strong, brutal-looking woman brought a good reference with her, forged by a friend of hers. She was fortunate that Mrs Thomas did not know about her background, since not only did she have a long history of drunkenness and dishonesty, she had also been imprisoned for theft, and given birth to a son born out of wedlock.

It did not take long before mistress and servant were at serious loggerheads at No. 2 Vine Cottages. Mrs Thomas scolded Kate for her incompetence, sloth and lack of cleanliness, and the sturdy, hard-faced Irishwoman more than once answered her back. Mrs Thomas made sure that Kate's term of employment would end by the last day of February. But still, as the weeks went by, the relationship between mistress and servant kept deteriorating. The nervous Mrs Thomas was becoming fearful that Kate would injure or murder her. When Kate asked to be allowed to remain in the house until 2 March, Mrs Thomas did not dare to refuse her this favour.

THE RICHMOND TRAGEDY.

KATE WEBSTER, THE ACCUSED.

"THE BARNES MYSTERY."

H. CHURCH, THE EX-HUSSAR.

RESIDENCE OF MRS. THOMAS AT RICHMOND.

Kate Webster and the Richmond murder house, from the *Penny Illustrated Paper*, 5 July 1879.

On that day, there was an angry quarrel between Mrs Thomas and Kate, after the latter had returned to No. 2 Vine Cottages quite drunk. Kate, who had a vocabulary like a Billingsgate fishwife, damned and blasted her employer with a hearty goodwill. A respectable, religious,

Portraits in connection with the murder of Mrs Thomas, from the *IPN*, 17 May 1879.

Kate Webster, from the *IPN*, 3 May 1879. The bottom right panel depicts the attempt to steal Mrs Thomas' furniture from the murder house.

former schoolmistress like Mrs Thomas is unlikely to have heard such horrid words from a woman before. The shaken old lady went to church, and several people saw that she looked very worried and upset, although they did not inquire what was the matter.

The execution of Kate Webster, from the *IPN*, 2 August 1879.

In spite of the terrible scene earlier in the day, Mrs Thomas, whose instinct of self-preservation appears to have been quite defective, returned to No. 2 Vine Cottages. Kate was waiting for her there, with murder in mind. Mrs Thomas tried to take refuge in her bedroom, but Kate followed her upstairs. She seized hold of her employer and flung her headlong down the stairs. Mrs Thomas landed with a heavy thud, and Kate seized her by the throat and throttled her to death. The Irish virago then dragged the limp body of her mistress into the kitchen, where she made use of a saw, a chopper and a knife to dismember it. She lit a roaring fire underneath the large kitchen copper, and as soon as the water boiled, she loaded various body parts into it. This was hot work, and Kate had to go to The Hole in the Wall pub to refresh herself at regular intervals, leaving what remained of her mistress boiling in the copper.

With admirable coolness, Kate Webster cleaned the murder house and the kitchen. She put the bones and some flaps of skin in a wooden box and a Gladstone bag. She answered the door to visitors and delivery boys, and seemed to be her regular truculent self. There is even a – hopefully apocryphal – story that Kate went round the neighbourhood offering two tubs of lard for sale, declaring them to be the best drippings; this was the residue left by her recent 'cookery' in the kitchen copper. With the help of a singularly unsuspicious boy, she managed to throw the box and the Gladstone bag into Thames. The box and its contents did not sink as she had expected, but was found washed up in shallow water next to the riverbank the very next day. It was spotted and recovered by a coal porter driving his cart past the Barnes Railway Bridge. After the discovery had been reported to the police, the remains were examined by a doctor, who found that they consisted of the trunk (minus entrails) and legs (minus one foot) of a woman. Around the same time, a human foot and ankle were found in Twickenham. Crucially, the incompetent doctor who examined these body parts erroneously attributed them to a young woman with dark hair, and nobody thought of old Mrs Thomas. The newspapers dubbed the unexplained murder the Barnes Mystery, and speculated that the body might have been used for dissection by some medical students.

Kate Webster stole everything valuable in the murder house but, before escaping to Ireland, she also wanted to sell the furniture. Passing herself off as Mrs Thomas, she contacted a former publican named John Church, who agreed to buy it. But when Church came to No. 2 Vine Cottages, he was spotted by Mrs Ives. She told him that since Mrs Thomas was in arrears with her rent, her furniture was not going anywhere. From her description of the original householder, it became clear to Church that the woman who had passed herself off as Mrs Thomas was in fact her servant Kate Webster. When he went through the clothes in the delivery van, he found a letter addressed to the real Mrs Thomas. The police were called in and searched No. 2 Vine Cottages. They discovered bloodstains, burnt finger-bones in the hearth, and fatty deposits behind the copper, as well as a letter left by Kate Webster giving her home address in Ireland. They immediately put out a 'wanted' notice giving a description of Kate and her son. She was arrested at her uncle's farm at Killanne near Enniscorthy, and taken back to Richmond via Holyhead.

The murder of Mrs Thomas caused a great sensation in London: when the news broke, many people travelled to Richmond to look at the murder house. Kate Webster went on trial at the Old Bailey on

2 July 1879, before Mr Justice Denman. The prosecution was led by the Solicitor General, Sir Hardinge Giffard, and Kate was defended by the prominent London barrister Warner Sleigh. Over the course of six days, the court heard a succession of witnesses piecing together the story of how Mrs Thomas had met her death. Kate attempted to implicate the publican Church and her former neighbour Porter, but both men had solid alibis and were cleared of any involvement in the murder. Kate's defence counsel sought to emphasise the circumstantial nature of the evidence and highlighted his client's great devotion to her son as a reason why she could not have been capable of the murder. A particularly damning piece of evidence came from a woman who told the court that Kate had visited her a week before the murder and had said that she was going to Birmingham to sell some property, jewellery and a house that her aunt had left her. The jury interpreted this as a sign that Kate had premeditated the murder, and convicted her after deliberating for about an hour and a quarter.

Hoping to avoid the death penalty, Kate pleaded that she was pregnant. Eventually the Clerk of Assize suggested using the archaic mechanism of a jury of matrons, constituted from a selection of the women attending the court, to rule upon the question of whether Kate was 'quick with child'; it turned out that she was not, and accordingly she was sentenced to death. Kate Webster was hanged at Wandsworth Prison on 29 July 1879, and buried in an unmarked grave in one of the prison's exercise yards. The venerable crime writer Guy Logan had a journalist colleague who was once imprisoned at old Wandsworth Gaol for the non-payment of rates. When he complained that his cell was particularly uncomfortable and spooky, the warder exclaimed 'Why, you ought to be honoured, you did! Blow me if they ain't been and given you Kate Webster's condemned cell!' There has been speculation among aficionados of South London ghosts that the 'Grey Lady of Wandsworth', a ghost still haunting Wandsworth Prison, is the apparition of Kate Webster.

The day after the execution, an auction of the property of Mrs Thomas was held at the murder house. John Church, the publican, managed to obtain the furniture after all, with numerous other personal effects including her pocket-watch and the knife with which Mrs Thomas had been dismembered. The copper in which the body of Mrs Thomas had been boiled was sold for 5s, and a woman bought the chopper that had been used with such gusto for 2s. Other visitors contented themselves with taking small pebbles and twigs from the garden as souvenirs. Since nobody would live there, the murder house remained unoccupied until

1897. But when the 'ghost-hunter' Elliott O'Donnell corresponded with the lady who had gone to live at No. 2 Vine Cottages in 1897, she assured him that there had been no ghostly manifestations, although the servants had been reluctant to work at such a notorious murder house. Guy Logan was always keen to point out that he had more than once passed the pretty little murder cottage in what was now Park Road. He even wrote that

> the majority of houses which have been the scenes of murder seem ever after to be under a cloud, and to shudder, as it were, from the public gaze, but this cannot be said of the neat and pretty little villa at Richmond, which was the locale of Kate Webster's horrid crime. I have passed it many times in the course of years, and anything less like the popular conception of a 'murder house' it would be hard to imagine.

Elliott O'Donnell, who edited the *Trial of Kate Webster* in the Notable British Trials series, did not share Guy Logan's murder house detective skills, since the careless ghost-hunter reproduced an alleged 'contemporary print' that clearly does *not* depict the murder house at what is today 9 Park Road. This valuable and well-kept house is in good repair and looks very much as it had done at the time of the horrible events back in 1879.

The details of the brutal murder of Mrs Thomas caused an immediate sensation and were widely reported in the press. Such was Kate Webster's notoriety that within only a few weeks of her arrest, and well before she had gone to trial, Madame Tussaud's created a wax effigy of her and put it on display for those who wished to see the 'Richmond Murderess'. When a friendly aunt took Guy Logan to Madame Tussaud's, he shocked her by demanding an immediate descent to the Chamber of Horrors. As Guy himself later expressed it,

> My depraved interest in the models of the notorious criminals was such, I have been told, that it was with difficulty I was persuaded to return to the 'central transept', where the waxen Kings, Queens, and other celebrities held court. I could not be induced to come away from Kate Webster, whose image I regarded with fascinated horror. There, in front of me and as large as life, was the waxen counterfeit of the dread woman whose crime had caused such a stir, and who looked capable, in my youthful imagination, of boiling half a dozen mistresses in as many coppers.

There was also a popular song about the Richmond Murderess:

> The terrible crime at Richmond at last,
> On Catherine Webster now has been cast,
> Tried and found guilty she is sentenced to die.
> From the strong hand of justice she cannot fly.
> She has tried all excuses but of no avail,
> About this and murder she's told many tales,
> She has tried to throw blame on others as well,
> But with all her cunning at last she has fell.

It is quite uncommon that women commit murder with dismemberment, but the fierce, coarse-looking Kate Webster was not particularly feminine. Elliott O'Donnell described her as 'not merely savage, savage and shocking ... but the grimmest of grim personalities, a character so uniquely sinister and barbaric as to be hardly human'. Her appearance and behaviour were seen as key signs of her inherently criminal nature. Her callous lying in court, and attempt to 'frame' Church and Porter also caused revulsion. Many Victorians who came to gawp at her statue at Madame Tussaud's viewed Kate Webster as the ultimate murderess: strong, ugly and brutal, and capable of every crime. The anti-Irish sentiments of the time were also fuelled by her crime; the denigration of Kate Webster was a part of the public perception of the Irish as innately criminal.

So, the *flesh* of Mrs Thomas was boiled in the copper, and her *bones* were dumped in the Thames. But what about her *head*? Well, the story goes that in 1952, the celebrated naturalist Sir David Attenborough bought a house situated between Vine Cottages and the Hole in the Wall pub. The old pub closed in 2007 and fell into dereliction but was bought by Attenborough in 2009 to be redeveloped. On 22 October 2010, workmen carrying out excavation work at the rear of the old pub discovered the skull of a woman. It had been buried underneath foundations that had been in place for at least 40 years, on the site of the pub's stables. It was immediately speculated that the skull was the missing head of Julia Thomas, and the coroner asked the Richmond police to carry out an investigation into the identity and circumstances of death of the skull's owner. Carbon dating indicated that it was dated between 1650 and 1880, but it had been deposited on top of a layer of Victorian tiles. The skull had fracture marks consistent with Kate Webster's account of throwing Mrs Thomas down the stairs, and it was found to have low collagen levels, consistent with it being boiled. It entirely lacked teeth, something that is of importance, since we know that Kate Webster stole Mrs Thomas' 'snappers' which contained a gold plate, to have them sold. In July 2011, the coroner concluded that the skull was indeed that of Mrs Thomas, and it was decently buried. Although the evidence for the skull's authenticity is far from conclusive, one can almost see the brutal Kate Webster exclaiming 'Good riddance to yer!' and giving the head of Mrs Thomas a mighty kick, sending it into the hole she had dug in the rear yard of the pub.

26. The Strange Case Of Jonathan Geydon, 1879

In June 1857, Mary White, an elderly housekeeper living at Chingford Hatch, Essex, was found murdered in the small farmhouse where she had been living with her sister and brother-in-law. Suspicion soon centred on a young ne'er-do-well named Jonathan Geydon. After being sentenced to 18 months in prison with hard labour for stealing a pony, he had recently emerged from Springfield Gaol in Chingford, looking as work-shy and mean-spirited as ever. The night of the murder, Geydon had been observed walking towards the murder house by a person who knew him; he had looked furtive and said 'Do not say you have seen me!' The master shoemaker of Springfield Gaol testified that the murder weapon, a large knife, had been stolen by Geydon while in prison.

The parents of Jonathan Geydon, who had been hounded out of Essex by their son's perpetual bad conduct, were tracked down in Gloucestershire, but Jonathan was not with them. Parties of police were searching suitable hideouts near Chingford, beating the bushes and looking into hollow trees, but without success. Notices advertising a £100 reward for the capture of Geydon were pasted up, with a description of

The portrait of Jonathan Geydon, with the murder house, from *IPN*, 27 September, 1879.

him: a very ugly, unkempt fellow, aged 26 and 5 feet 9 inches tall, with a dull countenance, small whiskers, and a number of nasty-looking boils on his neck. But the suspected murderer was nowhere to be found, and the Chingford Hatch murder was gradually forgotten about.

In September 1879, more than 22 years after the Chingford Hatch murder, a rough-looking tramp walked into Horsham Police Station, gave his name as Jonathan Geydon, and declared that he was the murderer of Mary White. He had knocked her down with a stick and stolen all valuables he could find, but when she tried to raise the alarm, he had cut her throat. Since the murder, he had been tramping the country for many years, and even been to India, working on board ship. But ill health, privations, and his conscience gnawing away for decades, had finally broken his determination to keep running from the law. Although not yet fifty years old, he looked quite decrepit, with grey hair and a stooping gait. When he was examined at the Waltham Abbey Petty Sessions, several people, including Miss White's brother-in-law, recognized him as the Jonathan Geydon they had known.

When tried at the Old Bailey, Geydon was defended by the young barrister Horace Avory, later to become a successful judge. The despondent-looking Geydon pleaded guilty, but Avory interposed to make him change his plea to 'not guilty'. After the prosecution witnesses had identified the prisoner as Geydon, and the evidence concerning the Chingford Hatch murder had been considered, Avory made a clever attempt to save his client. Several former soldiers identified the prisoner as Charles Wilson, a private in the 5th Fusiliers. Another individual testified that the original Jonathan Geydon had been suffering from a limp, and that he had burst himself at the wheel during forced labour while serving his sentence for horse-stealing. Surely, a limping man suffering from a hernia could not be accepted into the army, and it would be a dangerous thing for a jury to convict his client of a terrible crime.

But the equally clever Harry Poland and Montagu Williams, prosecuting, pooh-poohed this testimony, saying that all it proved was that Jonathan Geydon had served as a soldier for a short time, under an assumed name. Not a single Essex witness had denied that the prisoner was Geydon. And what about the prisoner's confession, and his acquaintance with every detail about the murder? The jury found the prisoner Guilty, and Sir Henry Hawkins, the notorious 'hanging judge', donned the black cap and sentenced him to death. But several jurymen, and quite a few humanitarians, brought up a petition that Geydon's sentence should be commuted to life imprisonment. Almost at the last minute, they had success, and Geydon was removed to Pentonville Prison in December 1879. The 1881 Census puts Geydon in the Woking Invalid Prison, but regular nourishment seems to have improved his health; in 1891, he was a convict at Dartmoor Prison, and he died in 1896 aged 65 at Parkhurst Prison, Isle of Wight.

The case of Jonathan Geydon was considered very singular at the time, and was commented on even in the *New York Times*. With more than 22 years passing between murder and conviction, he beat the aforementioned William Sheward, the Norwich wife-murderer, by nine years. In Victorian times, murder convictions after such a considerable period of time were possible only after the confession of the conscience-stricken killer. Today, advances in DNA technology have meant that murderers never can feel quite safe; there are many examples, on both sides of the Atlantic, of murderers being convicted after several decades.

27. The Widnes Murder, 1879

Patrick Tracey was a honest, reliable Irish labouring man, employed at Mr J. Muspratt's chemical works in Widnes just outside Liverpool. He lived at 60 Oxford Street, off the Lugsdale Road, in central Widnes; in stark contrast to the corresponding street in London, this was a humble suburban road filled with small working men's residences. Paddy Tracey had a wife named Mary Ann, and three children as well.

Mary Ann Tracey was very fond of her 'Darlint Paddy', but unfortunately this was not her husband, but the lodger Paddy Kearney, a younger and more attractive Irish labouring man. When Mary Ann got pregnant, the guilty pair decided to persuade the other lodger in the house, the Irishman Hugh Burns, into a conspiracy. They would purchase a revolver and shoot Paddy Tracey dead while he slept, and then fake a robbery and say that burglars had broken into the house. Paddy Tracey's life was already insured, but on the advice of Hugh Burns, who was quite a hardened wretch, Mary Ann went and purchased another life insurance premium on her hapless husband, meaning that if the three villains managed to get away with murdering Paddy, they would have £365 of insurance money to take with them to the Emerald Isle.

On the evening of 22 October 1879, the conspirators decided to set their plan in motion. Mary Ann sneaked out of the bedroom, and one of the lodgers came in and shot the sleeping Paddy behind the ear with the newly purchased revolver. Mary Ann then made an outcry that robbers had entered the house and gunned down her husband; they had broken open a box and

The murder of Paddy Tracey, from the *IPN*, 8 November 1879.

stolen £15 in cash, she claimed. But the experienced Liverpool detectives immediately suspected that the surviving inhabitants of 60 Oxford Street were lying. Mary Ann Tracey, who claimed to have slept next to her husband when he was shot, had no marks of blood on her nightgown, although poor Paddy's head was covered with blood, and the bed liberally sprinkled with gore. The two lodgers claimed to have seen or heard nothing of the murder, but the detectives did not believe them. Although Paddy Kearney was a good-looking youth, just 21 years old, the 30-year-old Hugh Burns was a shifty-looking cove, who had a police record for petty crime. The detectives promptly arrested all three suspects, and held them in jail as the coroner's inquest on Paddy Tracey was opened on 27 October.

Mary Ann Tracey had said that the burglars turned murderers had entered through a window, but here she fell victim to her indifferent application to her duties as a housewife: the windows were all dirty and full of cobwebs, indicating that no person had entered that way. The police had found the murder weapon, which matched the revolver purchased by Paddy Kearney and Hugh Burns beforehand. The detectives also found out about the large life insurance premium that Mary Ann had taken out on her husband a few days before he was murdered. The Widnes police court committed the three miscreants to stand trial for murder, and at the Liverpool Assizes, they were all found guilty and sentenced to death. Lord Coleridge, the Lord Chief Justice presiding, said that they had 'cruelly, deliberately, and ruthlessly – without any quarrel, without any kind of extenuation or excuse – murdered an unoffending and harmless man from the basest and wickedest of all base and wicked motives.'

The cowardly nature of the Widnes Murder was commented on by the local newspapers; it was considered 'not cricket' to shoot dead a respectable householder in his sleep, and the role played by the faithless Mary Ann in planning and executing the murder was deplored. The *Liverpool Mercury* exclaimed that 'For cool cruelty of premeditation, cunning of arrangement, and brutality of execution, the Widnes murder stands perhaps without a parallel in the dark history of crime.' As the three villains were held in prison, pressure was put on them to confess, but Hugh Burns maintained a sullen silence, and Paddy Kearney vociferously pleaded his innocence. As for Mary Ann Tracey, her pregnancy saved her from the gallows: she gave birth to her daughter Mary, who was promptly removed to the Widnes workhouse, in early March 1880.

Hugh Burns and Paddy Kearney were executed at Kirkdale Gaol in Liverpool on 2 March 1880. There was a heavy snowstorm, and the High Sheriff went to the wrong prison by mistake, meaning that the two men were kept waiting for several hours, before Marwood the executioner launched them into eternity. At the time of the 1881 Census, Mary Ann Tracey was languishing in Woking Convict Prison; she was still there at the time of the 1891 Census, and is likely to have ended her life in Liverpool in late 1901, aged 50.

28. The Murder of Sarah Jane Roberts, 1880

Mr Richard Greenwood was a 70-year-old retired business man, residing in a small semi-detached house at Westbourne Grove, Harpurhey, a small town just north of Manchester. In contrast to its busy London namesake, this Westbourne Grove was a lonely thoroughfare, without much of interest ever happening there. With Mr Greenwood lived his elderly invalid wife Mary Ann, and the 18-year-old servant girl Sarah Jane Roberts. Sarah Jane was the fifth child of Hugh Roberts, a respectable Oswestry maltster, who had later moved to Pembroke, South Wales. She went out into service at an early age, and went to join her brother in Manchester in 1878. The year after, she joined Mr Greenwood's household in Westbourne Grove. Sarah Jane Roberts was a sturdy, handsome girl with luxuriant black hair. Although by nature reserved, she was friendly and cheerful, and Mr Greenwood and his wife found her a very agreeable servant. They treated her almost like a member of the family, and to induce her to stay with them in their old age, Mr Greenwood made provisions for her in his will.

On 7 January 1880, everything seemed normal in the Greenwood household at Westbourne Grove. At midday, Mr Greenwood's business partner Mr Cooper came calling, and Sarah Jane Roberts opened the

The finding of Sarah Jane Roberts, and the murder house, from the *IPN*, 24 January 1880.

A portrait of Sarah Jane Roberts, and incidents from the arrest of the tramps Heald and Laycock, from the *IPN*, 7 February 1880.

door to him. He noticed a letter lying on the porch carpet, and said 'Hullo, Jane, here's a love-letter for you!' She examined the letter, which must have been delivered by hand since it had no stamp attached, and said 'Oh, no: it is for Mr Greenwood.' She gave the letter to her master, and he opened it, to read the lines:

Mr Greenwood, I want to take the land near the coal-yard, behind the druggist's shop, Queen's-road. I will pay either monthly, quarterly, or yearly, and will pay in advance, and will meet you to-night from five to six o'clock at the 'Three Tuns', corner of Churnet-street, and will tell you all particulars. I don't know your address or I would have posted it. Yours, &c., Oldham Road, W. Wilson.

He found it strange that, instead of calling at the house, the mysterious 'W. Wilson' had just pushed the letter underneath the door. And how could he claim not to know Greenwood's address, when the letter had been correctly delivered? Richard Greenwood was not particularly keen to part with the land by the coal yard, but his wife persuaded him that no harm would come from keeping the appointment at the Three Tuns, since some extra money in the household would come in handy. At 5 p.m., Richard Greenwood left his house and walked over to the Three Tuns to meet 'W. Wilson'. He was dismayed to find that no such person was present at the tavern. At 6.20, Mr Greenwood went back home, telling the barman that if Wilson belatedly appeared, he would have to come to Westbourne Grove.

While her husband was away, the invalid Mrs Greenwood sat in her room on the first floor, with the door open, enabling her to hear what was going on in the household. At 6.25 there was a knock on the front door, and she could hear Jane open the front door and let in some person who walked very lightly, like a woman. The kitchen door closed. There was silence for five minutes, and then a terrible scream rent the air. Mrs Greenwood limped out of her room and called out 'What's the matter, Jane?' The only answer was another bloodcurdling scream, and then dead silence. Mrs Greenwood hobbled down to the front door and screamed 'Murder! Murder!' Next door lived Mr Cadman, a Unitarian minister, and his wife. Mrs Cadman heard the screams emanating from the Greenwoods' kitchen, and she ran out to her front door, where she saw old Mrs Greenwood, who exclaimed 'There's something wrong in my kitchen!' Mrs Cadman and her servant entered the house and opened the kitchen door, finding Sarah Jane Roberts lying on the floor with blood trickling from her head. She was still breathing, and medical assistance was sent for, but the girl died within five minutes, without uttering a word. When Mr Greenwood returned home at 6.40, Sarah Jane Roberts was a corpse.

Mr Pinder, surgeon, was soon at Westbourne Grove, and he declared the cause of death to be repeated heavy blows to the head from a blunt instrument. The murder weapon was not found on the premises. Superintendent Bent took charge of the policemen working on the case. He was interested to find that the school board officer Mr E. A. Halling, who lived a few yards away from Mr Greenwood, had heard some person rush past his front door, and then splash through a deep clay pit across the road, through 3 or 4 feet of water. He had then heard the cry of 'Murder! Murder!', armed himself with a stick, and went over to Mr Greenwood's house. Had the murderer escaped from Greenwood's house through the back door, and waded through the water-filled clay pit? It was clear to Superintendent Bent that the letter from 'W. Wilson' had been intended to lure Richard Greenwood away from the house, leaving Sarah Jane Roberts alone with the invalid Mary Ann Greenwood. He was undecided whether the letter had been pushed under the door by a burglar, or whether Sarah Jane Roberts may have left it there herself, either intending to see her lover behind the back of the Greenwoods, or admit a burglar friend into the house. Mr and Mrs Greenwood retorted that Sarah Jane had always been a very good girl, who had shown no interest in the opposite sex; she had also been commendably loyal to her employers, and it was inconceivable that she would have let a burglar into the house. There was a good deal of gossip in Harpurhey, and it was said that Mr Greenwood had been very intimate with his servant, and that he might well have been involved in the murder. The police responded that Greenwood had a watertight alibi, having been at the Three Tuns shortly before the murder. The next man named and shamed was the business partner Mr Cooper, and there was idle gossip that he had given Sarah Jane the letter that lured Mr Greenwood away from the house. A milkman named Partington was also talked about as being involved in the murder, but the police established that he had been on a milk round half a mile away at the time of the murder. The police received several anonymous letters, and another one was sent to the *Newcastle Daily Chronicle* by some joker claiming to know the identity of the murderer, although he was unwilling to come forward due to some discreditable incident in his own past. The coroner's inquest on Sarah Jane Roberts returned a verdict of murder against some person or persons unknown.

Sarah Jane Roberts was buried at Christ Church, Harpurhey, on 10 January, three days after she had been murdered. Richard Greenwood, who had paid all expenses for the funeral, was present, as were Sarah Jane's mother Elizabeth, her brothers Robert and Hugh and their wives, and her sister Elizabeth. The coffin had the inscription 'Sarah Jane Roberts: died 7th January; aged 18 years. In Adam all die; in Christ shall all be made alive.' Just before the coffin was closed, the Manchester photographer James Mudd photographed the eyes from a close distance. Superintendent Bent ordered magnifications of these photographs to be manufactured, and they were closely examined in the hope of seeing the face of the murderer appear. Interviewed in the *Manchester Times*, Dr A. Emrys-Jones, honorary surgeon to the Royal Eye Hospital, did not believe that the stratagem of photographing the eyes of a person who had been dead for three days would produce results; instead, the eyes should have been removed as soon as possible after death, for examination by a team of eye specialists. And indeed, Superintendent Bent's examination of the eye photographs turned out to be entirely futile, although the persistent policeman told a journalist that he intended to submit the negatives to a man of science for further examination. Thus the earliest instance of eyeball photography in a British murder case ended anticlimactically.

In late January 1880, the two vagabonds Robert Heald and Thomas Laycock came tramping into Plymouth, where they lodged with a certain Mrs Sprague. They seldom left their room, and seemed to be hiding something. Mrs Sprague had read about the murder of Sarah Jane Roberts, and after Heald had told her that he had tramped all the way from Manchester, she suspected that she was hiding the murderer under her own roof. She went to the police, and the two vagabonds were arrested. It turned out that they were hoping to emigrate to Melbourne, Australia, and that Heald had applied for an assisted passage, giving his name as Watts and stating that he was unmarried. This was clearly untrue, since he was in fact married, with one child. Clearly, he had intended to leave Mrs Heald behind when decamping for the Antipodes. Robert Heald was a short, thin, insignificant-looking man, who appeared very gloomy and dejected; he certainly looked very unlike a brutal, cunning murderer. It turned out that he had a good alibi for the time of the murder of Sarah Jane Roberts, and although it was contemplated to prosecute him for his perjurious application for a passage to Australia, he was eventually released without charge. Hopefully, he took his wife and child with him to the Antipodes, instead of leaving them behind.

It would not appear as if the murderer of Sarah Jane Roberts was a stranger to her: after all, she had willingly let him into the house, and stayed with him in the kitchen for five minutes. Thus he could hardly have been a burglar, robber or old enemy, rather some person she knew and trusted. It is of course possible that she had planted the letter herself, to get Mr Greenwood away so that she could meet a secret lover, but I do not subscribe to that theory. Firstly, Mr Greenwood could have been home any minute, to catch the guilty pair; secondly, the murdered girl had turned out to be *virgo intacta* at the post-mortem; thirdly, it was not in character for her to deceive her master and enjoy a sordid intrigue. Another hypothesis discussed by the police, namely that Sarah Jane Roberts let a burglar friend into the house, after Mr Greenwood had been lured away, also seems unlikely, since she had always been a good girl, and devoted to her master and mistress; moreover, although the house had contained a good deal of money and valuables, nothing whatsoever had been stolen. The internet offers up an interesting wild card, alleged to emanate from a deceased local historian named as Mary Turner: it was the brother of Sarah Jane Roberts who had come calling at the murder house, and he had been a police suspect at the time. But this startling information is not backed up by any evidence, except that the brother is said to have escaped to America, and that his granddaughter informed the veteran local historian that according to a family tradition, he had fled to New York after murdering somebody. Two brothers of Sarah Jane Roberts, Robert and Hugh, were present at the coroner's inquest. There was a rumour locally that Robert Roberts had once tried to buy some of Mr Greenwood's land, but this was denied at the inquest. Interestingly, when Mary Ann Greenwood testified at the inquest, she said she had thought that the person Sarah Jane had let into the house was the wife of Robert Roberts, who apparently had visited her before. Since the murder was likely to have been committed by a strong, powerful man, due to the power of the blows delivered, it remains a mystery how the elderly, infirm Mrs Greenwood could have felt certain that the visitor was a woman. There was a Manchester local historian named Mary Turner, who died in 1989, but no contemporary newspaper mentions the brother of Sarah Jane Roberts as a suspect, and the internet account may still be a falsification.

As befitting a famous murder mystery, there were some later and anticlimactic 'developments' in the Sarah Jane Roberts matter. In February 1881, the soldier Edward Lynch, of the 4th King's Own Regiment and stationed in Calcutta, confessed to the murder, but he later retracted his confession after sobering up. In June 1882, the 33-year-old Manchester man William Nightingale Thomas gave himself up for the murder, but he was blind drunk and could not even tell the name of the murder victim. He was taken into police custody for a while, but it was soon proven that he was not the guilty man. As late as 1890, a man named John Williams, who had been arrested in Chicago for some other offence, confessed to the murder of 'Emma Roberts' in Leeds back in 1880, but again he was not believed. According to the crime writer Guy Logan, Mrs Greenwood never recovered from the shock of the murder of her servant girl, and she died shortly afterwards. Mr Greenwood left Harpurhey and went to live with friends. Only a rump of Westbourne Grove, off the Rochdale Road, remains today, and the murder house is long gone. The monument to Sarah Jane Roberts, in Christ Church Cemetery, Harpurhey, still stands: it has the inscription: 'In Memory of Sarah Jane Roberts, daughter of Hugh and Elizabeth Roberts, of Merlin's Cross in the Parish of St Michaels, Pembroke, born March 1st 1862, met with her Death by an Unknown Hand January 7th 1880.'

29. The Acton Atrocity, 1880

Mr John Shepherd was a successful builder and house decorator, who employed several workmen. He lived at 3 Herbert Villas, Cowper Road, Acton, with his second wife, his young son, and his four daughters. The oldest daughter, ten-year-old Ada, was reliable enough to take care of her younger sisters. On Friday 22 October 1880, Mr Shepherd and his wife went to visit Mrs Shepherd's mother, who lived at Norwood Junction. He took with him a large cheque for a house he had just sold, which he cashed in a bank on the way. Mrs Shepherd took the baby with her, but Ada was instructed to take the other three children to Mrs Perry's private school at 2 Churchfield Villas, where they were pupils, and to give them their lunch. George Pavey, a workman who had been in Mr Shepherd's employ for six months, was left in charge of the house, which doubled as Mr Shepherd's office. Pavey was a 'cripple' affected with partial spastic paralysis in one arm and leg, and he was supposed to be very grateful to Mr Shepherd, who had shown him much kindness in the past.

Just before 2 p.m., the three children came home to 3 Herbert Villas, where Ada made sure they were fed, before she escorted them back to school. But when some customers of Mr Shepherd came knocking at around 3–4 p.m., nobody answered the door. When the little children arrived home from school a little later, they were equally surprised

The discovery of the murder of Ada Shepherd, with a view of the murder house, from the *IPN*, 6 November 1880.

Ada Shepherd, and the apprehension of George Pavey, from the *IPN*, 6 November 1880.

that Ada was not there to let them in, and they went off for a stroll. Mr and Mrs Shepherd returned to the deserted house at 6.30 p.m., wondering where Pavey and the children had gone. In the kitchen, Mr Shepherd stumbled over a large object lying on the floor. He gave a cry of horror when he realized that it was the dead body of his daughter Ada, lying in a large pool of blood. Her face was covered with a handkerchief.

At first, the distraught Shepherds thought that their entire brood of children had been murdered, but the other three eventually turned up, none the worse for their late-afternoon stroll. Police Constable Walter Millar, who had been on patrol nearby when he heard an excited local shouting 'All of Mr Shepherd's children have been murdered!' as he ran

George Pavey, and other images from the Acton Atrocity, from the *IPN*, 13 November 1880.

George Pavey is sentenced to death, from the *IPN*, 4 December 1880.

along the pavement, went to Herbert Villas to investigate. He expressed relief when he saw the remaining children alive and well, and then horror as he was confronted with Ada's mangled corpse. The surgeon Mr Clement Murrell also arrived and examined the blood-soaked corpse, declaring that Ada had been brutally 'outraged' [raped] and then deliberately murdered with a deep stab wound to the throat. A bloodstained kitchen knife was found nearby. Ada's face was bruised and livid, as if her attacker had struck her, and held her in a stranglehold. She had been dead about three-and-a-half hours.

The question on everybody's lips was of course what had happened to the man Pavey, who was supposed to have been looking after the house. When Inspector Frederick Savage, an experienced officer from the Metropolitan Police, arrived at Herbert Villas to take charge of the murder investigation, it was clear to him that Pavey was the main suspect. After dispatching some constables to guard the murder house, and to search for Pavey and other suspicious persons locally, Inspector Savage went to the wanted man's last known lodgings, 31 Manchester Street, Notting Hill. Neither Pavey nor his wife were at home, however, and although the canny Inspector kept watch until 1 a.m., the suspect did not make an appearance.

The following morning, Inspector Savage ordered a general search for George Pavey, instructing that all hospitals and workhouses should report any suspicious new inmates, and that all low-class boarding-houses should be searched. It turned out that a young man had seen Pavey absconding from the murder house at 3.20 p.m., heading towards the Uxbridge Road. Ada Shepherd had last been seen alive at 2 p.m., by a confectioner from whom she had purchased a sugar-stick for her little sister, and at 2.10 by a greengrocer, from whom she had purchased halfpennyworth of nuts, obviously as a treat for herself once she had dispatched the younger children at their school. And indeed, some nuts had been found underneath one of Ada's lifeless hands. Inspector Savage suspected that Pavey had raped and murdered Ada soon after she had arrived home around 2.20 p.m. He had then broken open the door to Mr Shepherd's office, and searched it for the money his employer had spoken of receiving for the sale of a house. Finding none, since Mr Shepherd had not cashed the cheque but taken it with him to Norwood, he had stolen a pair of boots and various other articles, before skulking away towards the Uxbridge Road.

The days after the murder, there was uproar in Acton and its surroundings. Crowds of people stood gawping at the murder house.

Rumours abounded that all Mr Shepherd's children had been murdered, or that the entire family had been exterminated in a bloodbath. Still, the true facts of the case were horrific enough: nothing even remotely like the Acton Atrocity, as the rape and murder was called, had ever occurred in this quiet suburban neighbourhood. Rumours were flying about Pavey being arrested in Croydon, or with his parents in Brighton, possibly disguised as a woman. Unamused by such idle speculation, the police retorted that although several people had been taken into custody in different parts of London, they had all been able to explain themselves. Watch was kept at the railway stations, and at the main roads out of London, and all cheap hotels and lodging-houses were being searched by the police. The description of George Pavey, 5 feet 5 inches in height, of sallow complexion, clean shaven face, and walking stiffly due to being partially paralysed on the left side, was widely circulated. Local feeling against the suspect was greatly inflamed, and Inspector Savage was fearful that Pavey would be lynched if he was captured by the Acton vigilantes. The funeral of Ada Shepherd, at Hanwell Cemetery, was very well attended in spite of rainy weather.

On the evening of Sunday 24 October, two days after the murder of Ada Shepherd, a sore-footed vagabond came tramping into Hendon Workhouse. He was given some bread and butter, which he devoured with the rapidity of extreme hunger. The workhouse superintendent, who of course knew about the Acton Atrocity, came to see him. Since the tramp was lame in one arm and leg, and very much resembled the description of George Pavey that had been issued by the police, he gruffly called out 'Your name is Pavey!' The vagabond, who was chewing hard at the bread, swallowed convulsively, before meekly admitting 'Yes, it is.' He was promptly taken to the Paddington police station, where he was confronted by Inspector Savage. The detective showed him a large handkerchief, the one found covering the face of the murdered child, and Pavey said 'Yes, it is mine, I put it there!' He kept eating ravenously, consuming an entire loaf of bread, and drinking enormous quantities of tea, but he did not sleep all night.

On 25 October, Pavey was charged at the Hammersmith Police Court with the wilful murder of Ada Shepherd. A short, clean shaven man, he looked younger than his 29 years. His story was that around 2 p.m. on the day of the murder, an unknown man had come to 3 Herbert Villas, to say that Mr Shepherd wanted Pavey to go to the Uxbridge Road railway station at once. Without asking why, Pavey set off, but since he could not find his master, he returned to find that Ada had been murdered. Since Pavey has a criminal record for child molestation, he realized that he himself would become the main suspect, and absconded from the murder house. He had tramped round London for two days without anything to eat, and was in a state of near collapse, due to hunger and mental anxiety, when he decided to take refuge in Hendon Workhouse.

The police could soon verify that George Pavey had indeed 'been repeatedly convicted and imprisoned for horrible offences.' He came from a respectable Brighton family, and there was much sympathy for his poor parents. The police were working overtime to find additional evidence against him, and they soon had success: a pawnbroker's assistant named Henry Cross picked him out as the man who had pawned Mr Shepherd's boots, stolen from the murder house, for 7s. Pavey's shirt and trousers had been found to be stained with blood, and the forensic specialist Dr Thomas Bond declared that these stains came from human blood. The coroner's inquest on Ada Shepherd, held at the Station Hotel, Churchfield Road, [it still stands, but is today the Rocket public house], returned a verdict of wilful murder against George Pavey. According to a local newspaper, Pavey was quite optimistic about his chances at the Old Bailey, even making plans for his wife to sell his clothes to Madame Tussaud's when he had been acquitted.

On trial for murder at the Old Bailey on 23 November, things did not look good for George Pavey. His previous record of child molestation, the forensic evidence, and the clear and damning witness testimony all helped to bring the noose around his neck. He was prosecuted by the eloquent Harry Poland and Montagu Williams, and his own barrister Mr Frith could do little to combat the relentless witness testimony against him. The jury found Pavey guilty, and Sir Henry Hawkins put on the black cap, and delivered the following address:

George Pavey, it is impossible to conceive a more atrocious or a more cruel crime than that of which you have been convicted by the jury, who have listened patiently and very attentively to all that has been said on your behalf. God knows what can have possessed you to have committed that atrocious cruelty in violating the person of this poor little helpless unprotected child, and afterwards murdering her, as unquestionably you did, in the most cruel and brutal manner. It is difficult to find language to express one's sorrow at the barbarity of the act which you committed. For the crime of murder of which you have been convicted the law knows no sentence but that of death, and you must, young as you are, prepare to die, for your crime is of so barbarous a nature that I dare not hold out to you any hope that any mitigation of your sentence can be expected.

Sir Henry then pronounced sentence of death, and the prisoner, who remained perfectly calm during its delivery, was removed to the cells. While awaiting execution in Newgate, Pavey was twice visited by his wife, who took their young child along. He is recorded to have made statements to the warders that after he had been left alone in the house with Ada Shepherd, he felt strong urges to sexually molest her. Angered by her stubborn resistance, he then raped and murdered her. A garbled account of his dying speech and confession was widely hawked around the Acton streets. The Rev. Aaron Augustus Morgan, who had visited Pavey in prison, pointed out the prisoner's youth and paralytic affliction in a last-minute plea for mercy, but this document, which is still present in the police file on the case, is merely marked 'Nil'. George Pavey was hanged at Newgate on 13 December 1880, and a dark chapter in London's criminal history was at an end.

Both Harry Poland and Montagu Williams, who prosecuted George Pavey at the Old Bailey, wrote memoirs, but neither made any mention of their part in the conviction of the Acton child murderer. Instead, the famous Detective Superintendent Percy Savage, the son of Frederick Savage, pointed out the arrest and conviction of George Pavey as one of his father's greatest cases, instrumental in securing him the post as detective inspector in personal attendance on Queen Victoria. And just as the murderer himself had once planned, his effigy made an appearance at Madame Tussaud's, dressed in a suit of his own clothes, sold to Tussaud's establishment by Pavey's wife.

The question for the murder house sleuth, whether the house at 3 Herbert Villas, Cowper Road, is still standing today, was not immediately easy to answer. The reason is that all trace of the various 'Villas' and 'Terraces' in Cowper Road has disappeared, and the houses have been renumbered in a more conventional manner. Situated not far from Acton Central station, the houses in Cowper Road are numbered from the Churchfield Road end to the Shakespeare Road end, with even numbers on the eastern side, and odds on the western one. The houses closest to Churchfield Road on the eastern side are older in character, indicating that this part of the road was first developed. There is a terrace of four houses, and then a pair of semi-detached houses in a similar style. The third house in the terrace, formerly 3 Herbert Villas and now 6 Cowper Road, is the only house in Cowper Road to exactly fit the drawing of the murder house in the *IPN*; not even the windows appear to have been changed.

30. The Chislehurst Double Murder, 1880

Joseph Waller was a 24-year-old native of Chislehurst, who had gone to London and become a Metropolitan police constable. He had patrolled his beat in the City of London, being based at the Old Street police station, until he was dismissed for disorderly conduct. He went back to Chislehurst, where he supported himself through various odd jobs. The 74-year-old gamekeeper Edward Ellis had more than once employed him

Keeper's Cottage, a likeness of Joseph Waller, and the cottage where he lived with his parents, from the *IPN*, 13 November 1880.

Waller writing on the wall of his prison cell, and other features from the Chislehurst double murder, from the *IPN*, 20 November 1880.

as his assistant while patrolling the woodland looking for poachers. This veteran gamekeeper had been in the service of the local magnate Mr R. B. Berens Esq. for not less than fifty years, and his wife Elizabeth had been cook for Mr Berens for twenty years; their decades-long service had rewarded them with a home of their own on the estate, a humble two-storey house known as Keeper's Cottage.

On Saturday 30 October 1880, Joseph Waller was drinking hard at the Five Bells public house in Chislehurst. Since he was angry and argumentative in his cups, there was soon an altercation, and he was thrown out of the pub. After wandering about for a while, Waller took refuge in a pigsty, but the farmer spotted him and turned him out. The drunken young man then got the impulse to cause some serious mischief. The gamekeeper Ellis had refused to employ him recently, and Waller decided to teach him a hard lesson. He had a loaded revolver in his pocket, and after firing a shot into the night, he went up to Keeper's Cottage to tell the elderly gamekeeper that there were poachers in Pett's Wood. Although the time was 2.30 a.m., Edward Ellis got dressed, grabbed his lantern and truncheon, and followed Waller into the woodland. Once they were some distance away from the cottage, Waller shot the old gamekeeper down, and then finished him off with repeated blows from the truncheon.

The demented former policeman then returned to Keeper's Cottage, where he woke up Elizabeth Ellis and told her that her husband needed her urgently, since he had been injured in a fight with some poachers. Once the murderer had lured Mrs Ellis into the woodland, he attacked her with the truncheon and beat her to death. At 4 a.m., Police Constable Mackay saw Waller skulking outside Keeper's Cottage, but when asked what he was doing, the miscreant calmly replied that he was waiting for old Ellis, and the policeman walked off.

After the bloodbath in Pett's Wood, Joseph Waller returned to the rather dilapidated little Chislehurst house where he lived with his parents. He was dismayed to find a police constable waiting for him there, to take him into custody; this was not due to lightning-fast detective work concerning the double murder, but to the farmer who had caught him in the pigsty reporting him to the police for trespass. Waller was taken to the Chislehurst police station, looking very hungover and bedraggled. When he was searched by the police, they found the empty revolver and some loose cartridges. It was also noticed that he had blood on his hands, and that his clothes were bloodstained. All of a sudden, Waller said 'This is a good charge ... If you have a couple of stretchers and eight strong men, you can go to Ned Ellis's and there you will find two dead bodies.' When the startled Inspector Higgins asked who they were, Waller said: 'Ned Ellis and his wife,' before proceeding to tell the policemen exactly where the murdered people were to be found.

The mangled bodies of Edward and Elizabeth Ellis were found exactly where Waller had said they would be. The fingers of both victims were terribly broken, indicating that they had desperately tried to defend themselves against the ferocious assault with the truncheon. According to Waller, Ellis had tried to plead with him, saying 'I never did you any harm, Joe!' Although nothing had been stolen from Keeper's Cottage, the police presumed that robbery had been the motive for the murders, since Ellis was supposed to have hoarded money in his cottage. Waller denied having any animosity against the two Ellises, who had befriended him and never done him any harm. The murderer seemed quite mentally deranged after his terrible deed, and he scratched a drawing of Keeper's Cottage on the wall of his cell, with a crude picture of himself hanging from the gallows, with the caption 'Joseph Waller, murderer'.

The coroner's inquest on Edward and Elizabeth Ellis returned a verdict of wilful murder against Joseph Waller, and he was committed to stand trial at the Kent Winter Assizes. There was no doubt that he was the guilty man, but his sanity seemed questionable. Waller's father told a journalist that during his years as a police constable, Waller and his colleagues had once tried to capture some burglars inside a church. When Waller was lowered into a vault where the burglars were thought to be hiding, the rope broke and he landed on his head, sustaining a concussion and injuries to his spine. This accident changed his character, his father argued, and made him violent and obstinate. At the Kent Assizes, he was found insane and unable to plead, and was detained at her Majesty's pleasure. Waller was then removed, without making any remark or sign that he had understood what had just taken place. One internet writer claims that he was confined to Maidstone Gaol, but this can hardly be correct since that was no place for a lunatic; another writer puts him in St Luke's Hospital, a large London asylum; the correct version is that he was admitted to Broadmoor after his trial at the Maidstone Assizes, and that he died there in 1923. As for Keeper's Cottage outside Chislehurst, it still stands and looks entirely unchanged from the drawing in the *IPN* of 1880.

31. The Murder Of Mrs Reville, 1881

Hezekiah Reville was born in Linton, Cambridgeshire, in 1843, the son of the farmer John Mackintosh Reville. He became apprenticed to a butcher, and made good progress in his chosen trade. In 1874, he married Mary Ann Chudley at the London Street Chapel in Reading; both bride and groom were 21 years old. In or about 1876, he purchased a butcher's shop at Windsor Road in Slough, and set himself up as a master butcher. An *IPN* illustration shows him looking quite dignified, with a large bushy beard to match his venerable Biblical name. The Revilles had two daughters: Alice Jane, born in Slough in 1876, and Emily Gertrude, born in Eton in 1878. Mr and Mrs Reville were both steady, industrious people, and the butcher's shop made good progress. The shop opened at 7 a.m. and remained open until 8 p.m. Mrs Reville served behind the counter, kept the books and handled the accounts. In 1881, Mr Reville employed two young assistants: the 16-year-old Alfred Augustus Payne and the 15-year-old Philip Glass; both of them had been at the butcher's shop for around two years.

On Monday April 11 1881, everything seemed well at the little butcher's shop in Windsor Road. Hezekiah Reville and his two assistants were butchering away, and Ann Reville sold meat and hams behind the counter. The shop was a small one, about 18 feet by 12 feet, and equipped with a chopping-block and a counter with the scales. Behind the shop was a parlour, with a window to the shop; when doing the books, Ann Reville used to sit at a desk by this window so that she could see the customers coming into the shop. After a hard day's work, Hezekiah Reville went out around 8 p.m., to speak to some fellow tradesmen and empty a pint or two of beer. He told Payne to stay late at work, to rub salt into some

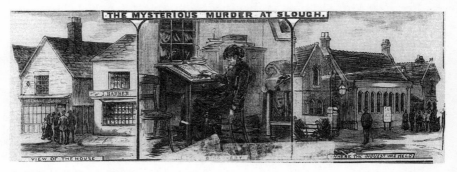

The butcher's shop, the corpse of Mrs Reville, and the hall where the inquest was held, from the *IPN*, 23 April 1881.

Drawings of Payne, Glass, Mr Reville and Superintendent Dunham, from the *IPN*, 7 May 1881.

hams. In spite of the late hour, the butcher's assistant obediently got to work. Glass left at 8.25 p.m., leaving Payne alone with Mrs Reville, and the two little girls sleeping in their bedroom upstairs. Payne claimed to have left at 8.32 p.m., Mrs Reville telling him to turn the gas down and shut the door before he went out. Just a few minutes later, Mrs Eliza Beasley, who lived next door but one to the Revilles, came to keep the butcher's wife company in the evening. She was horrified to find that Ann Reville had just been murdered with a chopper: there were two frightful wounds on the top of the head, breaking the skull open, and another deep wound in the neck.

Mrs Beasley ran out of the shop to summon assistance. She met a coachbuilder named George John Leight, who offered to stand guard at the shop while she ran to fetch a doctor; he later estimated that he

The shop at Slough in which the crime was committed.

The butcher's shop, from *Lloyd's News*, 13 October 1907.

reached the shop at 8.40 p.m., indicating that he had met Mrs Beasley at around 8.38 p.m. On her way to Mr Edward Dodd, the local surgeon, she met Police Sergeant Hebbes in the street, and explained to him what she had just seen. The experienced policeman consulted his watch when he reached the butcher's shop: it was 8.45 p.m., and he had met Mrs Beasley two minutes earlier. Mr Dodd also had a look at the clock in his consulting-room when the excited Mrs Beasley came to call: it was 8.45 p.m. The surgeon then made haste to Reville's butcher's shop, where he found Mrs Reville dead but still warm; she was far advanced in pregnancy, and sitting on the chair reclining backwards. He estimated that death had been instantaneous, due to the severity of the wounds, each of which had been sufficient to stun her. A bloody chopper was lying on the table, with a handwritten note.

Superintendent Thomas Dunham, of the Buckinghamshire Constabulary, who had been instrumental in the arrest of John Owen, the Denham mass murderer, back in 1870, was swiftly alerted, and he arrived at the murder shop as early as 8.45 p.m. Sergeant Hebbes pointed out that there an obvious clue to the identity of the murderer had been found: namely the handwritten note found on the table:

Mrs Reville: You never will sell me no more bad meat like you did on Saturday. I told Mrs Austin, of Chalvey, that I would do for her. I done it for the bad meat she sold me on Saturday last – H. Collins, Colnbrook.

This threatening missive was filed in a folder marked 'evidence', and some constables went to Colnbrook to find the man Collins, and to Chalvey to find Mrs Austin. By this time, Hezekiah Reville himself had been alerted by a boy sent to the White Hart nearby, where he had sat swigging from his pint glass of beer. Since Superintendent Dunham knew that the husband was often the guilty party in cases of wife murder, he considered the butcher as a prime suspect, but Reville was able to give a good account of his movements that evening, and he seemed genuinely distraught at the loss of his wife, to whom he had been devoted. When Reville was asked if he had any suspicions, he immediately mentioned the lad Alfred Augustus Payne, who had been suspected of stealing meat in the shop. Superintendent Dunham and Sergeant Hobbes went to see Payne, whose father kept the Royal Oak public house in Slough. Young Payne seemed strangely detached when the policemen told him that his employer's wife had just been brutally murdered, something they found odd and incriminating. They took Payne into custody, and ordered him to provide samples of his handwriting, for comparison with the writing of the note from 'Collins', which had clearly been written by the murderer.

On the afternoon of 12 April, Mr Frederick Charsley, the Coroner for South Buckinghamshire, opened the inquest on Ann Reville at the Crown Inn in the High Street. Captain Tyrwhitt-Drake, the Chief Constable of Buckinghamshire, and Superintendent Dunham, were watching the proceedings for the police. Philip Glass, the first witness, testified that he had been employed by Mr Reville for two years; Payne had been engaged some time before him. When Glass had left the butcher's shop at 8.25 p.m., Mrs Reville had been sitting in the back room, and Payne had still been on the premises. The saw and two steels had been on the block, but the chopper was nowhere to be seen. Glass had heard Mrs Reville complaining of Payne's conduct once or twice, and a month ago, Payne had been going to leave his employment, although Mr Reville persuaded him to stay. Hezekiah Reville testified that when he had left the butcher's shop at a little before 8 p.m, Payne and Glass had both been on the premises. He had pointed out some hams to Payne and ordered him to rub them with salt, but it later turned out that the careless butcher's boy had done the wrong ones. He had seen Payne writing on a piece of paper when he left the shop. He, Reville, had gone to see two fellow tradesmen named Wilmot and Green, before having a pint or two at the White Hart. Both he and his wife had more than once complained about Payne's work: in spite of his youth, he liked to go to the public house, leaving Glass to do all the work. Reville had once found a beefsteak hidden under a blade bone in the shop, and when he had told his wife that he would like to find out who was the thief, she had said 'Oh, you'll never do that. You have not seen half that I have.' Reville had been to see Mrs Glass, trying to ascertain who it was who had been stealing meat in the shop, and he had told both her and another woman that he was going to dismiss Payne. Mrs Reville had once said that if he did not dismiss Payne then she would do it, and the truculent butcher's boy 'had been greatly annoyed since, and there had been a great difference in his manner to his mistress.'

Mrs Mary Ann Glass confirmed that Reville had been to see her, complaining about losing a quantity of steak, and Philip Glass had been told why his master had come to call, although he denied mentioning this to Payne. Alfred Augustus Payne was the next witness: dressed in his blue butcher's frock, he seemed to be as cool as a cucumber. He merely confirmed that when he had left the shop at 8.32 p.m., at that time the chopper and other tools had been on the block, except the knife, which had been put by the scales and weights. The mysterious note from 'H. Collins' was read aloud in court, but police inquiries had showed that no such person was a resident of Colnbrook. There was a Mr Robert Collins in Chalvey, and he was a customer of Reville's, but he denied any knowledge of the note. The constables had found two Mrs Austins in Chalvey, but both of them denied knowing anything about a 'H. Collins', or any complaint about bad meat. Sergeant Hobbes testified that there had been a great deal of blood about the murder room, and that the kitchen table behind the murdered woman was liberally splashed with gore; the murderer's clothes were likely to have been equally stained with blood. When Payne's shirt had been examined, two stains of blood had been found on the left sleeve, but the butcher's boy said they had come from killing sheep the week before. The inquest was adjourned for a week.

The police belatedly removed all of Payne's clothes, for examination by an expert. They had time to compare the witness testimony, being amazed that the murder had clearly been committed between 8.32 p.m., when Payne left the shop, and 8.38 p.m., when Mrs Beasley discovered the murder; a short interval indeed for some murderous individual to burst into the shop and make use of the chopper to dispatch the butcher's wife. It was also noteworthy that she seemed to have been struck down from behind: had the murderer entered the house through the side entrance and sneaked up to her from behind? If some thief or old enemy had come running into the shop, Mrs Reville would have been unlikely to remain sitting on her chair, since she had a good view of the shop through the window. She had been given a florin by a customer, and put it in her dress pocket, but this coin could not be found at the scene of the crime, so it had probably been stolen by the murderer. Some small coins were strewn on the floor, and Mrs Reville's watch lay in front of her. It also turned out that one of Mrs Reville's little daughters had walked downstairs for some water, and heard the shop door slam, most probably by the absconding murderer; the girl had then seen her mother sitting in the chair dreadfully injured, and giving a choking noise as she breathed her last. The frightened little girl had run back up to bed and hid underneath the bed sheets, shivering with terror all night. Ann Reville was buried on the evening of 14 April. The neighbouring shops were closed, and all blinds had been drawn. Hezekiah Reville and his fellow tradesmen followed the coffin on its hearse, with Philip Glass carrying a basket of primroses and violets. The Rev. P. W. Phipps conducted the service as Mrs Reville was laid to rest in St Mary's Churchyard at Upton, where her headstone, albeit very worn, is still legible. Many people attended the funeral, and in the coming days, numerous London murder enthusiasts travelled to Slough to see the murder shop in Windsor Road, and Mrs Reville's gravestone.

When the coroner's inquest resumed on 19 April, Mr Reville's memory had improved, and he delivered some further hostile testimony against Payne, including that his wife had once said 'If you do not get rid of Payne, I will, for I know that he is robbing us.' Payne could swing a heavy chopper with alacrity, Reville said, and in spite of his youth, he was an expert on killing sheep. Importantly, the witness Kate Amelia Timms testified that she had met Philip Glass in the High Street at 8.28 p.m.; she had met Alfred Augustus Payne a few minutes later, and he had been walking rather hurriedly. When she had come home to her lodgings, the time had been 8.36 p.m. The brickmaker George Roll, who knew Payne, had seen him coming out of the Reville butcher's shop at around 8.30 p.m.; he had wished him 'Good night' and Payne had returned the compliment. Then it was time for the London graphologist Mr Charles Chabot to give evidence. He had been provided with handwriting samples from Mr Reville, Payne and Glass, and compared them with the 'H. Collins' note. Chabot was 66 years old, and he had 30 years of experience in his chosen field. He declared that the handwriting on the

'Collins' note was that of Alfred Augustus Payne, although the miscreant had clearly tried to disguise his writing. As a result of Chabot's confident identification of the handwriting, the inquest returned a majority verdict of wilful murder against Alfred Augustus Payne, and he was committed to stand trial for murder at the Aylesbury Assizes.

The mills of justice ground at a more rapid pace in those days, and already on 28 April 1881, the trial of Alfred Augustus Payne opened at the Aylesbury Assizes, before Mr Justice Lopes. The prosecution was led by Mr J.C. Lawrance and Mr Bullock, and Payne was defended by Mr Walter Attenborough and his junior Mr Whiteway. Hezekiah Reville, who was said to be deeply affected by the occasion, this time said that he had gone out at 8.10 p.m., leaving his wife and two children alone with Payne and Glass. He repeated his hostile testimony against Payne, but on cross-examination, he had to admit that although Mrs Reville had complained of Payne's slovenly work, this was a full month before the murder, and she had not found any faults with him since then. Mrs Maria Barber, whose husband had a dairy next door to Reville's shop, testified that she had a dog, and that this animal would have barked if some person had tried to approach the house through the side entrance. Mrs Beasley, Mr Leight and the surgeon Mr Dodd repeated their evidence from the inquest, without any addition, as did the important witness Kate Amelia Timms, who had met Glass and Payne the evening of the murder. Then it was the turn of the star witness Charles Chabot to perform, but the peppery Mr Attenborough soon had him in serious difficulties. It turned out that Chabot had been looking at an accounts book where some entries were by Payne; others he had merely assumed to have been written by the butcher's boy, although this could by no means be proven. Nor could Chabot deny that graphology was far from an exact science, and that he himself sometimes made mistakes.

Mr Attenborough concluded with an eloquent speech for the defence. Although at least a florin had been stolen from the murdered woman's pocket, not a farthing of money had been found in the prisoner's possession. Both Mr Dodd the surgeon and Sergeant Hebbes had given evidence that the clothes of the murderer must have been extensively bloodstained; yet an expert had found no trace of blood on Payne's clothes, apart from the minor stains on the sleeve of his shirt. The prisoner had not been in Reville's shop for any felonious purpose the evening of the murder, but he had merely been doing his duty for his master. Since Payne knew that R. Collins, of Chalvey, was a bona fide customer of Reville's, why would he sign his forged letter 'H. Collins, Colnbrook'?

The note had been written by an uneducated person, who could not spell; yet in a letter Payne had written while in police custody, his spelling was very good. The handwriting evidence had very little value, he assured the jury, and he himself had seen several words in the 'Collins' note that very much resembled the handwriting of Mr Reville! Mr Justice Lopes delivered a scrupulously fair summing-up, warning the jury that if the circumstantial evidence presented in court did not establish the guilt of the prisoner, then they must acquit him. The jury was out for 25 minutes before returning a verdict of Not Guilty, and Alfred Augustus Payne was a free man.

The police investigation of the murder of Mrs Reville was completely deflated by the acquittal of Alfred Augustus Payne, and in spite of a £100 government reward, there was never any further progress. The police would seem to have thought Payne a lucky lad to get away scot free at the Aylesbury Assizes, thanks to the muddled evidence from the elderly Mr Chabot, and the exhortations of a first-class barrister. Payne joined the army later in 1881, enlisting in the King's Royal Rifle Corps. He later remained in Slough for many years to come, and left butchery alone to become a general labourer; he married in 1890 and had a daughter. He served gallantly in the Great War, and was promoted to sergeant, finally dying in 1941 at the age of 77. As for Hezekiah Reville, he was presented with a purse containing £64 10s. collected by the Slough vicar, postmaster and coroner, among other benevolent local worthies, as 'practical proof of the sympathy felt for him in the town and neighbourhood'; it is noteworthy that Superintendent Dunham was another of the contributors. Reville remarried in 1883 and moved to Brighton, where he ran a small bakery, and later worked as a bath chair attendant. He remarried again in 1913 after the death of his second wife, and died in 1933 aged 91. Both the Reville daughters married and had offspring. At regular intervals, the unsolved Slough murder was mentioned in alarmist newspaper articles about unsolved slayings in London and its vicinity. In 1907, a *Lloyd's News* journalist went to Slough, where he found the butcher's shop in Windsor Road still standing, and not much changed since the murder back in 1881. Today, most of central Slough has been carted off by developer's lorry, however, and the murder shop is long gone.

In an analysis of the murder of Ann Reville, it is important to note that the murder was clearly premeditated. The murderer took care to write the 'Collins' note, before attacking Mrs Reville and putting the note next to the bloody chopper on the table. This means that the 'usual suspects' can be excluded: tramps, thieves, robbers and lunatics. The murderer was either Philip Glass, Alfred Augustus Payne, Hezekiah Reville, or some unknown enemy of Mrs Reville. As for Glass, he was just 15 years old at the time of the murder, he did not have any motive, and he left the shop prior to Payne, being spotted by a witness walking away from the butcher's shop; to my mind, he can be excluded as a suspect. As for Payne, he was a slovenly worker and a suspected thief; if we are to believe Mr Reville, he disliked Mrs Reville and was seen writing on a piece of paper prior to the murder. The police thought him guilty, from his callous reaction when informed of the murder. At the inquest, Glass had testified that Payne had told him that he would be staying another half-an-hour to rub the hams; yet according to his own version of events, he left just five minutes later. Chabot may well not have been a leading light in his profession, but at the coroner's inquest, he declared himself certain that the 'Collins' note had been written by Payne. The idea that such a note would divert police suspicion away from the real murderer is a preposterous one to a grown man, but perhaps not to an adolescent. The motive for Payne to murder Mrs Reville might well have been a combination of revenge against her, and against her annoying husband. Payne was physically capable of committing the murder, being a strong and sturdy lad, and experienced at killing sheep.

In Payne's defence, it must be objected that after all, the lad was just 16 years old. Was he capable of planning and executing the perfect murder? Well, some adolescents are clever sociopaths who can keep their cool even under trying circumstances, and the mass murderer Graham Frederick Young poisoned his first victim when he was just 15 years old. Most of the incriminating evidence against Payne came from Mr Reville, who might well have had reasons of his own to inculpate his young assistant. At the trial, Mr Attenborough pointed out that money had been stolen, and that Payne had no money on him when he was arrested, but he could have hidden the money, or thrown it away. Mr Attenborough successfully challenged Chabot's evidence, however, and it must be admitted that the elderly graphologist made a most unsatisfactory impression in court; he clearly was a sick man, and would in fact die the following year. Importantly, Payne's clothes were not bloodstained, whereas those of the murderer would have been hit by blood-spatter when he struck his victim down from behind. It is difficult to think of any stratagem by which Payne could have avoided getting blood on his clothes. Moreover, Payne was just an ordinary man, who did nothing newsworthy or interesting before or after the murder, whereas the murderer was clearly a person of superior cunning and cleverness.

In 1929, the crime writer Guy Logan suggested that Hezekiah Reville was the guilty man: he had entered the butcher's shop through the side entrance, murdered his wife, and then deliberately tried to incriminate Payne. The crime writer Jack Smith-Hughes agreed, pointing out that although Reville had been seen by several people, calling at fellow tradesmen, and visiting two pubs, his alibi was far from rock solid. It would have been possible for him to return to the butcher's shop, either through the front or the side entrances, murder his wife, and then return to the White Hart to fake an alibi. The motive might well have been that he secretly resented his wife, and wanted to remarry, as he did in 1883. Neither Logan nor Smith-Hughes seems to have appreciated that Mrs Reville was heavily pregnant at the time of the murder, however; what kind of monster would murder both his wife and his own unborn child? Furthermore, Reville seems to have lived perfectly happily with his wife, and he was an ordinary man who did nothing interesting neither before nor after the murder. The police thought him innocent, and there is nothing to suggest that his clothes were stained with blood.

Finally, we have the scenario that a secret enemy of Mrs Reville committed the murder, waiting outside until Payne left, and then negotiating an entry through the side door, and striking Mrs Reville down from behind. There was a dog next door, however, and its owner testified that this animal made it its business to bark at people trying to make use of the passage between Reville's shop and that of the dairyman Barber. Moreover, Reville testified that this door was kept locked, and any person with an ambition to open it had to understand a system to retrieve a key suspended with a piece of string. The murder of Mrs Reville is one of twelve unsolved murder mysteries in this book, and it is the most enigmatic of the lot. It is possible to narrow down the search to just two credible candidates, namely Payne and Mr Reville, but both of them have multiple arguments in favour of their innocence, in particular a lack of both motive and technical evidence. If either Payne or Mr Reville managed to get away with murder, they did so with impressive coolness and cunning, in a cataclysm that lit up an otherwise perfectly ordinary and humdrum existence. It is noteworthy that neither of the prime suspects did any further butchery after the murder; did Payne flinch at the crushing sound as a sheep's skull was broken, or did Reville abhor the weight of the chopper in his hand? Personally, I would favour Payne as the murderer, with a narrow margin; if this otherwise model citizen, with gallant wartime service, was really the guilty man, he would have been able to write a murder story that would outshine Agatha Christie, based solely on his own experiences back in 1881.

32. The Case Of Dr Lamson, 1881

The Rev. William Orne Lamson was an American clergyman resident in New York City. Coming from a well-to-do family, he devoted himself to

Dr Lamson, from a drawing by P.B. Whelpley reproduced by H. L. Adam, *The Trial of George Henry Lamson.*

DR. LAMSON.

A drawing of Dr Lamson, from the *Penny Illustrated Paper*, 11 March 1882.

Dr Lamson at Bow Street, from the *Penny Illustrated Paper*, 14 January 1882.

charity work, with his wife Julia. In 1852, they had a son, George Henry, born in New York on 8 September. The New York State Census for 1855 lists the then 30-year-old William O. Lamson, his wife Julia and his two young sons George H. and Robert S. In 1858, the Lamson family moved to Paris, where the Francophile clergyman had found employment at the American Chapel in Rue Bayard. In 1865, the Rev. Mr Lamson

"THERE, MY DEAR PERCY, TAKE THIS PILL," SAID LAMSON.
Vol. IV.—No. 42.

Percy is given a pill, from *Famous Crimes Past & Present*.

is recorded to have held an impressive service there after the death of President Lincoln. George Henry Lamson became a medical student in Paris, making good progress through the courses. At the outbreak of the

The trial of Dr Lamson at the Old Bailey, from *Graphic*, 18 March 1882.

Franco-Prussian war, the Rev. Mr Lamson became the chaplain to the American Ambulance, and George Henry was sworn in as an assistant surgeon. Both distinguished themselves in helping the sick and wounded: the Rev. Mr Lamson was made a Chevalier of the Legion of Honour, and young Lamson was rewarded with the Bronze Cross for his bravery.

At the time of the 1871 Census, the Lamson family was on a visit to Ventnor in the Isle of Wight. The now 45-year-old Rev. William Lamson was now the father of three children: the 18-year-old medical student George H., his younger brother Robert S. and his much younger sister Julia. George Henry continued his medical studies in Paris after the war. In 1872 he went back to the United States, where he graduated as a Doctor of Medicine at the University of Pennsylvania. He practised medicine for a while, moving from Ferry Town in New York, to Lancaster in Pennsylvania, where he supplemented his income by 'cramming' medical students for their exams. The musical doctor was organist and choirmaster of Christ Church, Lancaster, and a member of the Lancaster Medical Society. In late 1876, the Rev. Mr Lamson was sent to Belgrade as the emissary of the League in Aid of the Christians of Turkey. The philanthropic clergyman sent for his adventurous son, who left American soil and enlisted as a surgeon in the Serbian army. He saw much service in the Moravian valley, and had a rib broken by a stray shell, before being appointed to lead the military hospital at Semendria. He received

The execution of Dr Lamson, from the *IPN*, 6 May 1882.

a gold medal for his bravery, and a hero's welcome at a function for the League in Aid of the Christians of Turkey in London.

In 1877, after the outbreak of the Russo-Turkish War, the Rev. Mr Lamson became the agent for the British Benevolent Association for the Care of the Russian Wounded, and he went to St Petersburg to oversee matters there. George Henry Lamson went to Bucharest as the head of an English military hospital. He was at Plevna on transport service, and returned conveying Turkish prisoners, suffering terrible privations after being snowed up for six days without any food. When he returned home in March 1878, he was awarded the Star of Romania. After passing his medical exams in Edinburgh, and gaining a licence to practice in Britain, Dr Lamson set up practice in Rotherfield, Sussex. In October 1878, he married Kate George John, who belonged to a wealthy Welsh family hailing from Swansea. Her parents, the linen merchant William John and his wife Eliza, were both dead, as was her younger brother Sydney, but her sister Margaret Eliza had married the civil service clerk William Greenhill Chapman in 1877. Kate also had two living brothers: Hubert William John, born in 1861 and afflicted with tuberculosis, and Percy Malcolm John, born in 1863 and paralysed in the legs due to severe curvature of the spine. When Kate married Lamson, the inheritance from her parents was paid out, and it soon found its way into the doctor's pockets. After his marriage, George Henry Lamson settled in Rotherfield outside Tunbridge Wells. In 1879, his brother-in-law Hubert William John died mysteriously during a visit to Lamson's house, aged just eighteen. As a result, Mrs Lamson received another generous legacy, which the doctor soon spent on his various amusements.

Dr Lamson later purchased a practice at 1 Beaumont Terrace in Bournemouth for £400, but in spite of his gallant wartime service abroad, he was an indifferent doctor in civilian life, and a bad business man. The Bournemouth locals preferred the local doctors to this transatlantic interloper, and the practice never took off. Moreover, Lamson had become addicted to morphine after his service abroad, and he took it in increasing quantities, becoming quite haggard and irritable. The local doctors disliked this out-of-town competitor, and they accused him of making use of medical degrees to which he was not entitled. Lamson spent much money on his travels, visiting Paris and London, and more than once going to the United States. In April 1881, he sold his Bournemouth practice and went to America, leaving his family behind. By this time, the Lamsons had a little daughter named Agnes, born in 1879. The police file on his case contains several letters from Lamson's creditors in Bournemouth and elsewhere, who were utterly at a loss to understand his silence, as they expressed it. Bailiffs were called in, and the doctor's remaining effects were seized and auctioned off. Lamson was something of a hypochondriac, and very worried about his chronic constipation. In a letter to his mother, he complained bitterly about the 'stoppage of his bowels', as he expressed it. In a letter to a certain Mrs Millett, sent from New York City in June 1881, he wrote that although his health had improved, it was not wise or prudent to take up a practice like the one in Bournemouth; instead, he was planning to join his father in Florence and spend the autumn and winter there.

The crippled Percy Malcolm John had been deposited at Mr Bedbrook's Academy at Blenheim House, situated at 1–2 St George's Road, Wimbledon. The unfortunate lad was much older than the other pupils, but still he appears to have been well liked. Two wheeling chairs were kept on the premises, one on the second floor, where Percy slept, and the other on the ground floor; the schoolboys took turns to carry him up and down stairs in the morning and in the evening. He took part in the lessons as well as he could, and even tried to play sports with the other pupils, seated in his wheelchair. Apart from his scoliosis, Percy was in good physical health, albeit often despondent about his prospects in life. His brother-in-law William Greenhill Chapman, who had become his guardian, considered Mr Bedbrook's Academy a cheap and convenient place for him to live.

When Dr Lamson returned from America, he was in dire financial straits, and he had to borrow money from the other passengers to be able to purchase victuals. Once back in London, he tried to obtain money from some dubious-looking cheques, without success; on 24 November, he had to pawn his watch and a case of medical instruments. His bank account was overdrawn, and he had no money at all. On 1 December, he successfully cashed a dud cheque for £12 10s and made plans to travel to Paris and Florence. The same day, he wrote a letter to Percy Malcolm John, to the effect that before travelling abroad, he wanted to come to Wimbledon to see his brother-in-law.

On the morning of 3 December 1881, Percy Malcolm John was carried downstairs in the usual manner. After tea, he was employed looking through another boy's examination papers. He then received a message that Dr Lamson had come to see him. When he had been carried upstairs to a reception room, he saw Dr Lamson and Mr Bedbrook speaking together. 'How fat you are looking, Percy, old boy!' exclaimed the jovial doctor. 'I wish I could say the same of you, George, 'the crippled lad replied, referring to Lamson's thin and haggard looks. Mr Bedbrook poured some glasses of sherry, and the doctor produced some slices of Dundee cake, which all three ate with relish. He gave Mr Bedbrook some American gelatine capsules, which he said would come in handy for giving the boys medicine. He filled one of them with sugar, and exclaimed 'Here, Percy, you are a champion pill-taker; take this! Show Mr Bedbrook how easy it is to take!' Percy obediently swallowed the capsule.

Not long after, Dr Lamson said he would be leaving, since he wanted to catch the train for Paris. When Mr Bedbrook showed him the way out,

Lamson said that he did not think poor Percy would last much longer, an observation that surprised the schoolmaster since Percy's general health had appeared perfectly good. Ten minutes after the doctor had left, Percy complained of a heartburn, and feeling generally ill, just as he had done on a previous occasion when Dr Lamson had given him a pill to take. His condition soon deteriorated: he vomited and was seized with terrible convulsions. Two competent doctors soon arrived, and their diagnosis was the boy had been poisoned. The likely suspect, Dr Lamson, had successfully made his escape. Nothing could be done for the dying boy except to give him morphine to ease his pain. When poor Percy died at 11 p.m., the police were immediately notified about the grave suspicion that the lad had been murdered.

Dr Lamson went to Paris just as he had planned. Already on 5 December, he could read about himself in the London newspapers: both the *Pall Mall Gazette* and the *Daily News* were able to cover the 'Mysterious Death in Wimbledon' in their late editions, indicating Lamson as the main suspect sought by the Scotland Yard detectives. The coroner's inquest on Percy Malcolm John was opened on 6 December, and Mr Bedbrook gave evidence concerning the luckless lad's hasty collapse soon after he had been given some cake, and a pill, by Dr Lamson. On December 7, the globetrotting Rev. Mr Lamson sent a telegram from Florence to William Greenhill Chapman, Percy's guardian, saying that his son George Henry, who was lying ill in Paris, was quite overcome by the news of the sudden death of his young brother-in-law. Dr Lamson's wife, who had remained in England, was also in a precarious state of health.

On 8 December, George Henry Lamson gave himself up at Scotland Yard, saying that he was deeply pained by the report of the death of his young brother-in-law, and the mentioning of his own name as a suspected murderer. He had nothing to hide and had committed no crime, he asserted. He was arrested and taken to the Wandsworth Police Station. Described by a *Morning Post* journalist as a tall, dark-complexioned young man with a languid appearance, he was charged at the Wandsworth Police Court with murder, before the magistrate Mr Paget. The schoolmaster and the doctors gave evidence, and the magistrate remanded Lamson in custody and refused him bail. When the prisoner was led into his cell, he entirely lost his composure and screamed 'I will go mad!' in a terrible voice. On 8 December, the remains of Percy Malcolm John were interred at Wimbledon Cemetery; it is sad but true that very few people were present, and that neither of the sisters of the deceased attended.

The coroner's inquest returned a verdict of wilful murder against George Henry Lamson, and he was committed to stand trial at the Old Bailey. The trial opened on 8 March, before the old 'hanging judge' Sir Henry Hawkins. The evidence against Dr Lamson seemed impressive indeed. The forensic chemists Thomas Stevenson and Auguste Dupré had found traces of aconitine, a vegetable poison from the monkshood root, in Percy's remains. Lamson had purchased some aconitine shortly before the murder, and used it to fill the capsule he had given to the luckless lad. Some pills given to Percy by Dr Lamson were found inside one of the murdered boy's boxes: they also turned out to contain aconitine. The motive for the murder was obvious: upon Percy's death, no less than £3 000 of the John family's capital would be divided between Mrs Lamson and her sister, and thus £1 500 would become available to her penniless husband, enabling him to make a new start in life. Lamson was defended by the eloquent Montagu Williams, who tried his best to confound the medical witnesses for the prosecution, but without much success. His speech for the defence lasted for the greater part of two days. The evidence against Lamson was overwhelming, and after the jury had been charged by Sir Henry Hawkins, they were absent for half-an-hour before returning a verdict of Guilty. Sir Henry addressed the hapless prisoner with the following words,

> George Henry Lamson, the jury having convicted you of the crime of wilful murder, the law commands me to pass upon you the sentence of death. It would serve no good were I to recapitulate the harrowing details of your cruel, base, and treacherous crime; nor is it part of my office to admonish you how to meet the dread doom which awaits you ...

Considering the callous and cowardly nature of the crime of which he had been convicted, surprisingly many people tried to save Dr Lamson from the gallows. The execution was even postponed, for affidavits regarding the prisoner's mental health to be procured from the United States. But all the efforts from the Rev. Mr Lamson, his family and friends were in vain: no respite was forthcoming, and Lamson was to be executed on 28 April. In a letter, he practically admitted murdering Percy John, although denying any responsibility for the sudden death of his brother Hubert two years earlier. He also admitted his drug abuse, and hoped that his brain would be examined after death, for the collapse of his mental powers to be elucidated. On the morning of 28 April, Lamson rose early and had a hearty breakfast of coffee, eggs and toast, before praying with the Chaplain until the bell tolled at Wandsworth Prison. Lamson said goodbye to the Chaplain in a fairly firm voice, but when the executioner Marwood led him onto the drop and put on the white hood, he nearly collapsed. Marwood swiftly launched him into eternity, however, and he died without a struggle.

As for poor Mrs Lamson, she is said to have been entirely devastated when her husband was executed for the murder of her brother. Montagu Williams greatly admired her constancy and devotion to her husband. There were persistent rumours that in spite of his firm denial, Dr Lamson had also written one of his 'prescriptions' for her other brother Hubert William John, and it certainly seems a strange coincidence that this young man should die suddenly and mysteriously two years before Percy was poisoned. It turns out that it was Lamson himself who had signed the death certificate, at his own residence at Horse Grove, Rotherfield. His wife and his sister-in-law Mrs Margaret Eliza Chapman had also been present at this family gathering, and the latter came in handy as the informant on the certificate. Lamson wrote that Hubert William John had died from 'Pulmonary consumption 3 years, Amyloid degeneration 3 months, certified by Geo. H. Lamson MD'. He did not specify what organ (the kidneys?) were afflicted by the amyloidosis, a diagnosis that today demands a microscopic examination of a biopsy. According to Sir Harry Poland, the detectives thought Lamson had murdered Hubert William John as well, although there was insufficient evidence to prosecute him.

The crime writer Walter Wood had heard that Mrs Lamson had opened a boarding-house under an assumed name, and eked out the remainder of her days in obscurity. Charles Kingston, another prolific old crime writer, who made it his business to investigate the fates of criminal celebrities after the verdict, found out that Mrs Lamson had opened a small boarding-house in a town 60 miles from London. Once, she was recognized there by one of the members of the Lamson jury. She died in Devonshire, still under an assumed name, and her daughter Agnes went to the United States, where she was supported by Lamson's friends and relatives, and later married a prosperous estate agent. Unfortunately, these stories turn out to be fantasies: Kate Lamson changed her name to Kate G. George and took charge of a convalescent home in Westgate-on-Sea. 'Agnes George', as she was known, died there from tuberculosis in 1899, aged just 20. Kate herself lived on until 1910, expiring at her home in Hastings, and leaving her assets of £1,701 and change to her sister Margaret Eliza Chapman.

As for the philanthropic Rev. William Lamson, father of the murderer, he seems to have fallen upon evil times in his old age, since the *New York Daily Tribune* records that in May 1907, an old man was found wandering aimlessly around the streets of New York, pursued by a mob of men and boys who were laughing at him. The old man could not give an account of himself, but from some letters found in his bag, he was identified as William O. Lamson D.D., former rector of the Holy Trinity Church in Harlem, who had later held a living at Nyack, New York. He spoke confusedly about his daughter running off with an Italian nobleman, and afterwards shutting the door of her home in his face. A doctor diagnosed him with 'paresis' and he would be sent to Bellevue on 1 June, unless friends called for him. Dr Lamson's brother Robert Schuyler Lamson had predeceased him in 1876, and his sister Julia had married an Italian nobleman in 1890.

In some aspects, George Henry Lamson was an unlikely murderer. A young man from a respectable family, with a good medical education and brave service as an army surgeon abroad, he should certainly have had sufficient knowledge of the Hippocratic Oath not to poison his relatives. The verdict in the case of Hubert John remains open, but I would not put it beyond the cunning, ruthless doctor to poison this hapless youth to get his hands on the inheritance. In the case of Percy Malcolm John, the evidence against Lamson is rock solid. The reason Lamson chose aconitine as the method to poison at least one of his brothers-in-law is said to have been that he had been taught, while a medical student, that this poison could not be detected, but forensic science had made advances since Lamson's student days, to the detriment of the murderous doctor. This theory explains why Lamson thought he could have got away with murder even though Percy had expired as a direct result of eating victuals supplied by himself, and also why he returned to London instead of making his escape to continental Europe. It can only be speculated what event in Lamson's life had destroyed his moral responsibility, and made him into a cool, calculating murderer. He may well have seen scenes of carnage and bloodshed during his wartime service abroad, but so had many other military surgeons, without developing any murderous tendencies. Lamson may well have been right when he himself blamed his escalating drug addiction: the dependence on morphine had taken away his self-respect and undermined his moral sense, and in the choice between admitting his addiction and failure in life, and committing a cowardly and premeditated murder, he had chosen the latter alternative.

33. The Ramsgate Tragedy, 1882

Mr Charles Wagner was a German immigrant who had built up a flourishing butchery empire in West Ham. The 1881 Census lists the 39-year-old Charles Wagner as living above a butcher's shop at 104 Victoria Dock Road, with his second wife Caroline, who had also been born in Germany, and their young children Rosa, Bertha and George. There was also an elder son named Charles John Wagner, born in West Ham in 1865, who worked as an assistant to his father. There were two young butchers at work in the Wagner butcher's shop, and also a servant girl; the wealthy German immigrant also owned another large butcher's shop at 55 Victoria Dock Road, and a third shop at 114 Albert Road, North Woolwich.

On Saturday 1 April 1882, Charles Wagner Sr gave his son Charles a bag containing £150 in gold, with orders to take it to his bank in Stratford; he was given three pennies to pay his train fare, and left at 1.45 p.m. An apprentice butcher named James Walters, employed in the shop at 104 Victoria Dock Road, saw and heard Wagner Sr send young Charles to the bank. Since they lived in the same house and worked in the same shop, Walters and young Wagner must surely have known each other, but the true nature of their relationship remains a mystery. Walters had been employed on the premises for five weeks, but since his work had been unsatisfactory, he had recently been given notice. But Charles Jr did not return from the bank, nor was Walters anywhere to be found.

Charles Wagner Sr went to the bank at 5 p.m., where he was told that young Charles had not made an appearance. Mr Wagner was worried both about the well-being of his son and the whereabouts of his £150, and he suspected that the lad James Walters may well be involved in the mysterious disappearance. On Monday 3 April, he confronted Walters in the butcher's shop and asked him 'What have you done with Charlie?'

Vignettes from the Ramsgate Tragedy, from the *IPN*, 22 April 1882.

As cool as a cucumber, the apprentice butcher replied 'Mr Wagner, I have not seen your son since he left the shop on Saturday.' Charles Wagner Sr had seen in the newspapers that the body of a young man had been found under the East Cliff, Ramsgate, by a coast guardsman. Mr Wagner travelled to Ramsgate by train, and identified the dead youth as his son. Since witnesses could report that Charles had come to Ramsgate with another young man answering the description of Walters, the apprentice butcher was arrested by the West Ham police. Much money in gold, and a valuable gold watch, were found in his possession. Walters protested his innocence, saying that on Saturday, he had gone to Dalston with an old sweetheart. When told that young Charles Wagner had been found dead in Ramsgate, and that he was at risk of being charged with a much more serious offence than that of stealing £150, he said: 'You don't say so … It is a bad job!' In the prisoner's van, in spite of being cautioned, he exclaimed 'I have not yet said anything I know … It is so thundering black against me, the boy is found dead.'

A number of witnesses had observed Walters and young Wagner together, descriptions that certainly gave food for thought. A man had seen them hastily walking away from the Wagner butcher's shop, together, without Walters restraining the young man in any way. On Saturday afternoon, at 2.45 p.m., these two had entered the tailor's shop of Mr Thwaites, near Victoria Station. Since young Wagner seemed very shy and timorous, and 'all of a tremble', Mr Thwaites had said 'The young man is not well; let him sit down.' Walters had ordered a new pair of trousers for his companion, whom he introduced as his wife's brother, and a new coat for himself, giving young Wagner his old one. The timorous Charles Wagner had seemed quite unwilling to change his trousers, but Walters had his way. The apprentice butcher had then paid for the clothes, pulling up a fistful of gold sovereigns from his pocket. The two young men had then taken the last train from London to Ramsgate. Here, they had bought three collars in a High Street shop after 10 p.m., before walking off towards East Cliff. Walters had been overheard saying that he was sending 'the lad' to Paris. A number of witnesses had seen James Walters alone after Charles had plunged to his death: on the train to Canterbury, he had remarked that even though he had only been in Ramsgate for a day, he had already seen a man fall off a cliff, although it was not a person known to him. In Canterbury, Walters ate and drank well, and spoke of his visit to Ramsgate together with a 'friend' whom he had since 'lost'. He paid for his food and transportation from a large bag full of gold sovereigns.

When James Walters was charged with murder at the Town Hall in Ramsgate, the court was crowded to capacity. The coastguard described finding the body, and the local surgeon said that death had been due to internal haemorrhage. From the post-mortem and the analysis of the stomach contents, there was nothing to suggest that young Wagner had been drunk, and a fit and sober person was unlikely to fall off a cliff. There were no marks on the body indicative of an assault, and the hand still held a pipe, as if he had been in the process of lighting it. When Charles Wagner gave evidence, describing his business and the situation in his household, the solicitor Mr Metcalfe, representing the prisoner, objected that young Charles had in fact been very unhappy, since he had not got on with his stepmother, and not been allowed to dine in the parlour. After the London, Ramsgate and Canterbury witnesses had told their stories, James Walters was committed to stand trial for murder at the Kent Summer Assizes.

On trial for murder in Maidstone, before Mr Justice Hawkins, James Walters was well defended by the barrister Mr Kemp. The prosecution case was that after young Charles Wagner had agreed to rob his father and escape from the household, Walters had taken charge of the stolen money and taken him to Ramsgate, a town he knew well. He had lured young Wagner up East Cliff, and pushed him over the edge, afterwards telling various untruths to Charles Wagner Sr and the police. The defence argued that there was no conclusive evidence that murder had been committed at all, since the medical witnesses did not find evidence the lad had been assaulted, and since the cliff was a steep and perilous one. Although the actions of James Walters had been wholly blameworthy, he had been contemplating robbery, not murder, and he hoped the jury would give him the benefit of the doubt. After Mr Justice Hawkins had delivered a scrupulously fair summing-up, the jury was out for not less than an hour and a half, before returning a verdict of Not Guilty. Walters had hardly time to draw a sigh of relief before he was re-arrested and committed for trial for stealing £150. This time, the evidence against him was rock solid, and he was sentenced to seven years of penal servitude.

The origin of the Ramsgate Tragedy would appear to have been that young Charles Wagner was unhappy with his father and stepmother, and that he wanted to escape abroad. James Walters, who must have resented Charles Wagner Sr for sacking him, persuaded the lad to steal the £150, which he took charge of himself. After purchasing new clothes to disguise themselves, the two fugitives went to Ramsgate. It may well be that young Wagner's courage had evaporated by this stage, and that he wanted to return to his father with the money. Walters lured him up onto East Cliff, and most probably pushed him over the edge. He later made various confused statements about seeing a man perish, or losing his friend. It is in his favour that instead of absconding to Paris himself, he returned to London to 'face the music', even though he was aware that the body had been found; it is to his detriment that he lied to Charles Wagner Sr, denying any knowledge of young Charles, and to the police, saying that he had been to Dalston. The murder of young Charles Wagner was a both stupid and pointless crime, because the victim would be found, missed and recognized, and since several witnesses had seen the two together; yet murder I believe it was, and James Walters was very lucky to escape as lightly as he did. It can only be speculated whether there had been a homosexual relationship between the two main actors in the Ramsgate Tragedy, or whether Walters had made use of a more conventional stratagem to bring young Charles under his influence.

The bereaved butcher Charles Wagner Sr again made the news in July 1883, for all the wrong reasons, being prosecuted for selling diseased meat in his shop, and fined £100. He and his remaining family are not listed in the 1891, 1901 or 1911 Censuses, indicating that he moved abroad, perhaps returning to his *Vaterland* after the meat scandal. As for the desperado James Walters, he would appear to have served his prison sentence and then disappeared into obscurity, without hatching any further extravagant plots to murder feeble and unsuspecting young lads. It is up to the late-night wanderer on East Cliff to experience the climax of the Ramsgate Tragedy of 1882: a youthful, timorous soul debating whether to return to his father, and how he would get to Paris, a coarse cry of 'Well, yer could try *flying*!'; a push, a muffled scream, and a heavy fall, and then silence as the wild-eyed murderer makes his escape.

34. The Fulham Tragedy, 1882

Richard George Wells was a Woking solicitor's clerk, a married man with two grown-up daughters. In 1881, when he was 47 years old, he started an intrigue with Mrs Lina Keyzor Sykes, a flashily dressed, middle-aged Jewess with a very dubious past. She claimed to be 29 years old, although she was really in her mid-forties. In the 1860s, she had been the mistress of the yachtsman Sir Gilbert East, and she had appeared as the principal witness after he had drowned mysteriously at Ryde in 1866. Richard Wells was quite infatuated with Lina, however, and he left his wife to go

Scenes from the Fulham Tragedy, from the *IPN*, 10 June 1882.

A portrait of Richard George Wells, from the *IPN*, 10 June 1882.

to London with her, under the names of Mr and Mrs Wallace. Since both of them had independent means, they did no work at all, and they drank and partied to excess.

In early 1882, Richard Wells and Lina Keyzor Sykes were living in an elegant terraced house at 6 Moore Park Road, Fulham. On May 26, they went to Epsom in a cab to see the Oaks. They drank a good deal of beer, champagne and whisky, and had some bets on the horses. They met the sturdy, 32-year-old idler John Carlisle, who had also eaten and drunk well, and invited him to share their cab back to London, stopping at several pubs on the way, for some more liquid refreshments. Carlisle was very polite to the fickle Lina, and Richard Wells resented that he put his arm around her. When they reached Moore Park Road, Wells held out his hand to Carlisle and said 'If we part now, we part as friends, but if you enter my house, we shall be enemies!' If Carlisle had heeded this thinly veiled threat, much mischief would have been averted, but Lina insisted on inviting their guest in for another glass of whisky or two. When Wells objected, she called him a dirty beast and threatened to have him evicted from the house.

A whisky bottle was produced, and in spite of having drunk hard all day, the two men lurched into the back garden to have a few glasses. Lina also wanted a glass of whisky and water, and Carlisle poured her one, but the angry Wells snatched the glass away and dashed it against the garden wall. The men fought fiercely, Carlisle hitting Wells hard in the face, and kicking him in the ribs. Lina ran into the house and locked herself up in the water closet, and the charwoman ran out to get a police constable. When Constable Arthur Flawn arrived at 6 Moore Park Road, the two combatants had calmed down. John Carlisle showed the constable a bruised and swollen hand, the result from a blow with a poker. Richard Wells was lying on a bed upstairs, with a black eye and bruised ribs. When Lina asked the constable to evict Wells from the premises, he sullenly retorted that he was the person paying the rent. Thinking the fracas just a brawl between two mindless drunks, Constable Flawn took no further action.

Just half-an-hour later, the police were again called to 6 Moore Park Road. Sergeant George Bartle was aghast to find that this time, John Carlisle was clearly badly injured. He was bleeding from the head, and exclaimed 'Oh, policeman, come on, he has stabbed me this time!' As the sturdy Carlisle staggered forward, he suddenly collapsed and fell, toppling over the police sergeant as he went crashing to the ground. Although a doctor was swiftly called, the injured man expired just minutes later. Sergeant Bartle had seen Richard Wells lurking in hallway, behind Carlisle, without trying to help the dying man. When questioned, Wells admitted lurching downstairs, in the hope that Carlisle had gone. When he saw his rival sitting in the drawing-room, he had seized up a large whisky bottle and hit him hard over the head with it. 'If I have killed him I don't care!' he callously exclaimed. He denied stabbing Carlisle, however, saying that this must have been done by the faithless Lina. When the police searched the house for the murder weapon, they found a bloodstained poultry knife in the kitchen.

Richard George Wells was arrested by the police, and after the coroner's inquest on John Carlisle had returned a verdict of wilful murder against him, he was committed to stand trial at the Old Bailey, before Mr Justice Stephen. Harry Poland and Montagu Williams prosecuted, and Mr Wildey Wright and Horace Avory defended. The principal prosecution witness was Lina Sykes, who had been in the house throughout the fracas between Wells and Carlisle. She described herself as a married woman living apart from her husband, with the benefit of a private income of in excess of £600 a year. She had seen Wells enter the drawing-room, seize the whisky bottle without saying a word, and crack Carlisle over the head with it, exclaiming 'Take that, you bastard!' Carlisle did not go down for the count, but reeled out towards the hallway. She had then run to the water closet to lock herself up, and from there she heard Carlisle exclaim 'Oh, he has stabbed me this time!' This evidence sounded relatively coherent, and agreed roughly with what the charwoman and policemen had testified, but Mr Wright soon had Lina in difficulties. An elegantly dressed, Jewish-looking woman, she claimed to be 29 years old, but Mr Wright had found out that she had been a witness at the coroner's inquest on Sir Gilbert East back in 1866; had she then been just 13 years old at the time, and was it true that she had cohabited with Sir Gilbert as man and wife for more than eight years, since when she had been just five years old? Lina had no truthful answers for these questions, even when the Judge threatened her with an indictment for perjury if she did not tell the truth. In his summing-up, Mr Justice Stephen instructed the jury that since the evidence from 'the woman Sykes' had been of such an inferior quality, the prisoner could not be convicted of murder, so the case was one of manslaughter. The jury found Wells guilty of manslaughter, and Mr Justice Stephen sentenced him to imprisonment for life. As he left the dock, Wells angrily exclaimed 'I never stabbed that man, by God! That woman stabbed him, by God!'

At the time of the 1891 Census, Richard George Wells was in HM Convict Prison, Medway. He was out of prison by 1898, when he remarried. He is likely to have died in 1914, aged 80. When Mr Henry Cecil Sykes, the estranged husband of Lina Keyzor Sykes, read about the 'Fulham Tragedy' in the newspapers, he brought for a suit for divorce. When the case was heard in May 1883, Mr Sykes claimed that during their married days, she had been drinking, driving about in cabs, and running him into debt. After she had left him, she had been consorting with various dodgy 'gentleman friends', the convict Richard George Wells one of them. And indeed, the former solicitor's clerk was brought into court, dressed in his convict's uniform, to confirm that he and the faithless Lina had been living together as man and wife. Mr Sykes, who had formerly been a theology student, but who was now working as an omnibus conductor, was granted his divorce; her court appearance was the last newsworthy action of his former wife. Due to her habit of regularly changing her name, nothing further can be discerned about the subsequent career of that Fulham *femme fatale*.

In spite of his denial, it seems very likely that Richard George Wells murdered John Carlisle, however, and he may well have been lucky to escape an encounter with the hangman. Sergeant Bartle saw Wells standing in the hallway behind Carlisle when he collapsed; he made no effort to help the injured man, but merely slammed the door. Whatever we think of the moral standards exhibited by Lina Keyzor Sykes, she had no motive to murder Carlisle, and although this madly vain woman told untruths about her own age, there is nothing to suggest that she lied about her activities on the evening of the murder. A modern housing development today stands on the spot of the murder house at 6 Moore Park Road, although the opposing terrace, consisting of houses in a similar style, still remains.

35. The Plumstead Poisoner, 1882

Louisa Jane Scott was born in Scotland in or around 1848, the daughter of a sergeant-major in the Royal Artillery. In 1878, when she was 30 years old and working as a milliner, she married the 39-year-old divorced customs officer Thomas John Taylor, and they moved into a suburban house at 5 Little Heath, Charlton. Mr Taylor retired from the customs not long after, being the recipient of a monthly pension of £5. He died

A portrait of the Plumstead Poisoner, Louisa Jane Taylor, with vignettes of some of the notable characters from the trial, from the *IPN*, 30 December 1882.

unexpectedly in early 1882, at the age of just 43. His family suspected foul play, and spread rumours that he had been poisoned. They could hardly believe that Louisa Jane was really his wife, but she silenced them by producing their marriage certificate, and took possession of all the furniture and household goods.

In August 1882, Louisa Jane Taylor went to see an old friend of her late husband, the retired customs officer William Tregellis, who lodged on the first floor at 3 Naylor's Cottages, Plumstead. Tregellis had been married to a very angry, mean-spirited woman, whose conduct had driven him to enter a lunatic asylum; while he was incarcerated there, the wife had died, and in late 1879, he had remarried his second wife Mary Ann. Both the Tregellises were elderly: he was 85 years old and she 80, and they lived in two small upstairs rooms in a house owned by a Mr Ellis. William Tregellis was quite pleased to see Louisa Jane Taylor, the wife of his old customs colleague. When she suggested that for the sake of her health, she ought to move in with them at Naylor's Cottages, they willingly agreed. Old Tregellis slept in one of the rooms, and the other served as bedroom to his wife, who shared a bed with Louisa Jane Taylor.

William Tregellis was physically fit but mentally quite feeble; his wife was hale and hearty for her age. One day, when Mary Ann Tregellis and Louisa Jane Taylor went to town to do some shopping, a thief tried to snatch the old lady's bag, but since she held on for dear life, she was pushed over and cut her eye. Dr John Smith, the local practitioner, of 89 Plumstead Road, was called in to see her. In the weeks following this incident, Mrs Tregellis seemed to be getting seriously ill, however. She complained of sickness, cold shivers, throat-burn and stomach pain, and Dr Smith diagnosed her with a combination of ague and debility from old age, and he prescribed some pills and mixtures for her. Louisa Jane Taylor took on the role of nurse, and helped Mrs Tregellis take her medicines.

Louisa Jane Taylor was visited, at regular intervals, by a man named Edward Martin, who described himself as a watercress merchant. To forestall suspicion from the landlady Mrs Ellis, he introduced himself as the nephew of Mr Tregellis, although he was in fact Louisa Jane's boyfriend on the side. Martin came and went at Naylor's Cottages, as he liked it, and he helped Louisa Jane to buy some medicine for Mrs Tregellis. The old lady showed no signs of recovering, however, and Dr Smith noticed that her teeth were very black, and that she was becoming increasingly emaciated. He still maintained his diagnosis that old age was behind the patient's deterioration, and prescribed some mixtures and tonics. Louisa Jane Taylor nursed the old woman devotedly, and made sure that she took her medicines as prescribed. The police file on the case contains a letter sent by Louisa Jane Taylor to Dr Smith on 20 September, on heavily black-edged paper, in a similarly black-edged envelope with the Queen Victoria halfpenny blue stamp intact; the old lady was still not well, she wrote, and Dr Smith should not worry about his unpaid bills. Old Mr Tregellis was astounded when Louisa Jane told him that she had received a legacy of £500, and that she had written a will leaving everything to him and his wife. When Mrs Tregellis had died, she suggested to the feeble old man, she would look after him in a nice house, where he could live rent free. When Tregellis objected that his wife was not yet dead, this sinister woman replied that she soon would be!

In early October, William Tregellis went to draw his pension. He got his best suit out of the pawnshop, but then the forceful Louisa Jane Taylor took care of the remainder of the money, saying that she needed it for her patient. But old Tregellis never saw this money again, nor did his wife. Becoming suspicious, he made an inventory of the household goods, and found that two dresses, a petticoat, a shawl and a pair of boots had gone missing. When challenged with stealing and pawning these items, Louisa Jane was evasive and guilty-looking, so Tregellis called in a police constable who took her into custody. When she was searched at the Woolwich police station, ten pawn tickets were found.

In the meantime, the 'overworked' practitioner Dr Smith, who had seen poor Mrs Tregellis several times, started using his brain, an organ he appears to have left unconsulted since his first visit to the Naylor Cottages sickbed. What obscure condition could it be that blackened the teeth and gums, and caused irritation to the digestive tract? The answer came to him, either like a bolt from the blue, or through careful consulting of his dusty old medical textbooks: it was lead poisoning! Dr Smith was appalled to find that Louisa Jane Taylor had several times purchased sugar of lead (lead acetate) from his own surgery, either attending herself or sending the creature Martin along. When Dr Smith asked the local police surgeon for a second opinion, they both saw and appreciated the characteristic line of blue discolouration of the gums that is pathognomonic for lead poisoning. Mrs Tregellis, who was well-nigh dead by this time, said that Louisa Jane Taylor had given her repeated doses of a milky white medicine that tasted very bitter. It was clear to the two doctors that this was a case of slow poisoning, and that Mrs Taylor, who had inveigled herself as a family friend of the Tregellises, was the main suspect.

On 10 October, Louisa Jane Taylor was remanded in custody by the Woolwich Magistrates Court, on a charge of administering poison. Mrs Tregellis died on 23 October, however, and the case was now one of murder. The coroner's inquest returned a verdict of wilful murder against Louisa Jane Taylor, and she was committed to stand trial at the Old Bailey. The trial began on 11 December, before Mr Justice Stephen, with the eloquent Harry Poland and Montagu Williams prosecuting, and Mr Walton and Mr White defending. William Tregellis testified as to the thefts from his humble household, and his wife's protracted illness and eventual death. Dr Smith and his wife testified as to the ultimate diagnosis of lead poisoning, and the prisoner's purchases of sugar of lead. The celebrated analyst Dr Thomas Stevenson described the finding of quantities of lead salts in the murdered woman's inner organs. Although the defence objected, the damning death-bed deposition from Mrs Tregellis was read aloud in court. Edward Martin made a brief appearance in court as a witness, but the defence missed out on their opportunity to further probe his relationship to the prisoner. In his summing-up, Mr Walton could not deny that Mrs Tregellis had been murdered through lead poisoning, but he suggested that Mr Tregellis, who was 85 years old and had been in an asylum for seven months not long ago, had given his wife the poison by accident. He also questioned the alleged motive for the murder: what sane person would murder the wife of an 85-year-old man, in order to steal his pension? After Mr Justice Stephen had delivered a scrupulously fair summing-up, the jury withdrew for twenty minutes before returning a verdict of Guilty, without any recommendation to mercy. Mr Justice Stephen sentenced her to death for what he rightly described as a cruel, treacherous and hypocritical murder.

The usual squeamishness with regard to executing women in Victorian times did not apply to poisoners, and there was no chance for Louisa Jane Taylor to obtain a reprieve. She was executed at Maidstone Gaol on 2 January 1883: Marwood gave her an 8 foot drop, and she appeared to die instantaneously. The newspapers were puzzled by the apparent lack of motive for the murder: why spend much time and effort poisoning an elderly woman, for the purpose of sharing lodgings with her 85-year-old husband, who clearly would not live for much longer, and cheating him out of his pension? It might be speculated that Louisa Jane was a sadist who derived some perverted pleasure from seeing her hapless victim die slowly and inexorably. And was Mrs Tregellis perhaps not the first victim of the Plumstead Poisoner? It is notable that, in the words of the *Newcastle Courant*, who probably quoted some London paper,

> A report is current in Woolwich that, if the woman Taylor had escaped conviction on the charge of poisoning Mrs Tregellis, she would, in all probability, have been accused of other crimes equally heinous. Her husband died suddenly on March 18th last, and a physician who was called in expressed a strong suspicion that he had taken poison. Taylor was a very hearty man, and some of the symptoms of his illness were very similar to those apparent in the Tregellis case.

Thomas John Taylor's relatives more than once alluded to his sudden and mysterious death, and it turns out that his death certificate gives the cause of death as 'chronic nephritis, uncertain Coma 45 hours', a vague description indeed. The deaths of two young women, one at Woolwich and the other in the country, were also linked with the poisonous career of this Plumstead Borgia, whose familiarity with sugar of lead was such that she had once been charged with attempting suicide by taking it!

36. The Walthamstow Tragedy, 1883

In 1883, the 26-year-old blacksmith William Gouldstone lodged in a small terraced house at 8 Courteney Place, near the St James's Street railway station in Walthamstow. He was a quiet man of abstemious habits: he did not smoke, and used to drink nothing stronger than beer. He worked for a firm in Upper Thames Street, in the City, and commuted to work each morning, leaving his wife and three little sons behind. A gloomy, morose man, he often complained of headaches, and of a painful rupture, and he sometimes told his workmates that he wished he was dead. He got on well with his wife, and never complained about their unpromising living accommodation, with a large family sharing two tiny rooms. He worried about not being able to support his family

The murder of a Family at Walthamstow, from the *IPN*, 18 August 1883.

The murderer William Gouldstone, from the *IPN*, 25 August 1883.

one day, and sometimes upbraided his wife for giving birth to so many children.

In 1883, William Gouldstone had three children, namely Charles aged three, Herbert aged two, and Frederick aged little more than a year. He was fond of his little boys, and a good father to them. In August 1883, Mrs Gouldstone gave birth to healthy twin boys. She was delighted with these new additions to her family, although her gloomy husband kept worrying about two more mouths to feed, on his meagre salary. One of the other lodgers in Courtenay Place, the monthly nurse Mrs Ada Hamilton, moved in with the Gouldstones to help take care of the children. She noticed that Gouldstone seemed to be a troubled man: one evening, he drank to excess, and she twice saw him sit crying, as if he was utterly desperate. On Wednesday 8 August 1883, William Gouldstone came home from work early, without explaining why. When his wife asked him if he had told his workmates about the twins, he gruffly answered in the negative. He picked up his young son Frederick and withdrew to the kitchen, before returning to the bedroom and asking Mrs Hamilton to withdraw, since he wanted to talk to his wife in private. The nurse dutifully made herself scarce, but all of a sudden, there was an outcry of 'Murder!' from the bedroom: when she opened the door, she could see that William Gouldstone had attacked the twins with a hammer, killing them both. 'What have you done, you wicked man?' the horrified nurse exclaimed. Gouldstone replied 'All the children are dead now! I shall be hanged, and you will be single. You wished them dead, and now they are!' And indeed, the three older boys were found drowned in the kitchen cistern.

The Walthamstow Tragedy, as it was called, attracted widespread revulsion all over Britain. The coroner's inquest on the five murdered children, held at the Lodge of Walthamstow Cemetery on 10 August, was widely reported in the press. After Ada Hamilton and some other Courtenay Place witnesses had given evidence, Police Constable William Cheeseman graphically described going to the murder house and seeing the bodies of the children. The demented Gouldstone had seemed proud of what he had accomplished, exclaiming 'Good evening, policeman; I have done it; now I am happy! I am ready for the rope!' and 'I did it like a man, too!' A police surgeon detailed the injuries suffered by the murdered children. When the inquest was resumed on 13 August, the jury returned a verdict of wilful murder against William Gouldstone. At the Stratford police court, he was committed to stand trial for murder at the Old Bailey.

William Gouldstone stood trial at the Old Bailey on 14 September 1883, before Mr Justice Day. The nurse, the Courtney Place witnesses, the police constables and the doctors outlined the case for the prosecution, as described earlier. Mrs Gouldstone, who was still broken down with sorrow after losing her entire family, did not give evidence. Mr Thomas Gouldstone, father of the prisoner, was the first defence witness. He stated that his wife, William Gouldstone's mother, was of indifferent mental health, and that she had once tried to strangle herself with a scarf. William Gouldstone's sister Emily corroborated this evidence, as did Dr William Sunderland, of Thaxted in Essex, who had attended the mother professionally. William Gouldstone's brother Robert testified that William had suffered a serious internal rupture, and that he often complained of the severe pain. A number of workmates corroborated this evidence, some of them adding that they thought Gouldstone quite odd in the head. Dr George Henry Savage, a physician at the Bethlehem Hospital, who had examined Gouldstone, thought him weak-minded and slow-witted, but responsible for his actions. He had a latent tendency to insanity, the doctor pontificated, which had been provoked by the fear of ruin after his family had increased. After a brief summing-up from Mr Justice Day, pointing out that the jury had to determine whether the prisoner had known the nature and the quality of the act when he killed the children, the jury was only out for a quarter of an hour, before returning a verdict of Guilty. Mr Justice Day assumed the black cap and sentenced the prisoner to death. William Gouldstone stood with his hands on the front of the dock while sentence was passed; he seemed to want to say something, but the attendant warders instantly removed him to the cells.

As William Gouldstone was awaiting execution, a surprising number of people made exertions to save him from the scaffold. Excerpts from his trial had been published in newspapers all over the country, and they were pondered by members of the legal and medical professions, as well as by many journalists. Since the medical evidence had pointed in the direction of insanity, it was considered harsh to sentence Gouldstone to death, particularly since the extreme brutality of his crime made it impossible to believe that it could have been committed by a sane person. The London correspondent of the *Leeds Mercury* wrote that the Gouldstone case was clearly one for the attention of the Home Secretary, and his competent medical advisors. Dr George Henry Savage wrote to the *Lancet*, depicting Gouldstone as a weakly man with heredity for insanity on both his father's and his mother's side. Severe chronic headaches, and a large double hernia, had combined with anxiety over his increasing family, to exploit this incipient tendency to insanity, and sent him over the edge. If he were to be hanged, it would be a scandal to law and justice.

Having recovered from her nervous prostration, Mrs Gouldstone spoke out in the *Daily Telegraph*, saying that since her unfortunate husband had always been most affectionate to herself and the children, he must be saved from a shameful death. William Gouldstone himself wrote a confused and illiterate letter to his wife, which was reproduced in several newspapers; in an unfortunate sentence, he hoped that she was 'Happey' and that 'all at home are quite Well'; he was conscious of the death penalty, and hoped to see her in Heaven one day. Impressed with the amount of letter-writing on behalf of William Gouldstone from the legal and medical professions, the Home Secretary, Sir William Harcourt, began to stir. In late September 1883, he ordered Dr Orange, the Superintendent of Broadmoor, and the London alienist Dr Clarke, to go to Chelmsford Prison and examine the convict William Gouldstone, and to make out a report directly to himself. The execution was postponed for the medical evidence to be pondered. On 10 October, the High Sheriff of Essex received a communication from the Home Office that Gouldstone had been certified to be of unsound mind; the prisoner is said to have reacted with deep gratitude then he was told that his life had been saved.

William Gouldstone was incarcerated in Broadmoor, where he was employed in the shops as a handyman. He was said to have performed his duties conscientiously, as the months, years and decades went by in that living tomb, isolated from the remainder of humanity. Did the wretched Broadmoor inmate curse his fate, and wish that the do-gooders and busybodies had stayed away back in 1883, so that he could have expiated his terrible crime on the gallows; or had he become a hospitalised wreck of a man, grateful for every day of sunlight, every bowl of porridge, and every kind word from his supervisors? In the 1920s, he became too old to work, and had to retire from the shops. When he finally expired, from pneumonia and senile decay, in January 1935, the headline of the *Chelmford Chronicle* exclaimed 'Fifty Years in Broadmoor!'

37. The Stoke Newington Murder, 1884

John Broome Tower, a native of Stockton-on-Tees, received a good education, and in 1883, when he was 19 years old, he became a clerk with a firm of underwriters in Great Winchester Street. On New Year's Eve

The finding of the body, and other vignettes of the Stoke Newington Murder, from the *IPN*, 12 January 1884.

A portrait of John Broome Tower, and other vignettes from the coroner's inquest, from the *IPN*, 19 January 1884.

SCENE OF THE MYSTERIOUS STOKE NEWINGTON MURDER.—[See "Law and Crime."]

A view of the Stoke Newington reservoir, from the *Penny Illustrated Paper*, 12 January 1884.

1883, he went to call on his friend, the merchant's traveller Ernest Sidney Cogden, and they took a tram from Moorgate to Stoke Newington, where Codgen lodged at 9 Portland Road. They stayed at his rooms until 8 p.m., when they went to the house of Mrs Earle in nearby Green Lanes, to see her daughter, to whom John Broome Tower was engaged. They had quite a jolly time, and both drank a couple of glasses of whisky. At 10.30 p.m., they went to St John's Church, Highbury Vale, with Mrs Earle and her two daughters, to attend a 'watch service' to see in the New Year. They left the church at 25 minutes past midnight, escorted the ladies back to their house in Green Lanes, and then walked up to the crossing of Green Lanes and Portland Road, where they parted at 1.05 a.m. Cogden knew that Broome Tower usually walked down Green Lanes, then to the left into Lordship Park, then Queen Elizabeth's Walk to the right, on his way to his lodgings at 9 Dynevor Road, Stoke Newington.

On the afternoon of 1 January, a lad named William Johnson found a man's hat and coat in waste land off Queen Elizabeth's Walk, not far from the great New River Reservoir. He took them to a police constable, who believed that somebody had got into the reservoir and drowned there. The following day, a police patrol dragging the reservoir found the body of John Broome Tower. A handkerchief was tightly bound round his neck, his pockets were turned out, and his money and watch and chain were missing. His glove had been ripped open, and a diamond ring stolen. His coat was torn and his hat flattened, as if he had been in a desperate struggle before being strangled to death. The police had no doubt that this was a brutal murder, probably for the sake of robbery. Broome Tower had carried about £8 in coins when he was attacked. The police speculated that he had been waylaid by a pair of sturdy robbers, who had knocked him out after a furious fight, strangled him with the handkerchief, and thrown the body into the reservoir. There were signs of a scuffle, and footprints leading up to the reservoir. John Broome Tower had been a very respectable young man, and although he had enjoyed a few glasses of whisky to celebrate the new year, Cogden had thought him perfectly sober when they parted.

The coroner's inquest on John Broome Tower opened on 4 January, at the Parish House of St Mary, Stoke Newington, before Sir John Humphreys, the Coroner for the Eastern Division of Middlesex. The first witness was the mother of the deceased, Mrs Eliza Broome, resident of Stockton-on-Tees and wife of the schoolmaster John Broome. The reason John had the surname Tower was that he had been born before her marriage to Broome. John had been a short, thin young man, just 5 feet 6 inches tall, with dark hair and a waxed and curled moustache. Since he had a good salary, he had never applied to her for money. Miss Alice Goodwin Drage, the landlady at 109 Dynevor Road, said John paid £3 per month for his lodgings, money that had always been paid promptly and in full. He was engaged to marry Miss Earle, and she had never seen him with any other female companion. Ernest Sidney Cogden then described his rambles with John Broome Tower on New Year's Eve, adding that John had seemed in excellent spirits when they parted. When directly asked by the coroner, he had to admit that in addition to his steady girlfriend Miss Earle, John had been corresponding with a certain Maggie Waller, who lived in the North of England. The surgeon Mr R. C. Whites, who had inspected the body of the deceased, and the forensic specialist Mr Bond, who had performed the autopsy, agreed that the body had a number of lacerations to the nose, lip and ear, caused before death. The cause of death was homicidal strangulation. The inquest was adjourned until 7 January.

There was a good deal of newspaper speculation about the mysterious Stoke Newington Murder. Firstly, it was rightly pointed out that unless the robbers had carried John Broome Tower's body some considerable distance, he must have taken a left turning into Queen Elizabeth's Walk, the wrong way if he had been going to his lodgings. Had he arranged a clandestine meeting with some person near the reservoir? There was a story that part of a woman's linen cuff had been found in the dead man's hand, and that a brooch and an earring had been found nearby, but this was denied by the police. John Broome Tower was buried at the Abney Park Cemetery on 5 January: his parents were both present, as were Ernest Sidney Cogden and the landlady Alice Goodwin Drage, as well as the late schoolmaster and some former schoolfellows of the deceased.

When the coroner's inquest was resumed on 7 January, the lad William Johnson described finding Broome Tower's hat and coat in the waste land near the reservoir; the hat had been much battered, and the coat had two buttons missing, as if it had been forcibly torn off. The landlady Alice Goodwin Drage identified the hat and coat as belonging to Broome Tower, and she also identified two pins, the bar of a watch chain, a cigar-cutter, a ticket purse and a sleeve link, which had been found near the reservoir, as belonging to him. A number of police constables described the dragging of the reservoir and the finding of the body, and one of them had found two distinct sets of footprints nearby, one of them fitting the narrow, pointed boots worn by the deceased. A woman's earring and brooch had been found nearby, it was once more alleged. Summing up, the coroner pointed out that since John Broome Tower's money and watch and chain were missing, his pockets turned inside out, and his handkerchief thrice knotted around his neck, this was clearly murder and not suicide. The jury duly returned the verdict that the deceased had been wilfully and maliciously murdered by some person or persons unknown.

On 9 January, a man named Thompson, alias Simms, was arrested in Watford, since he had a black eye and a wound on the nose, and was wearing a chain similar to that belonging to John Broome Tower. He could not explain why he was carrying a press cutting about the Stoke Newington Murder. It turned out, however, that Thompson had a solid alibi, since he had spent New Year's Eve with a friend in the neighbourhood of the Strand. He was sentenced to seven days in prison for being drunk and disorderly. On 15 January, the *Globe* newspaper had some startling news: the employer of John Broome Tower had examined the books of which he had been in charge, and 'very serious discrepancies were found to exist, of which the latter must have been cognisant.' This of course raised the possibility that he had actually committed suicide, and the police detectives viewed this as a possibility, but the medical experts pooh-poohed this notion, and the coroner would not have the verdict of murder quashed.

In January 1886, two years after the Stoke Newington Murder, a man named George Thackray, alias King, who had been arrested at Grimsby on a trivial charge, confessed that he and a man named Sullivan had murdered a man in Queen Elizabeth's Walk, Islington, and thrown the body into the adjacent reservoir. They had spotted Broome Tower in Whitechapel Road, and followed him all the way to Stoke Newington, where they had waylaid and murdered him. But John Broome Tower had not been anywhere near the Whitechapel Road on New Year's Day, and Thackray alias King was well known as a liar. In January 1887, a Londoner named George Charles Wilson confessed to the Stoke Newington Murder, but he was found to be of disturbed mind, and was dealt with as a wandering lunatic.

So, what is the truth about the Stoke Newington Murder? I definitely think it was a case of murder, as indicated by the medical evidence, in spite of Broome Tower's faulty bookkeeping being exposed post-mortem. Either he was murdered by a pair of unusually brutal and violent robbers, who thought nothing of attacking a young and fit victim, or he was done to death by a secret enemy who had lured him to a late-night meeting near the reservoir, and attacked him in a furious rage. If Broome Tower had been walking his normal route home, he would have been attacked quite far from the reservoir, and it would not have made sense for his attackers to carry his body through the streets for quite some distance, to dispose of him into the reservoir. No, Broome Tower clearly had some reason to turn left instead of right into Queen Elizabeth's Walk, and to approach the reservoir. Although Portland Road is today Portland Rise, and houses have been built in the wasteland near Queen Elizabeth's Walk, the situation of Green Lanes, Lordship Park and Queen Elizabeth's Walk have not changed since the sketch of the murder site in the *IPN*. There were signs of a struggle in wasteland near the reservoir, indicating that Broome Tower had walked there of his own free will, the wrong way if he had been going to his lodgings. It is peculiar that a woman's brooch and earring were found nearby, and this raises the possibility that Broome Tower was seeing another lady friend on the side, only for her other boyfriend, who had of course followed her to her late-night assignment, to attack and murder him. But would 'the woman in the case' not have become upset that her swain had been done to death, and contacted the authorities? The Stoke Newington Murder, one of London's forgotten mysteries, may well have a more colourful solution than a pair of brutal robbers turned murderers.

38. The Man They Could Not Hang, 1885

John Lee was born in Abbotskerwell, an agricultural village near Torquay, in August 1864. He had an sister named Amelia and an older

+ Window of the Room in which the body of Miss Keyse was found.
RESIDENCE OF MISS KEYSE AT BABBICOMBE.
[SEE "TERRIBLE TRAGEDY NEAR TORQUAY."]

The Glen, from the *Penny Illustrated Paper*, 22 November 1884.

half-sister named Elizabeth Harris, his mother's illegitimate daughter. In 1878, John Lee joined the household of Miss Emma Keyse, a wealthy 62-year-old spinster, at her property 'The Glen' situated on Babbacombe Beach. Since John did not appreciate being a lowly servant, he joined the Royal Navy in 1879, initially making good progress in his training to become a sailor. In 1882, he recovered from a dangerous bout of pneumonia, and was invalided out of the navy as a result. After trying various menial occupations with little success, he managed to become footman to Colonel Brownlow in Torquay. In 1883, he was charged with stealing a quantity of silver plate from his employer, and was sentenced to six months imprisonment, with hard labour.

John Lee, from the *IPN*, 29 November 1884.

Vignettes on the Babbacombe Murder, from the *IPN*, 29 November 1884.

Portraits concerning the Babbacombe murder, from the *IPN*, 6 December 1885.

Since Emma Keyse was a naïve and kindly woman, she wrote to the prison governor after hearing of young John Lee's disgrace, offering to employ him in her household when he was released from prison. Having no other option, Lee accepted the offer of temporary

More vignettes about the murder, from the *IPN*, 6 December 1885.

employment as a footman, for a token wage, while Miss Keyse attempted to find him steady work elsewhere. But since no other person was willing to employ a convicted thief, Lee would remain at The Glen for several months to come. He showed Miss Keyse little gratitude, and used to refer to her as 'the old woman' and in other terms of disrespect. He became engaged to marry the local dressmaker Kate Farmer, but since Miss Keyse paid him a very low salary, they were not able to get married. Lee seemed to blame Miss Keyse for all his misfortunes, whereas in reality, his own thieving was the cause of his downfall. When the parsimonious Miss Keyse reduced his wages from half-a-crown to just two shillings per week, John Lee was bitterly disappointed, but he could do nothing about it since, as a convicted thief, he was unlikely to find employment elsewhere. Furthermore, Miss Keyse was feeling too old to live in the large house on Babbacombe Beach, and she was making preparations to sell the Glen and move into a more manageable property. Under these circumstances, she would no longer need a manservant.

Apart from Miss Keyse herself, the household at The Glen consisted of two elderly maidservants, the sisters Elizabeth and Jane Neck, who had been employed by Miss Keyse for nearly fifty years, John Lee the footman, and his half-sister Elizabeth Harris who worked as the cook. On the evening of 14 November 1884, the inhabitants of the Glen went to bed just as usual. The security-conscious Miss Keyse made sure that all doors were bolted and all windows shuttered. Her own bedroom was on the first floor, as were those of Elizabeth Harris and the Lock sisters, but John Lee slept in the pantry downstairs. After 3 a.m. on 15 November 1884, Elizabeth Harris woke up with a start, since smoke was coming into her bedroom. She gave a scream and alerted the Lock sisters, and they all made their way downstairs through the smoke-filled house. John Lee came out of the pantry fully dressed, saying that he had just been

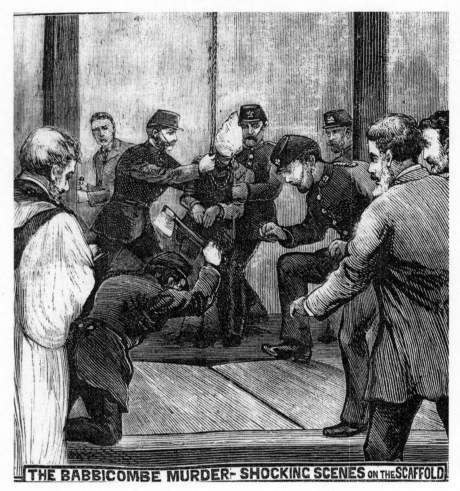

THE BABBICOMBE MURDER- SHOCKING SCENES on the SCAFFOLD

The bungled execution of John Lee, from the *IPN*, 28 February 1885.

woken up by the commotion. They found Miss Keyse dead in the hall, with a broken skull and he throat cut from ear to ear. The murderer had attempted to destroy the body by dousing it with paraffin and setting it alight.

After the murder, John Lee behaved most peculiarly. Although he had said that had been asleep when roused by his fellow servants, he had come bounding out of the pantry fully dressed. He then broke a pane of glass in one of the downstairs windows, in order to help the smoke escape, as he expressed it, cutting his arm in the process. When a hatchet was needed by the firemen, Lee fetched one that was likely to be the one used in the attack on Miss Keyse, as if he well knew where it was kept. He was then sent to the nearby village of Compton,

PRICE SIXPENCE.

THE MAN THEY COULD NOT HANG

THE LIFE STORY OF JOHN LEE

PUBLISHED AT 17 AND 18 HENRIETTA STREET. LONDON. W.C.

John Lee's autobiography.

to inform Miss Keyse's half-sister of what had happened. When he returned, Police Sergeant Abraham Nott had examined the crime scene and made some important deductions. Neither the elderly Neck sisters nor the pregnant Elizabeth Harris could have committed the murder, since considerable force had been used to strike Miss Keyse down and cut her throat: the murder had clearly been committed by a man, and John Lee had been the only man in the house. When Lee returned from Compton, he was taken into police custody, and frog-marched to the Torquay police station.

The coroner's inquest on Emma Keyse opened on 17 November, in the music room at The Glen, before Mr Sydney Hacker, the Coroner for South Devon. The solicitor Isadore Carter represented the Crown, and his colleague Reginald Gwynne Templer looked after the interests of the prisoner John Lee. The Neck sisters described their experiences the night of the murder, as well as they could. The London analyst Dr Thomas Stevenson had examined Jane Neck's nightdress, and found it to be stained with blood where John Lee had held her by the waist as he helped her out of the burning house; thus his hands had been stained with blood already, before he broke the window. The evidence from Elizabeth Harris was very much against her half-brother John Lee, since she said that he had once threatened to murder Miss Keyse, by pushing her down a cliff, after she had found faults with his work. Another time, he had threatened to burn down the house if Miss Keyse did not give him a character reference. He had been very angry when his wages had been reduced to just 2s per week. A postman named William Richards, who had known John Lee six years, had heard him say that he was quite fed-up with his menial work at The Glen, and that if Miss Keyse did not find him a better job soon, she would regret it.

A number of fire-fighters and policemen gave evidence about the fire at the Glen, which had been started using a can of paraffin, and about the suspicious behaviour of John Lee, that had led to his arrest. The medical evidence, from the two doctors who had performed the post-mortem examination of the murdered woman, indicated that she had been struck down with a hatchet found in the murder house, before her throat had been cut with a table knife, which had also been found on the premises. The aforementioned Dr Stevenson identified stains of mammalian blood on both weapons. John Lee's cotton shirt was found to be much bloodstained, more so than could be expected from a small cut on his arm. His socks were stained with earth, mineral oil, and blood, and had several hairs, matching those of the murdered woman, stuck on them.

His trousers were also stained with blood and mineral oil. The coroner's inquest returned a verdict of wilful murder against John Lee, and he was committed to stand trial at the Devon Assizes.

John Lee spent what must have been a miserable Christmas and New Year in Exeter Prison, awaiting being tried for his life. The trial opened at Exeter Castle on 30 January 1885, before Mr Justice Manisty. The prosecution was conducted by Mr Collins, QC, and Mr Vigor. The evidence against him seemed formidable indeed. According to Elizabeth Harris and the postman Richards, he had held a grudge against Miss Keyse, and made threats against her. She had clearly been murdered by a man, and John Lee was the only man in the household; the house had been locked up and the windows shuttered, and there were no signs of a break-in. There was hair and blood on John Lee's clothes, and the blood found on Jane Neck's nightdress indicated that his hand had been bloodstained before he broke the window and cut his arm. Some matches found near where the fire had been started matched those in the possession of John Lee. The paraffin can used to start the fire was normally kept near John Lee's bed in the pantry, where no other person could have got hold of it without waking him. Prior to the murder, he had stolen and pawned a guitar belonging to Miss Keyse. For the defence, Mr Walter Molesworth St Aubyn, MP, suggested that Lee's clothes had become bloodstained when he helped to carry Miss Keyse's corpse out of the burning house. There had been no motive for him to murder her, and the talk of his previous threats was just idle gossip. He had not escaped after the murder, although he had every opportunity to do so. Elizabeth Harris was pregnant, indicating that she had been seeing a lover during her stay at The Glen; might she have let this individual into the house the night of the murder? The jury was out for thirty minutes before returning a verdict of Guilty, and John Lee was sentenced to death by Mr Justice Manisty.

Awaiting execution, John Lee was incarcerated in the condemned cell at Exeter Prison. He wrote his parents and sister some letters indicating that his impending death had given him a sense of religion, although he still stoutly maintained his innocence, and accused Elizabeth Harris and the Lock sisters of perjuring themselves. The Vicar of Abbotskerwell wrote a petition to the Home Secretary, pointing out the youth of the prisoner, and the lack of a motive for him to commit murder, but it was ignored. The appointed time came on 23 February 1885. The executioner James Berry had come to Exeter, and the scaffold and drop had been made ready. John Lee was pinioned and hooded, the noose was put round his neck, and he was moved to the trap. But when Berry pulled the lever to open the trap, it did not move. The executioner pulled the lever twice more, with the same result. There was panic on the scaffold as Berry removed the noose and hood and pulled Lee aside to be able to inspect the mechanism. Finding nothing wrong with it, he made sure that Lee was pinioned for a second time, and the cap and rope were put into position, but again the trap refused to open. The rope was again removed, and the mechanism inspected. Lee was then placed on the trap for a third time, with the noose around his neck, but once more, the mechanism failed to operate, although the desperate Berry tried to force the trap by stamping hard on it with his foot, risking a heavy fall along with his victim. It was decided not to make a fourth attempt, and John Lee, who had maintained an admirable coolness throughout his ordeal, was taken back to the condemned cell. In a letter to his sister, he thanked God for saving his life, describing a prophetic dream the previous night, that he would not be executed since the scaffold was not ready.

When Queen Victoria heard of John Lee's ordeal on the scaffold, she sent a telegram to the Home Secretary, Sir William Harcourt: 'I am horrified at the disgraceful scenes at Exeter at Lee's execution. Surely Lee cannot now be executed. It would be too cruel. Imprisonment for life seems the only alternative.' This Royal Command was duly heeded, although a hardcore newspaper faction criticised the Home Secretary for allowing a cruel murderer to live. John Lee had to look forward to a very long time behind bars, but he endured the prison regime with great fortitude. His early imprisonment was solitary confinement at Pentonville and Wormwood Scrubs, but in October 1885 he was transferred to Portsmouth Prison, where he was worked hard in the wash-house. In 1892, he was moved to Portland Prison, where he was kept busy in the quarry. In 1905, on the twentieth anniversary of the bungled execution, there were rumours that Lee's release was imminent, but he would remain in prison until December 1907, when he was released on ticket-of-leave and reunited with his elderly mother in Abbotskerwell. He sold his life story to the *Lloyd's Weekly News*, and it was later reissued in pamphlet form as 'The Man they could Not Hang', enjoying good sales both in Britain and in the United States. Lee gave a graphic picture of the hard and unrelenting work, and the unappetizing prison 'grub': he likened his 22 years behind bars to a 'living death'. In January 1909, Lee married the workhouse attendant Jessie Bulled, and they soon had a healthy young son. Lee made a career of working as a barman in various pubs, where the customers were keen to see the Man they could Not Hang as a curiosity.

In 1911, John Lee emigrated to the United States, taking with him Adeline Gibbs, a barmaid from the pub where he had been pulling pints, but leaving his pregnant wife and son behind to face destitution. He settled down in Milwaukee, where he found work as a shipping clerk for a motor vehicle company. He remained faithful to his new 'wife' Adeline, and they had a daughter named Evelyn who died accidentally in 1933, from asphyxiation by naphtha fumes. Lee himself did nothing newsworthy during his lengthy residence in Milwaukee: he lived quietly in a succession of houses and flats, and enjoyed some peaceful years of retirement. He died from heart failure in March 1945, surviving his encounter with the gallows by no less than 60 years. His 'widow' Adeline lived on until as late as 1969, reaching the age of 96.

Over the years, the debate concerning the guilt of John Lee has continued. There have been rumours that a local fisherman held a grudge against Miss Keyse, that a wealthy builder living nearby had committed the murder, that a smuggler was the guilty man, that the unnamed lover of Elizabeth Harris was the real murderer, or that a Torquay solicitor had murdered Miss Keyse. But in real life, there is very little doubt concerning the guilt of John Lee. There have also been conspiracy theories that the real murderer had saved the life of John Lee the day he was to be executed, by sabotaging the drop or bribing the hangman. But it is unlikely that Berry would take bribes when he risked losing his job if the execution was bungled, and no convict labour had been involved in erecting the scaffold and preparing the drop. If the drop was sabotaged, it was done by one of the regular workmen at Exeter Prison, who risked being fired from his job if exposed, and who had no other motive than general mischief-making. A more likely explanation for the failure of the drop to operate properly, favoured by Gerald de Courcy Hamilton, the Chief Constable of Devon, is that the planks swelled up due to rain in the days preceding the execution. John Lee remains the only person in the world whose execution was prevented by the malfunction of the drop, and technically at least, he was the luckiest of all the murderers in this book. Not much is known about his subsequent life in Milwaukee: in particular whether he was tormented by regular nightmares of a burning house and a mutilated body, a judge donning a black cap, and standing on the scaffold with a noose around his neck. But Lee appears to have been a stolid, unimaginative, materialistic character, who was not inclined towards morbid musings and gloomy contemplation of death; in his Milwaukee exile, he must have enjoyed some tasty burgers and hot dogs instead of the prison 'grub', a comfortable American bed instead of a prison bunk, and light duties as a clerk rather than forced labour in a quarry.

When the contents of The Glen were sold at auction after the murder, several hundred collectors of souvenirs and criminal curiosities attended, and the house was so crowded that the sale had to be held out on the beach. There was less enthusiasm with regard to the Babbacombe murder house itself, in spite of speculation that Madame Tussaud's would make a bid for it. The Glen failed to attract an opening bid of £2 000 when put up for sale at auction in August 1889, although it did sell in June the following year. It was eventually demolished in 1904, and the cellar and part of the foundations became part of the Babbacombe Beach Café. A scarce postcard was printed to commemorate 'John Lee's Cellar', all that remained of the old murder house. When the café burnt down in 1928, another one was built on the spot, and it stood until demolished, with cellar and all, in 1974.

39. The Camden Town Shooting Case, 1885

In March 1885, the widow Maria Hammond kept a small lodging-house at 7 Caroline Street, Camden Town. Occupying the kitchen and one room herself, she let the remaining five rooms to various needy characters. One of her favourite lodgers was the 31-year-old coachbuilder Charles Wheaton, who had occupied the back parlour on the ground floor for no less than three years. A quiet, industrious man, he had shown no intention at all to move into more salubrious accommodation, preferring to stay in his little room with a cage of 'fancy birds' as his only companions. Another, more adventurous lodger in the same house was the 35-year-old John Rose, who described himself as an author and a journalist. He had already published one book, and was completing the manuscript of another, he claimed. When Mrs Hammond was incredulous, knowing Rose only as a seaman, he produced the book manuscript with a flourish, saying that the publishers would pay him £400 for it, money he would make use of to go to Australia to seek his fortune.

On the early morning of March 6 1885, Rose left his first floor room and walked downstairs, fully dressed. Without explaining what he was up to, he went into Wheaton's room and very soon after, Mrs Hammond heard four shots and a cry of 'Murder!' Bleeding profusely from the head and chest, Wheaton came bursting out from his room. He ran out into the street 'in a state of nudity' and kept running at speed 'through

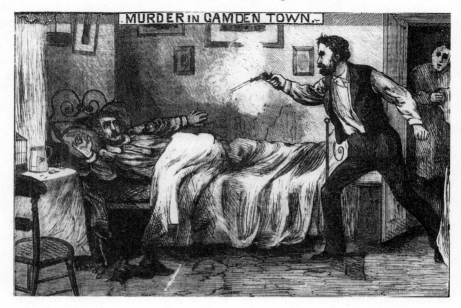

John Rose shoots Charles Wheaton, from the *IPN*, 28 March 1885.

Caroline-street, Hamilton-street, Bayham-street, Camden-road and Kentish-town-road, to the North-West London Hospital, the blood streaming from his wounds.' Mrs Hammond followed him, screaming 'Murder! Murder!' until she was quite out of breath. Some neighbours also tied to keep up with the wounded man desperately running through the Camden Town streets.

Once he safely arrived at the hospital, Charles Wheaton's wounds were bandaged by the house surgeon. Since no bed was available, he was transferred to the North London Temperance Hospital, where three bullets were extracted from his head, chest and belly. In the meantime, the police had gone to 7 Caroline Street, to find Rose still there. He seemed quite excited, giving a rambling account of being invited into Wheaton's room to see his birds. When he got into the room, Wheaton had pulled a revolver on him, and Rose had made use of his own weapon to kill him in self-defence. No revolver was found in Wheaton's room, however, and Mrs Hammond denied that her timid lodger had ever possessed any firearm. It also turned out that for many years, Rose had been far from sane. He had more than once been in asylums, but he had escaped from one of them, becoming a sailor and travelling the world. No less than £39 in gold was found in his room. How he had earned that money remains a mystery, for his yarn about being a journalist was completely untrue according to

Mrs Hammond, and no book was published under his name at the relevant time.

For a while, Charles Wheaton seemed to recover, but one of the bullets had perforated the small intestine, and he died painfully from peritonitis. At the inquest, the verdict was wilful murder against John Rose. From his rambling statements, the former sailor seemed quite insane. On trial at the Old Bailey, be was found to be of unsound mind, and was incarcerated at Broadmoor. The 1891 and 1901 Censuses list him as an inmate of Gloucester Second County Lunatic Asylum in Barnwell, and according to Broadmoor records, he was permanently transferred to Long Grove Asylum in January 1920. The murder house at what is today 7 Carol Street still stands today.

40. Murder In Brecknock Road, 1886

In 1886, the ground floor of the house at 165 Brecknock Road, Kentish Town, contained a large chemist's shop that doubled as the local sub-post office. On 20 June that year Mr Hardy, the chemist, was not on the premises, but his daughter Frances acted as postal clerk, and the shop assistant John William Bowes looked after the druggist's counter. A local youth, 19-year-old George Vincent Finch, who had been loitering outside the shop for several hours, suddenly ran into the post office and seized hold of the cashbox that Miss Hardy had left on the counter. 'Stop thief!' cried the assistant Bowes, leaping out to intercept Finch, but the demented youth pulled a revolver and shot him at nearly point-blank range. Miss Hardy heard the shot and came running into the shop, giving a scream when she saw that Bowes was badly wounded. Finch took a pot shot at her as she stood just inside the shop door, but missed. He then ran away, clutching the cashbox, pursued by a lad named Alfred Partell, who had seen him fire at Miss Hardy.

It turned out that Bowes had received a revolver shot in the head, which had killed him instantly. As the shop was filling up with police constables, the brave lad Partell came running up to tell them that Finch had taken refuge at 15 Ospringe Road nearby [the house remains]. Since this was actually Finch's mother's address, Chief Inspector Millward and his men realized that they were hardly dealing with a master criminal. The police burst into the house, but initially, they could find no trace of Finch. His mother became quite hysterical when she realized that her son was a murderer. In the meantime, the police found a hidden trapdoor inside a closet, leading to a small hiding-place where the demented Finch was lurking. 'Give me the revolver, Finch!'

Murder and robbery in Brecknock Road, from the *IPN*, 19 June 1886.

Chief Inspector Millward ordered. 'It was entirely an accident!' a muffled voice replied from the hideout, presumably alluding to the murder of Bowes. The police kept negotiating with the hidden gunman, trying to persuade him to surrender his weapon, but Finch said he would only give it to a detective. The exasperated policemen began pulling up floorboards to get to grips with the hidden murderer, but before they were done, Finch meekly handed his revolver over to Detective Sergeant Miller. A sturdy policeman seized his hand, and he was unceremoniously dragged out of his hideout.

George Vincent Finch's mother freely gave interviews to the press, declaring that in spite of his shabby appearance, her son had received a superior education, and aimed to become an artist. Recently, he had been behaving very strangely, getting involved with private theatrical performances. After he had sold tickets to a play, to be staged at Kilburn Town Hall, the audience was disappointed when the actors went on strike because he had no money to pay them with. Mrs Finch had seen better days, she claimed: her late husband had been an officer, related to the Earl of Aylesford. Now, she was reduced to living off a small income, and letting rooms to lodgers. George Vincent had been a worry to her with his strange behaviour, which had deteriorated after he had fallen off a bicycle in Highgate Road, and landed on his head. Once, he had pushed down a small boy who had annoyed him, and made to beat him with a walking stick. One of his uncles had died in an asylum, and his cousin went insane from too much study, or so Mrs Finch alleged.

The journalist George R. Sims, who was quite a murder house enthusiast, read about the Brecknock Road murder in the newspaper, and he immediately set out to have a look at the scene of the crime. In his 'Mustard and Cress' column in the old *Referee* newspaper, he wrote that,

> The chemist's shop, a bright, handsome suburban house, was the last place in the world one would connect with a tragedy. The whole neighbourhood seemed to rise superior to a bloody deed. The surrounding houses were elegant, bay-windowed, aesthetically-curtained, flower-boxed abodes of gentility that would have blushed in every brick at the mention of the 'Newgate Calendar'.

Apart from a little girl who tried to peep through the keyhole of the murder shop, to see the murdered man in there, the locals seemed to view the recent murder with quiet detachment; even an aristocratic pug that was taking exercise with a maidservant did not even stop to sniff at the doorstep of the shop.

At the coroner's inquest, George Vincent Finch cut a sorry figure. Described as an unmanly-looking youth with a prominent nose, he sat grinning inanely at the witnesses describing the post office shooting tragedy. When asked if he had anything to contribute himself, he stood up and theatrically exclaimed: 'I simply know nothing about it, your Worship. I don't know the gentlemen who have come here. I don't remember being in the chemist's shop. That is all what I wish to say, thank you!' By the time of the trial of George Vincent Finch at the Old Bailey, he had been examined by Mr Gilbert, the surgeon at Holloway Prison, and the physician Dr Bastian, attached to King's College Hospital, and they were both of the opinion that the prisoner was quite insane and unfit to stand trial. Finch was committed to Broadmoor, and the 1891 Census lists him as one of the inmates there. He was released in 1922, into the care of the Salvation Army, and there is good reason to believe that he expired in Brentwood, Essex, as late as 1951. The murder house at 165 Brecknock Road is still standing, and has barely changed at all since the time of the shooting tragedy back in 1886.

41. The Penzance Triple Murder, 1886

James Hawke was born in Penzance in 1835, the son of a carpenter. He had a brother named George who emigrated to New Zealand, and a younger sister named Mary. James himself became a tin man's

Triple Murder and Suicide at Penzance, from the *IPN*, 14 August 1886.

apprentice, but he soon tired of the Cornish seaside town and went to sea, serving on various vessels. After being refused when trying to enlist in the Royal Navy, he went to Australia, where he worked as a storekeeper and a sheep shearer. He had a deep, booming voice and was fond of making recitations to his Australian colleagues. In the 1880s, he became a published poet of doggerel verse in the Sydney *Town and Country Journal*, under the pen-name of 'Boss' of 'Balala', the shearing station where he worked. He was married for a while, but not particularly happily:

> I'd freely give half-a-crown
> To one who'd take my wife;
> For she's the terror of this town,
> I'm sick of married life.

When the wife expired from some unspecified Antipodian malady not long after, he honoured her with an epitaph:

> Here lies Madame Boss, so let her lie,
> She's at rest, and so am I.

In late 1885, James Hawke returned to Penzance after having spent many years in Australia. He moved in with his sister Mary, who had married the shoemaker Charles Uren, at 1 Marine Terrace, a small street near the bottom of Queen Street, next to the still extant Navy Inn. He stayed with the Urens, who had seven children, for a while, and then went to Bristol. A short, thick-set man, scruffily dressed in nautical attire, he seemed gloomy and apprehensive, and drank hard at the local taverns, although he did not need to work since he had saved money in Australia. In June 1886, James Hawke came back to the Urens, who again allowed him to lodge in the crowded little house. On Wednesday 28 July, James went on a boating excursion with the landlord of the Navy Inn, before returning to the tavern for some liquid refreshments. He was neatly dressed in a blue serge suit. Having emptied his tankard of beer, he spoke to a young man named Daniel Williams at the end of Marine Terrace, before going back to the little house where he lodged, and walking upstairs to his room.

When James Hawke came lurching downstairs, his sister and brother-in-law gave him a glass of beer. Suddenly and wordlessly, he pulled a large revolver, which he had brought home from Australia, and shot Mary Uren in the mouth. She collapsed, on the spot, and James went on to gun down his brother-in-law. Mrs Elizabeth Gerrard, the wife of a neighbour, who had been helping Mrs Uren with the laundry, ran out of the house with a scream, but James shot her down from the doorway. The lad Daniel Williams heard the shots and came running up, seeing Mrs Gerrard lying dead on her back, and James Hawke standing in the doorway holding the revolver. Screaming 'Don't come near me, or I will kill you too!' James Hawke pointed the revolver to his temple and blew his brains out. When Captain Holbrook, who lived in a larger house with its back to Marine Terrace, heard the four shots and went out to investigate, he found all four people stone dead.

There was grief and amazement throughout the town as news spread of the triple murder and suicide. As the *Royal Cornwall Gazette* expressed it, 'Penzance was shocked on Wednesday afternoon by a tragedy surpassing in horror anything which has happened in the county for a lengthened number of years.' Police Constable Cliff and Superintendent Nicholas were soon on the spot, and the local doctor declared all four people dead. A local journalist, who came to see the crime scene, was struck with the effusion of blood and the horribly contorted faces of the murdered people. The two Urens left behind a family of seven children, and Mrs Gerrard, who was pregnant at the time of the murder, had six living children. James Hawke had seemed just as usual the day of his murderous rampage, and there was much speculation what had driven him to murder his sister and brother-in-law, who had given him food and shelter, and to gun down the blameless neighbour as well. There was a debate as whether Hawke had really been able to save money in Australia, or whether he had returned home penniless. There was also speculation that the 52-year-old Hawke had wanted to marry Mrs Uren's illegitimate daughter, born before her marriage to Charles Uren in 1875, but it was clearly quite unconventional for a middle-aged man to aspire to marry his own niece, who was barely out of her teens. Nor was it clear why these consanguineous aspirations would prompt the normally quiet and sociable James Hawke to become a triple murderer, before taking his own life.

42. The Hoxton Murder, 1887

Around the year 1870, Mrs Ann Green leased the large terraced house at 8 Baches Street, Hoxton. She lived in the basement kitchen with her three young daughters, and let all the other rooms to various needy slum dwellers in this very rundown part of London, notorious as a cesspit of vice and crime. Sometimes, families of five could share a single room in the house, which had neither a bathroom nor an indoor water closet. Ann Green was a tough woman, however, and hardened by years of adversity: she successfully brought her three daughters up to adulthood. The eldest daughter Alice married a man named William Thomas Gauntlett in 1884, and had a baby son with him, but the husband died prematurely in 1886, and Alice had to move back into 8 Baches Street with her little son. The middle daughter, Lydia, fell in love with Thomas William Currell, a soldier in the Royal Middlesex Fusiliers. They became engaged to be married when Lydia was 19 years old.

Thomas William Currell had a liking for military life, and was promoted in due course to corporal, but his army career soon ground to a halt, leaving him to face civilian life with neither a trade nor an education. He became a journeyman sponge-trimmer, employed by wholesalers to trim their sponges to make them ready for sale. This

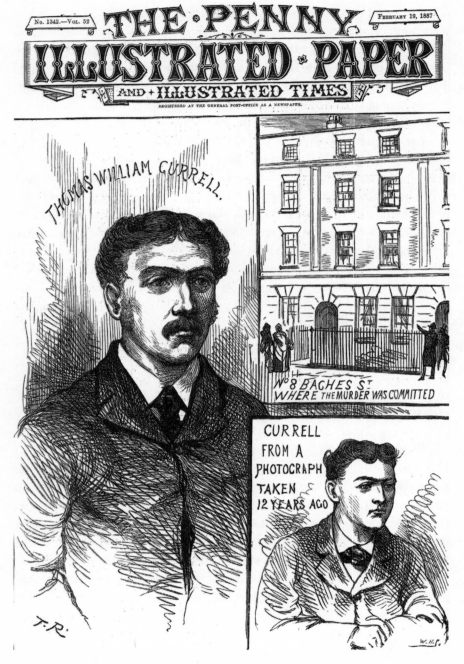

Currell and the murder house, from the *Penny Illustrated Paper*, 19 February 1887.

Features from the Hoxton Murder, from the *IPN*, 2 April 1887.

dreary and menial employment seems to have soured Currell's character in a permanent manner. His father was a retired drug-grinder, and his mother was lame with rheumatism; he had to share their humble lodgings when he could not afford a room of his own. Currell's only pleasure in life was drinking beer and gin in various Hoxton public houses, and since he preferred loafing around on a drunken bender to trimming sponges, he was soon in dire financial straits. Ann Green and her daughter Lydia were not pleased with this state of affairs but, in 1886, after being sweethearts for more than ten years, Currell was still engaged to Lydia. However, they sometimes quarrelled angrily about his work-shyness and heavy drinking, and about her suspected unfaithfulness with other men.

"MURDER WILL OUT": CURRELL, MURDERER OF LYDIA GREEN, IN HIS CELL BEFORE EXECUTION.

Currell in the death cell, and a portrait of Lydia Green, from the *Penny Illustrated Paper*, 23 April 1887.

By early 1887, Thomas William Currell had become a pathetic figure: a penniless vagabond without employment; although just 31 years old, he was well known to the police as one of the most notorious drunks lurching around in the Hoxton slums, from one public house to the next. His faithful Lydia still stood by him, although the remainder of the world had allowed him to sink. As for Lydia herself, she worked full time in a Walthamstow factory for surgical instrument cases, earning 18s per week, of which she handed over 10s to her mother for household expenses. She also helped her overworked parent to look after the ramshackle old house and its multitude of lodgers. Although Lydia's position in life was vastly preferable to that of her boyfriend Currell, she was hardly leading a life of luxury: she shared a parlour and a bedroom on the ground floor with her sister Alice and her baby. Ann Green and her youngest daughter Amy shared the first floor back bedroom, and the remaining rooms were all let to lodgers: two old women and their granddaughter, two married couples, and a young family with three children and a niece. This amounted to a total of 18 people living in a house without a proper bathroom or 'convenience' – 'Good Old Days' indeed!

On Friday 4 February 1887, all seemed well at 8 Baches Street. Lydia Green went to bed in the shared bedroom as usual. Her sister went out early in the morning, leaving Lydia alone with the baby. All of a sudden, there was a bang and a heavy fall, which alerted much of the crowded household. Mrs Caroline Sinclair, who lodged on the second floor, was woken up by the loud bang early in the morning; she then heard her landlady cry out in an excited manner for her daughter. John Thomas Day, who lodged on the third floor, also heard the bang, which he thought was caused by some street ragamuffins invited in by the lodgers on the first floor, but his wife Matilda was fearful that something serious had happened, and made her way downstairs to see what was up. Ann Green herself also heard three loud banging sounds in quick succession, as if something very heavy had fallen down. When she went into the bedroom shared by her two eldest daughters, she found Lydia lying on the floor, flat on her back, with some blood on her head and face. The baby was crying dreadfully in its cot.

Dr Davis, the local practitioner, came to 8 Baches Street, where he declared Lydia to be dead. He speculated that Lydia must have fallen over and broken her neck. When it was pointed out to him that Lydia's body had been bleeding from injuries to the right hand and the side of the throat, and that her right eye was very black and bruised, he said that she might also have been stabbed, and ordered a post-mortem to be performed. Ann Green wept bitterly at the death of her daughter. Since the case was considered suspicious, the police were alerted at an early stage. The lodger Thomas Attrell told them that when he was going to his bricklaying job early on Saturday morning, he had met Thomas William Currell not far from the house. Although it was 7.30 a.m., Currell invited Attrell to the Crosby Head public house nearby, to have half a pint of mild ale. Currell bought a pennyworth of gin to mix into his friend's ale, saying that this would give the bricklayer courage when going up on a high roof. He then said that he had left some things behind in Mrs Green's kitchen, which he wanted to remove without disturbing the family. Knowing Currell as Lydia Green's long-term boyfriend, Attrell lent him his latch key to the front door, drank up his ale, and went off to work.

At the post-mortem, it was found that Lydia Green had been shot dead with a small-calibre revolver: one bullet was lodged in her brain, and another one in her jaw. The wounds on her neck, which the careless Dr Davis had suspected to be the result of stabbing, were the entry marks of the two bullets. This was clearly a case of murder, and the obvious suspect was Lydia's long-term boyfriend, the drunk Thomas William Currell. When his latest lodgings were searched, a box of pin-cartridges were found, matching the bullets that had killed Lydia Green. The police suspected that Currell had been lying in wait for the lodger Attrell, who knew him as Lydia's boyfriend, and borrowed his latchkey to be able to enter the house and shoot Lydia dead. 'Wanted' posters were pasted up all over London, using an old daguerreotype portrait found at Currrell's lodgings as his likeness.

The Hoxton police were out in force, searching the local pubs where Currell used to hang out. They knew the murder suspect as a person of low intellect and dissipated habits, and hoped to capture him within a matter of hours. But it turned out that Currell had left the Hoxton area behind. He had visited the factory where Lydia had been working, and cashed in her unpaid earnings from an unsuspecting clerk who did not know about the murder. There were unconfirmed sightings of him from Hampstead, Kensington, Bloomsbury, North Finchley, Dalston and Richmond, and several men were arrested, although they were all able to prove that they were not the Hoxton fugitive. The police tracked down a landlady named Mrs Smith, of 25 Flask Walk in Hampstead, where Currell had been staying the night, under the name of Cole. The fugitive had eagerly read the newspaper reports of the Hoxton Murder, before hastily leaving the lodging-house, without warning. On Saturday 12 February, a week after the murder, Lydia Green was interred at Ilford with much pomp. There was an open hearse, with many wreaths and decorations sent by Lydia's friends and workmates, and two mourning coaches. A large crowd congregated in front of the Baches Street murder house, and throughout the neighbourhood, blinds were drawn and shops closed. A party of police were present to keep order, as the funeral cortege left for the Ilford cemetery, but they were not needed, since the crowd was orderly and respectful.

On Monday 14 February, Currell was still on the run. The police detectives were becoming worried that after leaving the Hampstead lodging-house, the fugitive had escaped from London through some stratagem or other: either purchasing a one-way train ticket or going off on the tramp. But on the following day, Inspector Peel, of the 'G' or Islington division, received an unstamped letter, allegedly coming from Currell, and stating that he would be giving himself up at St Mary's Church in Islington the following day. The Inspector made sure that there was a police presence at the church, and he shrewdly ensured that a constable named Mather brought with him a man named Oram, who knew Currell well, and was on patrol near the church. Currell did not give himself up, but all of a sudden, Oram spotted the fugitive in Upper Street, at the corner with Florence Street. He called out to Mather, and although Currell made an attempt to run away, he was soon in police custody. He did not struggle when he was taken off to the Upper Street police station, in handcuffs, but merely said that he had been intending to give himself up all along.

The police were astounded that Currell had been able to stay on the run, in the crowded streets of London, for no less than ten days. It had benefited him that the daguerreotype photograph the police had got hold of was a very old and indistinct one; it had also helped that Currell had sobered up after the murder, shaved and made use of the wages money to buy some nice new clothes. If he had made a determined effort to escape to the countryside, and started a new life for himself, he might have got clean away. The police found out that prior to the murder, Currell had purchased a revolver and ammunition in a shop; he had been very drunk at the time, and narrowly escaped injury when the weapon was accidentally discharged in his pocket. He was charged with murder and committed to stand trial at the Old Bailey before Mr Justice Grantham. The evidence against him seemed quite formidable: the purchase of the revolver, the bullets which matched those that killed Lydia Green, the clandestine borrowing of the latchkey to gain entrance to the murder house, and the escape after the murder. The defence made much of the lack of eyewitnesses to the murder, and the lack of a motive, but it might be argued that in his chronically drunken condition, Currell did not need any motive for his rash act. The jury found him Guilty, and Mr Justice Grantham sentenced him to death.

While awaiting his execution, Currell made a full confession to the murder. After some heavy drinking, he had got the sudden impulse to shoot Lydia with the revolver he had bought a few days earlier. After she had said 'Tom, what do you come here so early for!', he discharged the weapon at her twice, before making a swift escape. He threw the revolver into Regent's Canal, and then cleaned himself up, shaved and bought some new clothes, since he realized that the police were looking for a tramp. He was executed on 18 April 1887, within the walls of Newgate; death appeared to be instantaneous, and he did not struggle at all. Those who saw him thought he looked ten years older than at the time of the trial, the result of much mental suffering during his final weeks alive, pondering his pointless and motiveless crime, his ten days on the run in London, and his impending execution. Baches Street still exists, an insignificant little street between Chart Street and Brunswick Place, but no older houses remain; the Hoxton Murder of 1887 is also well-nigh forgotten by all but a few crime buffs.

43. Triple Murder at the Rue De Montaigne, 1887

Marie Regnault, the daughter of a bailiff in Chalon-sur-Saône, left home at an early age to become a courtesan in Paris. A very beautiful girl, she had considerable success in the Parisian *demi-monde*, being 'kept' by a succession of wealthy lovers. She called herself Regine de Montille, since it sounded better than her proper name. She was more prudent than the majority of her fellow courtesans, and was able to save money and build up a collection of expensive jewellery. In 1886, when she was 39 years old, Regine was able to move into a large second-floor flat at 17 Rue de Montaigne, which had previously been inhabited by an admiral. She had a maid named Annette Grémeret, who lived on the premises with her little daughter Marie.

On March 17 1887, the concierge at 17 Rue de Montaigne went to the Rue Berryer police station, to report that no person inside Regine de Montille's flat answered the bell, and that her two lapdogs were howling dismally. The police inspector on duty alerted a doctor and a locksmith, and entered the flat. Regine de Montille was found lying dead at the foot of her bed, with her throat cut, and the maid and her daughter had also

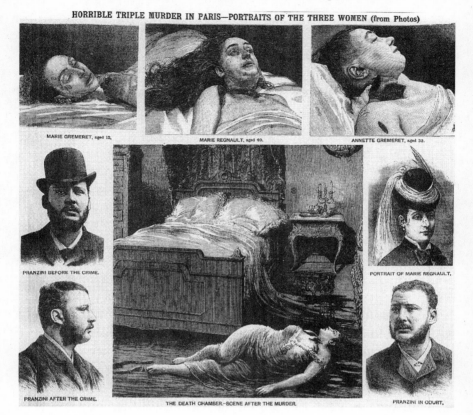

HORRIBLE TRIPLE MURDER IN PARIS—PORTRAITS OF THE THREE WOMEN (from Photos)

MARIE GREMERET, aged 12.

MARIE REGNAULT, aged 40.

ANNETTE GREMERET, aged 33.

PRANZINI BEFORE THE CRIME.

PORTRAIT OF MARIE REGNAULT.

PRANZINI AFTER THE CRIME.

THE DEATH CHAMBER.—SCENE AFTER THE MURDER.

PRANZINI IN COURT.

Pranzini and his victims, from the *IPN*, 23 April 1887.

been murdered in a similar manner. The motive for the triple murder had clearly been plunder, since money and valuable jewellery had been stolen, and a vain attempt had been made to force open an iron safe. Bloodstains on the washbasin in the dressing-room indicated that the murderer had washed his hands, and that he had injured himself during the triple slaughter.

It was clear to Superintendent Goron, who was put in charge of the murder investigation, that Regine de Montille had been murdered by one of her late-night male visitors. He had been let into the flat, and they had spent the night together, but in the morning, he had attacked and murdered her. Regine had desperately seized the bell-pull in her bedroom with her bloody hand, and the maid had woken up and come to the assistance of her mistress, only to be murdered herself; the killer had then completed his murderous orgy by cutting the throat of the sleeping little girl. No person had seen the murderer enter the flat, and he had made a clean escape. The immediate clue to his identity was a

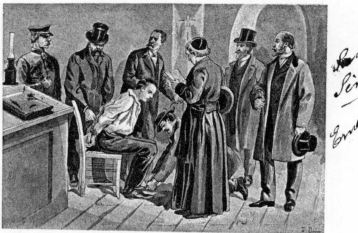

Pranzini — La toilette — 1887.

A postcard posted in Paris in 1905, showing Pranzini on his way to the scaffold.

belt left behind at the crime scene, marked with 'Gaston Geissler' in ink. When the detectives searched Regine's correspondence, a letter signed 'Gaston' asking for a *rendez-vous* was found. Every Geissler in Paris was questioned by the police, but the amorous Gaston could not be tracked down. Goron ordered that the search should be widened to Belgium and Germany. The closest the detectives came was a German named Georg Guttentag, who had called himself 'Gaston Geissler'. He had been taken into police custody in Paris, after attempting to destroy himself through leaping headlong into the Seine. A seedy character of questionable sanity, however, he was hardly the kind of man who would interest Regine de Montille.

On 21 March, M. Goron and his detectives received a very encouraging telegram from Marseille, namely that a man named Henri Pranzini had been arrested in possession of jewellery identical to that stolen from Regine de Montille. Pranzini had visited a brothel in the Rue Ventomagy, where he had sold two young prostitutes a gold watch and a pair of diamond earrings. They had told the brothel madam, who informed the police, and Pranzini was taken into police custody. The Paris detectives knew Henri Pranzini as a suave con artist, who seduced wealthy women and swindled them out of their savings. He had no history of violent crime, however, and the police initially suspected that he was merely the accomplice of the mysterious 'Geissler', who had taken the stolen jewellery out of Paris. When arrested in Marseille, he had posed as a Swedish doctor, on his way to Singapore.

Henri Pranzini was born in 1856, of mixed French and Italian parentage. He grew up in Alexandria, where he worked as a postal clerk until he was convicted of theft and sentenced to nine months in jail. He later worked as a hotel waiter, a courier and an interpreter. At the Hôtel Caprani in Naples, he was dismissed for stealing money, and implicating the hotel bookkeeper, a man named Geissler, in the theft. In the Soudan War of 1885, Pranzini served as an interpreter in the British Army, for once giving a good account of himself, since he was fluent in both Turkish and Arabic. He then returned to Paris, living off wealthy women. A handsome, personable man, he enjoyed an affair with a countess, and also seduced a young American girl, who implored him to join her in New York and marry her.

Henri Pranzini protested his innocence, saying that he had bought the jewellery in Paris from a man named Geissler. The evidence against him kept mounting, however. The police tracked down the cab man who had driven him away from the murder flat, and the cutler who had sold him a large knife prior to the murders. He had fresh cuts on his hands when arrested and, after being arrested, he had made a half-hearted attempt at suicide in the Marseille prison. His mistress Madame Sabatier, whom he had expected to provide him with an alibi, said he had been away from her flat at 40 Rue des Martyrs all night when the murder was committed. Pranzini had been imprudent enough to speak about the triple murder in the Rue de Montaigne to complete strangers he met in a shop, providing details not known to the public at the time. It was suspected that he had planted the letter and belt marked 'Geissler' to confound the police, and implicate his old enemy the Naples hotel bookkeeper. It was strongly suspected that Pranzini had tried to swindle Regine de Montille, but that she had not fallen for his tricks, being a very prudent woman. Thwarted, he had planned to murder and rob her, and executed his sanguinary scheme to perfection.

On trial for murder in Paris, the evidence against Henri Pranzini appeared rock solid. Although he maintained an impressive coolness in court, and was admired by the journalists for his upright stance and elegant clothes, the outcome could only be one: he was found guilty and sentenced to perish on the guillotine. When he was executed at the scaffold in Place de la Roquette, in front of an enormous crowd, many of them women, he walked to his death with impressive *sang-froid*. When his body was dissected, an anatomist cut out a large square of skin from his back, to make a note-case for himself and two card-cases for his friends. Another anatomist, who thought this quite unprofessional conduct, wrote to a boulevard newspaper exposing the scandal. There was a good deal of publicity, and an appeal was made to the Minister of the Interior to take action to prevent the rogue doctors of Paris from mutilating the corpses of executed criminals, but nothing came of it in the end, and the anatomists would keep building up their collections of criminal memorabilia for many years to come. The murder house at 17 Rue de Montaigne still stands today. I wonder if the second-floor flat is haunted, and if, early in the morning, a visiting psychic might hear a terrible scream, a frantic ringing of a bell, and then a horrid gurgling sound?

44. The Bradford Ripper, 1888

In late December 1888, the epidemic of murder and mutilation that was rampant in the East End of London seemed to have spread to the Northern provinces. In Bradford lived the cheerful, inoffensive eight-year-old lad John Gill, the son of respectable working-class parents. No friend of lazy mornings in bed, young Johnny, as he was called, used to rise at 6 a.m. to accompany the local milkman William Barrett on his round, before going to school. On December 27, he went with Barrett in his cart just as usual, but he did not return home. Barrett told Mrs Gill that after helping him to deliver some of the milk, Johnny had left him to return home before the round was finished. Mr and Mrs Gill were immediately worried about their son, since they knew about his good conduct and regular habits. They contacted the police, and made sure that an advert was placed in the local newspaper:

> Lost on Thursday morning a boy, John Gill, aged eight. Was last seen sliding near Walmer-villas at 8.30 am. Had on a navy blue top coat (with brass buttons on), midshipman's cap, plaid knickerbocker suit, laced boots, red and white stockings; complexion fair. Home, 41, Thorncliffe-road.

In spite of the newspaper advertisement, nothing was heard or seen of John Gill for two days. But in the morning of 19 December, the butcher's assistant Joseph Buckle went to his master's stable in Thorncliffe Road, to attend to a horse. He saw a bundle in a corner outside the coach-house, and went to examine its contents: it was the horribly mutilated remains of John Gill. Both legs had been hacked off

DREADFUL MURDER AND MUTILATION OF A BOY, AT BRADFORD.

THE LITTLE VICTIM SEEN PLAYING ON THE ICE.

THE BOY OUT FOR A DRIVE WITH THE MILKMAN.

THE HORRIBLE DISCOVERY OF HACKED REMAINS.

The milkman William Barrett, and other features from the mysterious murder of John Gill, from the *IPN*, 5 January 1889.

and placed next to the body. The unfortunate lad had been murdered by two hard stabs to the chest; since his clothes, which were wrapped inside the bundle, had no corresponding stab marks, he must have been stripped before he was murdered. The abdomen had been ripped open, and the heart torn out and placed underneath the chin. One lung, and one ear, were found inside his stomach. Since there were no marks of blood in or near the stable and coach-house, the murder and mutilation must have happened elsewhere, before the body was dumped in the corner.

There was widespread revulsion in Bradford at this murder and mutilation of a blameless young local boy. Had Jack the Ripper travelled north from Whitechapel, to continue his sanguinary depredations in Bradford? As the London newspaper correspondents pointed out, one anonymous Ripper letter had said that the Whitechapel Fiend was planning to leave London, and another that he would be starting on the men after becoming fed-up with murdering women. There was also an alarming story from a Bradford tailor who had come home to find that his house just had been burgled. On the living-room table were two knives placed crosswise, with a note saying 'Half-past nine – look out – Jack the Ripper has been … I have removed down the canal side, please drop in. Yours truly, SUICIDE.' This ominous note unnerved the tailor's wife so badly that she would not stay in the house without constant company.

There is jubilation in Bradford when William Barrett is discharged by the magistrates, from the *IPN*, 12 January 1889.

But the Bradford police eschewed such idle pseudo-Ripperine speculation, relying on good old-fashioned policework instead. The last person seen with the deceased was the milkman William Barrett. He had told Mrs Gill that Johnny had left him before the milk round had been finished, but several witnesses had seen John Gill with Barrett towards the very end of his run. Then there was the matter of a young servant girl at the nearby Friendless Girls' Home at 11 Belle Vue, whose bedroom overlooked a stable at the rear of the property. Very early in the morning of 29 December, she saw a light in this stable, and heard a man whistling, hammering and sawing in there, as if he was working with some material that made a soft sound when handled. Had this been the murderer dismembering the body of John Gill? The police were encouraged to find that this stable belonged to Mr Wolfenden, the master of William Barrett, and that the milkman held the keys to this property, since he used to work in there.

The police took William Barrett into custody, and charged him with the murder of John Gill in front of the Bradford Borough police court. Their theory was that, for some reason or other, Barrett had murdered Johnny on 27 December and hidden the body in Mr Wolfenden's stable, returning there early in the morning of 29 December to dismember the body and carry it to the stable yard in Thorncliffe Road, where he dumped it. They searched the stable at the rear of Belle Vue, and sent samples of carpet and horse-cloth to the local analyst to be tested for blood and hair. They also searched Barrett's cottage and found a recently cleaned carving knife that matched the stab wounds in the boy's chest very well. William Barrett was just 23 years old, with a wife and a young baby. He had a good reputation, and most local people thought him innocent, preferring to speculate that some drunken out-of-town lads might have killed and dismembered the boy just for the fun of it, to emulate the recent Whitechapel murders.

After having endured three searching examinations before the Bradford Borough magistrates, William Barrett was released from custody on 16 January 1889. The police had found no technical evidence against him, nor were they able to suggest a motive for the milkman to murder his young helper. The degree of mutilation involved suggested that the crime had been committed by a madman, and Barrett was definitely fully sane. Outside the court, he was cheered by a large crowd of people. But the coroner's inquest on John Gill, which continued throughout January and early February, managed to accumulate some further evidence against the milkman. A man named Dyer had seen Barrett near the stable behind Belle Vue on 27 December, carrying a bundle. A number of witnesses said they had seen John Gill with Barrett at a much later time than the milkman would admit, and it seemed like if he had been lying when he said the boy had left him before his round had been finished. As the inquest ended, the coroner took three hours to sum up the case, and the jury was out for more than an hour, before finding a verdict of wilful murder against William Barrett, by twelve jurors against two.

William Barrett was again arrested, under a coroner's warrant. This turn of events came as a complete surprise to both the milkman and his neighbours, who threatened violence against the police when they came to take Barrett into custody. The milkman was removed to Armley Gaol before there was any rioting, to stand trial at the next West Riding Assizes in Leeds. He was refused bail, and had to spend several weeks behind bars before he was to stand trial. There was drama when the Grand Jury threw out the bill presented by the Treasury against William Barrett, due to insufficient evidence, but he still had to face the court on the coroner's warrant, charged with the same crime. When Barrett faced the West Riding Assizes on 13 March 1889, there were immediate legal difficulties, due to the finding from the Grand Jury. Defending William Barrett, the eloquent Mr Waddy, QC, heaped odium on the coroner's jury: they had acted most carelessly, and made their decision without hearing all the witnesses available. When brought up, William Barrett pleaded 'not guilty'. Due to the verdict from the Grand Jury, the prosecuting counsel offered no evidence against him, and the Judge told the jury that it was their duty to return a verdict of Not Guilty. Barrett was discharged, and never did anything newsworthy again. Since all the efforts from the police had focussed on inculpating Barrett, the murder of John Gill was never solved. There was an extraordinary statement from a Leeds man approaching the Rev. J. Whittaker, the vicar of Cononley, to claim that five boys had murdered John Gill, but the man said that since he was tracing the murderers himself, he would not be sharing his findings with the police, and nothing more came of this story.

In spite of the bombastic police declarations that suspicious staining had been found in the stables off Belle Vue, or on the Barretts' kitchen knife, no technical evidence was presented against the milkman; in particular, there is nothing to suggest that blood or hair matching that of John Gill was found inside the stable. William Barrett had no motive to kill his young helper John Gill, with whom he had always been on the best of terms; after the boy had disappeared, he had more than once gone to see the Gill family to ask if they had heard anything about the whereabouts of the boy. Barrett had an excellent reputation locally as an honest young labouring man, he did not drink to excess, and did not have a police record of any description. A recently married man with a young child, he is an unlikely candidate to have committed a brutal murder, just for the fun of it. Since the evidence against him was entirely circumstantial, and since no motive for the crime was suggested, it is quite amazing how the coroner's jury could return a guilty verdict against him. No older houses remain in Thorncliffe Road, but Belle Vue remains in good order, including the former girl's home at No. 11, and its rear outbuildings. Are they perhaps haunted by the ghost of a young boy, searching in vain for his severed ears?

45. A Swedish Murderess Beheaded, 1890

On 7 August 1890, the Swedish murderess Anna Månsdotter was beheaded inside the county prison of Kristianstad. The executioner Anders Gustaf Dalman, who had never beheaded any person before, although he had been practicing on wooden dummies, dealt the blindfolded murderess a heavy blow, but his aim was uncertain: the axe went through the neck and jaw, leaving part of the tongue and the chin still attached to the body. Dalman was still proud of his first proper 'job', and he claimed that Anna Månsdotter had moved her head just when he was about to strike her, causing him to miss his aim. People being judicially beheaded, women in particular, was news, and the execution of Anna Månsdotter made the *IPN* front page, with a prominent illustration:

The beheading of a woman is, fortunately, a very rare occurrence in Sweden, but the deed for which Anna Månsdotter has just paid the

Anna Månsdotter is beheaded, from the *IPN*, August 23 1890.

extreme penalty of the law is quite out of the common. This modern Phædra, who wrought her terrible fate with her eyes open, died because she had wilfully murdered her young and innocent daughter-in-law. The murder, says the Christianstad correspondent of *Galignani*, was the outcome of another even more revolting and unheard-of crime …

Anna Månsdotter was a peasant woman living in the small village Yngsjö, outside Kristianstad in southern Sweden. Her husband died young from tuberculosis, but they had a son named Per, to whom Anna was very attached. Per was keen to get married, but since Anna had a fearsome reputation as a mean-spirited, intriguing harridan, none of the local girls wanted her as a mother-in-law. In the end, Per consulted a local matrimonial agent, who recommended the 21-year-old Hanna Olsson, the daughter of a well-to-do farmer living 15 miles away. Not knowing Anna's reputation, Hanna agreed to marry Per, and her father consented to buy Anna a smallholding of her own, so that the young married couple would be rid of her. But before the wedding, Anna demanded that the wedding should never be consummated and her weak-minded son, whom she could completely dominate, agreed to her request. Not surprisingly, Hanna was very unhappy in her marriage to Per, particularly since Anna, who moved in with the couple, was up to her usual mean-spirited tricks, accusing Hanna of being barren, and urging Per to leave her and escape to America. The desperate Hanna ran away to her parents, but her father urged her to return to the side of her lawful husband, and to try to resolve her problems as well as she could.

Anna Månsdotter was quite disappointed when her daughter-in-law returned to the household, but she soon plotted with the weak-minded Per to make sure her stay would not be a lengthy one. Just a few days later, Hanna was found dead at the bottom of the basement stairs. Per said that she must have fallen down and broken her neck, but the neighbours noticed that there was a red weal around her neck, as if she had been strangled. Anna and Per were arrested, and after five days, the feeble Per admitted that he had murdered his wife, absolving his mother from all guilt. When asked how he could have dragged Hanna's lifeless body down the stairs alone and unaided, he exclaimed 'The Devil helped me!' However, the neighbours were certain the harridan Anna was the person behind the murder. Finally, Anna and Per confessed that they had planned and executed the murder together. They had attacked Hanna in her sleep, and Anna had throttled her, before Per had had hit her over the head with a bludgeon. The main reason for the murder was that Anna hated Hanna, and wanted Per for herself. Without difficulty, she had managed to convince her feeble son that his wife had been most unsatisfactory. Moreover, Anna and Per had been enjoying an incestuous relationship since the lad was 15 years old, and they were both fearful that Hanna would report their guilty secret to the authorities.

After standing trial for murder, both Anna and Per were found guilty and sentenced to death. They both applied to King Oscar II for clemency and, by what must have been a narrow margin, Per received a late reprieve. After his mother had been beheaded, he spent 23 years in prison, where he learnt the bookbinding trade. After his release in 1913, he moved back to the outskirts of Kristianstad in southern Sweden, where the locals accepted him; he died from tuberculosis in 1919, aged 56. As for the executioner Dalman, he beheaded four more people in the following years, without any more untoward incidents. The Swedes then decided to invest in a guillotine, purchased in France and made use of only once, for Dalman to execute the murderer Alfred Ander in 1910; this was the final judicial execution in Sweden. The guillotine is still kept at the Nordic Museum in Stockholm.

46. The Plumstead Tragedy, 1890

In 1890, the 20-year-old machinist Walter James Lyons lived with his mother and brother at 32 Conway Road, Plumstead. Two other men also lodged in the little terraced house, where Walter's mother, the recently widowed Mrs Ellen Lyons, was the landlady. On Friday 1 September 1890, Ellen Lyons behaved very much unlike a respectable middle-aged Victorian landlady. She went to admire some military sports on Woolwich Common, where she was introduced to Quartermaster Sergeant John Stewart, a sturdy middle-aged man she had never before met. They spent the afternoon together, and Ellen invited her military friend back to her house for some hanky-panky. This was not a particularly bright idea, considering the crowded state of the house. When her son Walter entered his mother's bedroom unannounced, to wish her a good night, he was horrified to find her in bed with the soldier.

The distraught Walter called his mother a bloody cow and a bloody bitch, before screaming, to no one in particular, 'Would you like to come home and find a man in bed with your mother?' 'No', Sergeant Stewart calmly replied, but the frenzied Walter threatened to cut his head off. He ran into the kitchen, where he was heard to rummage in the drawers.

Walter James Lyons stabbing quartermaster sergeant Steward, from the *IPN*, 20 September 1890. The Lyons family home at 32 Conway Road, seen in the panel to the right, is still standing. The Catholic Church has been built near the murder site, seen on the panel to the left.

Further scenes from the Plumstead Tragedy, from the *IPN*, 27 September 1890. The murdered sergeant at least got himself a grand funeral.

Fearful that Walter was arming himself with the kitchen knives, Ellen Lyons and Sergeant Stewart quickly got dressed and retreated from the house. When the frantic Walter returned, they were relieved to see that he had got his hands on nothing worse than a small hammer. When he threatened the sturdy soldier with this weapon, the sergeant just made fun of him, saying that since he had fought in proper battles, he would knock a weakling like Walter down with a single blow. Without replying, Walter returned to the kitchen, fuming with rage.

Scenes from the trial of Walter James Lyons, from the *IPN*, October 4 1890

His mother ushered Sergeant Stewart away as quickly as she could, towards the hoardings around the building site for the Catholic Church at the corner of Conway and Griffin roads. But her frantic son pursued them, screaming like a lunatic. As he ran past, Mrs Lyons tried to stop him by grabbing his coat-tails, but they came off in her hands and she fell backwards. With another yell, Walter attacked the soldier with a large knife, stabbing him hard. Attracted by Walter's screams of fury, two other witnesses saw him stab the soldier. Once the deed was done, Walter calmly turned to one of them, saying 'I have done what I intended to do. Call a policeman.' When a constable came to the scene, Walter handed him the knife, as he was taken into custody. At the Woolwich police station, he made a full statement about the crime he had committed, which was taken down. According to the *IPN*,

> His mother also has furnished the police with her testimony in writing, and converses freely on the subject with inquirers. She is deeply grieved for the consequences of her folly, and takes all the blame, without reservation, upon herself. So slight was her acquaintance with the murdered man that she could not at first say whether his name was Stewart or Sheppard.

At the coroner's inquest on John Stewart, held at Plumstead Workhouse, Mrs Lyons arrived three hours early to avoid the mob. After the various witnesses had given evidence, the jury returned a verdict of wilful murder against Walter James Lyons, although they hoped that the considerable provocation received would recommend him to mercy. Outside the workhouse, a large and rowdy mob applauded Walter James Lyons, described as a tall, thin youth in shabby attire. They then booed and hooted his wretched mother, who would have been lynched had she not been protected by the police.

When Walter James Lyons stood trial at the Old Bailey on October 20 1890 before Mr Justice Stephens, on a charge of murder, his eloquent barrister Mr Geoghean addressed the jury, reminding them that the law was made for the man, not the man for the law, and that an English jury should be kind and merciful: 'Nothing could exaggerate the nauseous horror of the tragedy. The mother dishonoured and degraded her late husband's memory and disgraced her living son's fame.' In his summing-up, Mr Justice Stephens reminded the jury that in the eyes of the law, this was either murder or manslaughter. Speaking as a human being, and not as a judge, he thought the provocation given by the mother was as great as could possibly have been given to a son. He had never heard a more painful and horrible story in court, and still he had heard as many horrible stories as anyone.

The end of the story of the Plumstead Tragedy, an unedifying tale if there ever was one, is that the jury found Walter James Lyons guilty of manslaughter and he was sentenced to seven years penal servitude. There was a remarkable amount of newspaper interest in this relatively obscure case of manslaughter. The *IPN* could of course not refrain from using the case for headline material, for three consecutive weeks, with appropriate illustrations.

47. The Murderous Mrs Pearcey, 1890

Mary Eleanor Wheeler, a sinister young woman if there ever was one, was born in Ightham, Kent, in March 1866. Her family moved to Stepney soon after and she spent her youth in East London. After her father's death in 1882, her mother went to Kentish Town, where Mary Eleanor found work at a sealskin factory. In 1885, she became the common-law wife of the carpenter John Charles Pearcey, adopting his name. She cohabited with Pearcey for three years, before she became the mistress of a well-to-do local businessman named Charles Creighton. In September 1888, he installed her in the ground floor flat at 2 Priory [now Ivor] Street, Kentish Town. Contemporary accounts agree that in spite of her indifferent moral qualities, Mary Eleanor was a quite attractive young woman, with long russet hair, fine blue eyes and regular features.

Mr Creighton, who was probably 'running' other mistresses as well, used to visit Mary Eleanor on Monday evenings, and sometimes during the weekends. Since she no longer worked, this arrangement left her with plenty of spare time. She had a piano in her front room, which she learnt

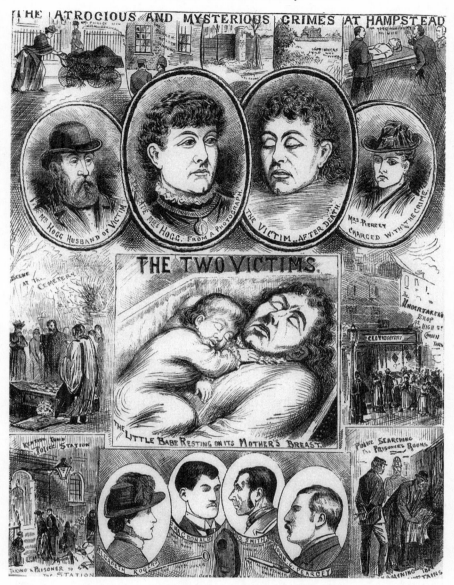

Portraits of all the main players in the Pearcey case, living or dead; from the *IPN*, 8 November 1890.

to play. She befriended some of the neighbours, particularly the family of a grocer named Hogg, who lived nearby in Prince of Wales Road. She became fond of Frank, the son of the family, who worked as an assistant in the grocer's shop, and gave him the key to 2 Priory Street. Frank knew that Mary Eleanor was a 'kept woman' and made sure he stayed away from her flat on Mondays.

The Hoggs, baby Tiggie, and a reconstruction of the murder, from the *IPN*, 13 December 1890.

As time went by, Mary Eleanor became increasingly fond of Frank. It is difficult to discern what she saw in him since he was described as a common-looking little man, with a large unkempt beard, a woebegone

Mrs Pearcey awaiting her doom, and a sketch of the murder house, from the *IPN*, 20 December 1890.

appearance, and ill-fitting clothes. Nor was his career exactly a success story: after the family lost their grocery, he had to work as a furniture-

Execution of the Ill-fated Mrs Pearcey, from the *IPN*, 27 December 1890.

carrier, relying on the kindness of his elder brother who owned a removal business. Frank's moral qualities were also found wanting: apart from visiting Mary Eleanor at 2 Priory Street, he was also 'walking out' with an accommodating young woman named Phoebe Styles. When Phoebe 'got in the family way' in November 1888, Frank felt obliged to marry her. They moved into lodgings at 141 Prince of Wales Road, and in April 1889, their little daughter Phoebe Hanslope, called 'Tiggie', was born.

Later in 1889, when Phoebe Hogg fell ill, Frank suggested that Mary Eleanor should nurse her. This unconventional arrangement seems to have had the desired effect, since Mary Eleanor took her duties seriously, and even bought fresh milk and eggs for the patient, who gradually recovered. But although Phoebe was hardly the most perceptive of women, she began to suspect that Frank had been motivated by immoral purposes, rather than concern for her own well-being, when he allowed Mary Eleanor to join their household. She deserted her worthless husband and moved out of 141 Prince of Wales Road, rejoining her own family and taking baby Tiggie with her. It was not until her brother had persuaded her that she could not afford a divorce, and that her reputation would suffer if she left Frank, that Phoebe was reunited with her cad of a husband.

In late 1890, Mary Eleanor became increasingly infatuated with Frank. Although he still visited her regularly, she sent him many love letters, begging him to come more frequently. But Hogg was under pressure from his family to stay with Phoebe and little Tiggie. He thought of going away, but did not have the willpower to do so. On 23 October 1890, Mary Eleanor paid a boy to take a note to 141 Prince of Wales Road, inviting Phoebe to come round for tea, and to bring the baby. Phoebe did not come, but when there was a similar message the following day, she put baby Tiggie in a large perambulator, left a note for Frank saying 'Shall not be gone long' and walked to 2 Priory Street, arriving around 4 p.m. Not long after, the next door neighbour heard glass breaking. She called out to Mary Eleanor, but there was no response, and the kitchen blinds were down. The upstairs neighbour at No. 2 heard a baby scream, and later what sounded like several people walking around and moving things about.

The evening of 23 October was cold and quite foggy. Still, several witnesses saw Mary Eleanor wheeling the large perambulator through the streets. Some of them added that although she was pushing with all her might, she had great difficulty moving the heavily laden vehicle. Nevertheless, the white-faced, breathless woman kept on pushing the perambulator through the endless streets, until she had reached Belsize Park more than 2 miles away. In an area where some houses had recently been erected, by the crossing of Adamson and Crossfield streets, she emptied the perambulator of its contents. The overloaded vehicle had broken, so she left it behind in a side street, before walking home. Another witness saw the exhausted Mary Eleanor return to 2 Priory Street, reeling asked if she was going to fall over at any moment.

Later the same evening, the corpses of a young woman and a baby were found near Adamson Road. Miss Clara Hogg, Frank's sister, saw the description in the newspaper, and suspected that this unidentified woman might be her missing sister-in-law. Although her relatives pooh-poohed her concerns, she wanted to have a look at the bodies. Mary Eleanor went with her to the mortuary. When the two women were taken into the presence of Phoebe Hogg's corpse, Mary Eleanor cried out 'It is not her! It is not her! Let us go!' and made to pull Clara Hogg away. But after a closer inspection, Clara identified the body as that of her missing sister-in-law, and proceeded to identify the baby and the perambulator as well. Mary Eleanor's strange behaviour had attracted notice, and after the two women had been taken home in a cab, the police kept watch on her house to make sure she did not escape. They found Frank Hogg, who collapsed when he heard his wife was dead, exclaiming that he knew that he himself was partly to fault. He then told them all about his illicit romance with Mary Eleanor.

Later that day, the police raided 2 Priory Street. Mary Eleanor let them in without demur. She sat by the piano in the front room, playing the piano loudly as the detectives inspected her kitchen. They found plenty of bloodstains on the walls, and signs that the floor had been recently cleaned. Mary Eleanor told them that she had been killing mice, but to produce such extensive bloodstains would have required a veritable massacre of the murine tribe. Her hands were very scratched and bruised, from a recent violent struggle. She was duly arrested, and at the coroner's inquest, a verdict of wilful murder was returned against her.

On trial at the Old Bailey before Mr Justice Denman, on 24 November 1890, Mrs Pearcey's solicitor Freke Palmer, and her barrister Mr Hutton, did their best to save their client. But the mass of evidence against her was too impressive, and an attempt to play the 'insanity card' did not have the desired effect. In his summing-up, Mr Justice Denman was severe on Frank Hogg, saying that no man had ever given himself a viler or more loathsome character. After an absence of an hour, the jury returned a verdict of Guilty, and Mr Justice Denman sentenced Mrs Pearcey to death.

There was a fair bit of sympathy for Mrs Pearcey in London society, resulting from squeamishness rather than from doubts about her guilt: surely, they reasoned, it was barbaric to execute an attractive young woman. Freke Palmer made a final attempt to save his client, by demanding that she should be examined by the controversial alienist Forbes Winslow. But instead, three other doctors visited Mrs Pearcey in Newgate, at the orders of the Home Secretary: their verdict was that she was definitely sane. On 22 December, Mrs Pearcey was visited one final time by her mother and her younger sister Charlotte Amy. She sent a letter to Clara Hogg absolving Frank Hogg from complicity in the murder. He had a rock-solid alibi, having been hard at work the entire afternoon, as verified by a number of witnesses. Mary Eleanor was very keen to see her dear Frank one final time, but true to his character, the coward refused to meet her. When urged to confess by the prison chaplain, she said 'The sentence is just, but the evidence was false.' She desired Freke Palmer to place an advertisement in a Madrid newspaper, with the enigmatic words 'Last wish of M.E.W. Have not betrayed.' When asked what she was alluding to, she said it was a secret marriage she had pledged herself never to reveal.

Mary Eleanor Pearcey was executed on 23 December 1890. Guy Logan and other crime historians have not doubted her guilt, but there has been suspicion that another person had been involved in the murder. In particular, the canny Guy Logan questioned how, alone and unaided, Mrs Pearcey had been able to pack the dead body in the perambulator with the presumably still living child. But people *in extremis* sometimes have surprising strength, and the perambulator was the only chance for the desperate woman to dispose of her victims.

Since Hogg had a rock-solid alibi, amateur criminologists have cast a wide net to find alternative accomplices for Mary Eleanor. It has been speculated that she belonged to a gang of burglars, or alternatively to a secret society of Spanish anarchists (or occultists), and that Phoebe Hogg had been murdered after she had threatened to denounce them. Other conspiracy lovers have implicated the mysterious first husband of Mary Eleanor, whom she married secretly at the age of just sixteen, and who later deserted her and presumably went to Madrid. These speculations have little foundation in fact, however. The motive for the murder was clearly Mary Eleanor's passion for Frank Hogg, and her jealousy of Phoebe. It is notable that she also murdered the innocent little Tiggie, who could not denounce any secret societies; she wanted to destroy not just Phoebe Hogg, but her progeny as well. As Mary Eleanor herself confessed to a wardress, the murder had not been premeditated, but the product of a sudden fury after the two women had quarrelled angrily.

In 1937, Priory Street changed its name to Ivor Street, for reasons unconnected with the murder. Guy Logan called this part of Kentish Town 'as dull, ugly, and lugubrious a portion of London as any I know' but Guy was fortunate to have been spared the horrors of 1960s and 1970s architecture. Indeed, today the relatively isolated area near the Camden Road railway station has a certain old-world attraction, with its cobbled streets and well-kept little terraced houses. When doing some murder house detection in the relevant archives, I noticed that the numbering of the houses on the north side of Ivor Street was more than a little odd. It began with 1, 1A, 2 and 2A, and 3, 4 and so on. Was this an attempt to disguise the identity of the murder house? No, it clearly was not, since three contemporary illustrations clearly show that Mary Eleanor Pearcey's house is the present-day No. 2 Ivor Street: a well-kept house subdivided into flats, still with the characteristic small cast-iron balconies intact. According to a now defunct internet page, a former resident of the ground floor flat found it to be haunted by the sound of a child screaming and bloodstains mysteriously appearing on the wall. She called the local vicar to have a ceremony of exorcism performed, and the haunting ceased.

48. The Murderous 'Gentleman Jim', 1892

James Banbury was born in Camden Town in 1868. At an early age, he was apprenticed to a carpenter, but since he turned out to be a quite vicious and unmanageable lad, his family sent him off to some relatives in Australia. Here, he robbed and nearly killed an old woman, and was sentenced to eleven months' solitary confinement. James Banbury emerged from the Antipodian prison as angry and mean-spirited as before. His family managed to provide him with a job as a clerk in a tramway company, but he embezzled a large sum of money and took to the bush. He lived rough for many months, hunting kangaroos and other animals, and working as a cowboy when he felt like it. After getting word that his father had died, he made haste back to England in September 1891, to make sure that he was not cheated out of his inheritance.

James Banbury made it all the way back to Camden Town and collected several hundred pounds. In high spirits, he made plans to really enjoy his sojourn in the Metropolis. He discarded his shabby Australian attire and bought some quality suits of clothes instead. Describing himself as 'a gentleman horse-gambler', he was fond of attending race meetings. He gambled hard, initially with good success. His flashy clothes and boastful

The Grosvenor Park murder house. Like the following two, this image is from the *IPN*, July 9 1892.

The pretty young Emma Oakley.

The sinister 'Gentleman Jim'.

All the major players in the Walworth Shooting Drama, and another sketch of the murder house, from the *Penny Illustrated Paper*, 9 July 1892.

affluence meant that he 'fitted in' very well with the raffish throng gambling on the horses. 'Gentleman Jim', as he soon became known, also acquired a mistress, the 18-year-old Emma Oakley, and he moved into her lodgings at 81 Grosvenor Park, Walworth. Emma was a pretty young floozy who had tired of working as a domestic servant. Instead she was 'kept' by a string of well-to-do lovers. She led a jolly life with the short, stocky, dapperly dressed 'Gentleman Jim' for several months.

But James Banbury's initial spell of good luck deserted him, and he gradually lost his money. When he was unable to pay the bills, Emma evicted him and he had to find alternative lodgings at 6 Brewer Street, Pimlico [the house still exists]. He had been genuinely fond of Emma, and drank hard to forget about his failing fortunes. On July 6 1892, 'Gentleman Jim' came lurching out of a public house at 2pm, drunk as a lord after a lavish luncheon. He hailed a hansom cab, finding that the driver, Henry Richard Briggs, was actually an old acquaintance of his, and a fellow racing enthusiast. Bragging that he had won £30 at Alexandra Park a few days ago, Banbury ordered him to drive to Walworth. They stopped at a pub on the way, to have a couple of glasses of gin each. At another pub in Walworth Road, the thirsty 'Gentleman Jim' emptied another glass of gin before wandering off, telling Briggs to wait for him. After twenty minutes, he returned, puffing at a large cigar. He ordered Briggs to take him to Charing Cross.

When they arrived at Charing Cross, they went off to another public house to have some more gin. Suddenly and unexpectedly, Banbury said 'Get down and have a drink as I am going to leave you. I have shot a girl'. Laughing, the equally drunk Briggs chaffed 'You have not got the pluck. You could not shoot for nuts!' But the cabbie became apprehensive when 'Gentleman Jim' pulled out a revolver, obviously a relic of his bush-ranging days in Australia, and said 'It is quite true. I loved her, and made up my mind no one else should have her!' Fearful that the weapon would go off by mistake when handled by the drunken gambler, Briggs snatched it away from him when he looked away. Much worse for wear from drink, Banbury was unable to reclaim his revolver by force; instead he cravenly begged for it to be returned to him, and even offered £50 for it. Again, Briggs thought he was just joking. But as they went back through the station, 'Gentleman Jim' struck him a hard blow on the neck. The sturdy cabbie returned the blow and frog-marched his inebriated opponent back to the cab. But when they went past Waterloo Place, Banbury suddenly jumped out of the cab and disappeared into the crowd, without paying his fare.

The cabman Briggs had thought that 'Gentleman Jim' had just been chaffing when he talked about shooting a girl in Walworth. But the next day, having recovered from his hangover, he read in the newspaper about the murder of young Emma Oakley. At the Carter Street police station, he gave a full account of his dealings with the sinister 'Gentleman Jim', handing over the loaded revolver to convince them he was telling the truth. Detective Sergeant Leonard and Police Sergeant Brogden knew all about the murder of young Emma Oakley, gunned down in her lodgings at 81 Grosvenor Park by an unknown assailant. They managed to track down Banbury's Brewer Street lodgings. He was not there, but another lodger told them that the evening before, 'Gentleman Jim' had been even more drunk than usual. He had talked about shooting a girl, but again the witness had not believed him. A few hours later, when Banbury had returned home, the two policemen kicked open the door to his room and took him into custody.

At the coroner's inquest on young Emma Oakley, the first witness was her father, the coachman Henry Oakley. Although he had known that she had not been in service for several years, he had not made inquiries what kind of life she was leading, since he thought her old enough to look after herself. The cabman Briggs told all about his expedition to Walworth with 'Gentleman Jim', and Detective Sergeant Leonard described the arrest of Banbury at his Brewer Street lodgings. The coroner's jury returned a verdict of wilful murder against James Banbury. They added that it was their opinion that the father of the deceased was deserving of severe censure for his most unmanly conduct towards his child, and that Detective Sergeant Leonard should be commended for his prompt arrest of the prisoner.

At the trial of James Banbury, the same individuals gave evidence. Furthermore, the landlady at 81 Grosvenor Park, Mrs Emma Foster, identified Banbury as the man she had seen running away from the premises after shooting Emma Oakley. The drunken 'Gentleman Jim' had confessed the murder to three different people, but none of them had believed him. Since it was clear to all that Banbury had murdered young Emma, the best the defence could do was to try playing the 'insanity card': his grandfather had been a little insane, it was claimed, and his great-aunt had died in a lunatic asylum in Australia. But the Holloway medical officer, who had observed Banbury there, gave the opinion that the prisoner was of sound mind. The jury retired for nearly two hours, before returning to deliver a verdict of Guilty, with a recommendation to mercy on account of the prisoner's age. But before the verdict was entered, there was farce when the Foreman pointed out that two of the jurymen were so deaf that they had been unable to hear the evidence. After the two men had readily admitted that this as the case, the jury was discharged. The case was reheard before another jury, with the same verdict. James Banbury was sentenced to death and executed at Wandsworth Prison on 11 October 1892.

While searching for the Grosvenor Park murder house, it soon became clear that the houses had been renumbered at some stage, perhaps after the murder. The present-day No. 81 does not at all match the drawing of the murder house in the *IPN*. Since the readers of this particular newspaper were often fond of gawping at murder houses, its illustrations were very accurate. And indeed, a search of the Post Office directories revealed that they houses had been renumbered a few years after the murder. The old No. 81 became No. 49, and the present-day No. 49 Grosvenor Park exactly matches the sketch of the murder house in the *IPN*. It remains virtually unchanged since the days of 'Gentleman Jim' and poor Emma, and apart from some yellowed newspaper clippings and James Banbury's revolver, which was deposited in the Black Museum, it is the sole reminder of a once notorious crime that has become almost completely forgotten. The police file on the case, which should have been at the National Archives, has been lost, but these archives do have a photograph of James Banbury and Emma Oakley together: she is standing up, looking quite pretty, whereas he is sitting on a chair, wearing a dapper-looking suit and a large bowler hat; a few weeks later, they would both be dead.

49. The Northampton Tragedy, 1892

Andrew George McRae was a married man with two sons, who worked as a grocer's assistant and lived in the Highgate Road, Birmingham. Next door lived a family named Pritchard, consisting of several orphaned brothers and sisters. Annie Pritchard, the eldest sister, became very fond of Mrs McRae, and they used to sing duets together in the parlour. Annie had once been engaged to a lithographer named Guy Anderson, but he had tired of her and moved away from Birmingham. She instead fell in love with Andrew McRae, and visited him clandestinely when his wife was away. In 1890, McRae got a job at Warwick, and Annie visited him there on many occasions. In March 1892, McRae became assistant to his brother Edward, who had a grocery business in Northampton. His duties included looking after a bacon warehouse in Dychurch Lane, to which he held the keys. Since Mrs McRae had remained in the family home in Birmingham, with the two children, Andrew McRae was able to install Annie Pritchard in lodgings at 33 St John Street, Northampton, where he lived with her under the names Mr and Mrs Anderson. Annie told her brothers and sisters that she was going to Liverpool to marry her old sweetheart Guy Anderson, and she made sure they got a letter from her, with a Liverpool postmark, saying that she was now married and on her way to the United States.

To begin with, Andrew McRae seems to have enjoyed his intrigue with Annie Pritchard, but after a few months, he began to tire of her. Annie was pregnant, and as a humble labouring man, he could not afford to raise one family in Birmingham and another one in Northampton. And what if his wife found out that he was 'carrying on' with Annie on the side? It cannot be excluded that he had entertained plans to do away with his paramour from a relatively early stage, and dictated the Liverpool letter for her to write, so that her Birmingham relations would not miss her. Annie Pritchard gave birth to a healthy boy on 23 June. On 18 July, Andrew McRae made sure all their belongings were moved to the bacon warehouse in Dychurch Lane, and two days later, they left the St John's Street lodgings. Annie Pritchard was last seen on her way to the bacon warehouse. The following morning, McRae came into the Lord Palmerston public house to have a few drinks, looking very tired and bedraggled. He told his drinking

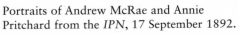

Portraits of Andrew McRae and Annie
Pritchard from the *IPN*, 17 September 1892.

Features from the Northampton Tragedy, from the *IPN*, 24 September 1892.

companions that his brother had ordered him to boil some bacon, and that he had been working hard all night.

A few weeks later, on 6 August 1892, a traveller on the high road between Rugby and Northampton noticed a nauseating smell coming from a large ditch. He saw that it emanated from a large package half submerged in water. When the police were alerted, it turned out that it was the doubled-up body of a woman, minus the head and arms. The sacking it was wrapped in had the label 'E. McRae, Northampton, L. and N.W.R.' The mutilated body was dressed in the usual female underwear, and two shirts. A doctor declared it the remains of a well-nourished woman, of between 5 feet and 5 feet 5 inches in height. A troop of police constables searched the nearby countryside, looking for the arms and the head, but found nothing. When Edward McRae the grocer was questioned, he denied any knowledge of the dead woman found wrapped in sacking from his company. He had sold some sacking to a tramp, he said, and it might well be that this person had committed the murder.

Led by Inspector Collings, the Northampton police began to suspect Andrew McRae, the brother of Edward, who had access to the McRae

Features from the trial of Andrew McRae, from the *IPN*, 31 December 1892.

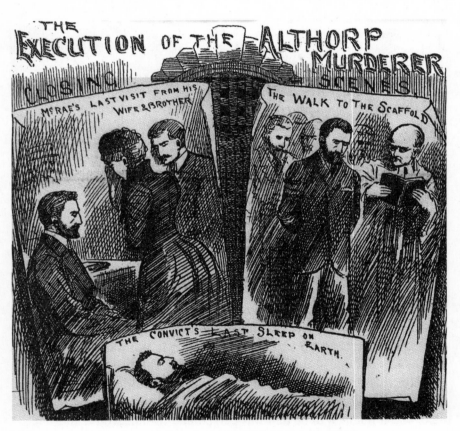

The execution of Andrew McRae, from the *IPN*, 14 January 1893.

grocery's sacking at the bacon warehouse in Dychurch Lane. It turned out that Andrew McRae had sold female apparel, and various other goods, to a dealer in late July, and that a neighbour had smelt a dense, offensive smoke emanating from the chimney of the Dychurch Lane bacon warehouse. A breakthrough came when the nurse who had delivered Annie Pritchard's baby was tracked down, since she could identify the two shirts found on the corpse as those worn by 'Mrs Anderson'. The landlady at 33 St John's Street was also found, as was Annie Pritchard's sister Lizzie, who identified a book and a glass sold by McRae as belonging to Annie Pritchard. A few days after Annie had been last seen, he had hired a pony and trap to transport something away from the bacon warehouse; when he had returned, the pony had been quite exhausted, like if he had been driving hard. In police custody, Andrew McRae denied any involvement in the murder, although the weight of evidence forced him to admit cohabiting with Annie Pritchard in Northampton, under an assumed name. He claimed that the faithless Annie had left him and gone off to Liverpool to marry Guy Anderson; thus the body found in the ditch could not belong to her. When the bacon warehouse in Dychurch Lane was searched, some calcified small bones, quite possibly from human hands, were found in the grate, and the police also discovered a bucket of a repulsive, oily substance, also containing some human hairs.

On trial for murder at the Northampton Assizes in November 1892, before Mr Justice Kennedy, Andrew McRae pleaded 'not guilty'. However, when it was discovered that Mr Asplin, one of the jurymen, had left the building to post a letter; the jury was discharged, and the defaulting juryman fined £50. In late December, the trial was restarted, this time with a more attentive jury. The prosecution argued that on 20 July, Andrew McRae had murdered both Annie Pritchard and their infant son, and burnt the infant's body as well as Annie's head and hands, before hiring the pony and trap to dispose of the rest of the body in waste land outside Northampton. The identification of the shirts worn by the mutilated body rendered it likely that the murdered woman was Annie Pritchard; the identification of the items sold by McRae after her death indicated that he had sold all Annie's belongings after the murder. It would of course have been wiser of him to have burnt all her clothes and other belongings, but McRae was a lowly paid workman to whom a few shillings would come in extremely handy. Edward McRae the grocer testified that the evening Annie Pritchard had disappeared, he had ordered his brother Andrew to get some bacon washed. Six or seven weeks before the body was discovered, he had sold two very similar pieces of sacking to a tramp. The defence went on to argue that Annie Pritchard was still alive: she had gone off to Liverpool to marry Guy Anderson, and the body was that of some other woman. It was a drawback for this version of events that neither Annie nor her husband had made themselves known, although the murder had been widely publicised in the newspapers, but perhaps they had gone to the United States. An even greater drawback was that Annie must have left her entire wardrobe, and all her other belongings including a much-treasured family Bible, in Northampton, to be sold for a few shillings by the covetous Andrew McRae.

After Mr Justice Kennedy had summed up the case carefully and impartially, the jury was out for an hour and forty minutes, before returning a verdict of Guilty. Donning the black cap, Mr Justice Kennedy sentenced McRae to death. There was a great cheer from the huge crowd outside the courtroom, to celebrate that a detested out-of-towner had been convicted for a brutal, cowardly murder. In the death cell, Andrew McRae maintained his innocence to the last, in letters to his mother, wife and brother, declaring that he was going to his death a murdered man. He was executed by Billington at Northampton Prison on 10 January 1893. Andrew McRae was the last murderer to be hanged in Northampton. Inspector Collings kept McRae's tobacco pipe as a memento, and his great grandson donated it to the Decorative Arts Gallery of the Northampton Museum, where it can be seen today. As for the murder warehouse in Dychurch Lane, it was still standing in the 1920s, when the murder house detective Guy Logan saw and photographed it, but it no longer exists today.

50. Murder By A Croydon Publican, 1893

For many years, Mr James Peckham had been landlord of the Oakfield Tavern, at the crossing of St James' Road and Oakfield Road, Croydon. In 1886, when he was 47 years old, he married the wealthy widow Sophia Thomson, who was eighteen years his senior, and settled down in a semi-detached house at 4 Quadrant Road, Croydon. This was an ill-conceived move, since the marriage seems to have been cursed from the start. Both the Peckhams were fond of drink, James more so than his wife. James was also fond of spending money, whereas his wife was very parsimonious. They were constantly at loggerheads, particularly when drunk. The only respite for poor Sophia came in 1891, when James was

James Peckham shoots his wife, from the *IPN*, January 14 1893.

admitted to Cane Hill Asylum, where he spent eighteen months suffering from 'melancholy mania'.

But James Peckham emerged from the asylum as angry as before. In spite of his eighteen months of forced abstinence from alcohol, he drank harder than ever after returning to the family home at 4 Quadrant Road, and his temper suffered as a result. The neighbours at No. 6 could hear the Peckhams quarrelling furiously, and James threatening to shoot his wife. This was no idle threat, since the former publican had access to a loaded shotgun, among other firearms. On 2 January 1893, the Peckhams were at loggerheads as usual. Alice Aldous, servant to Mr Veale who lived at No. 6, was fearful that James might injure his wife. She could hear tongs smashing against the kitchen furniture, and moments later, the now 71-year-old Sophia was forcibly thrown out of the house, still holding some formidable-looking tongs. When Alice Aldous went out to comfort her, she saw that apart from a swollen and bloody nose, Sophia seemed unharmed. She asked to be readmitted to No. 4, but James twice replied 'If I let you in, I'll murder you!' In spite of this dire threat, the foolhardy old woman, whose instinct of self-preservation was clearly not in good working order, once more went into the house. Moments later, an explosion was heard. Fearful that James Peckham had shot his wife, Alice Aldous ran to fetch a police constable.

But it turned out that Police Constable George Windus had also heard the shot. When he came trudging up to 4 Quadrant Road, James Peckham stood outside, dancing a jig. 'I have shot my wife!' he shouted to the police constable. 'Surely not?' he startled constable answered. 'I have, my bonny boy!' shouted James, who appeared very exhilarated. He showed the constable into the kitchen, where Sophia's lifeless body was lying on the floor. A large part of her head had been blown off by the gunshot, and she was quite dead. Indicating the shotgun, James said 'I shot her with the right barrel, and the other barrel is loaded!' There had been two other people in the house at the time of the murder: the lodger Louisa Woodhams, and Sophia Peckham's imbecile sister.

At the coroner's inquest on Sophia Peckham, Louisa Woodhams and Alice Aldous gave evidence about James's drunken ways. He had often shouted threats to injure or murder his wife and kept his arsenal of rifles and shotguns ready for use. It is remarkable, even by the standards of the time, that a person recently committed to a lunatic asylum for eighteen months was allowed to keep firearms, and a plentiful supply of ammunition. When asked for the motive of murdering his wife, James replied that it had all been an accident: the gun had gone off by mistake. At the Guildford Assizes, several people testified as to James's fierce, angry temper; his fondness for firearms and his strange and unreasonable behaviour. One man had been held at gunpoint at 4 Quadrant Road, and forced to execute an infantry drill until he nearly dropped from fatigue.

It was found that James Peckham had committed the murder in a state of insanity, and he was incarcerated in Broadmoor. He became a very difficult patient, known for his truculence and his foul language. A sturdy, corpulent man, nearly 6 feet tall and weighing 16 stone, he was a force to be reckoned with when seriously annoyed. Broadmoor records indicate that James Peckham remained a patient for 20 years, before succumbing to diabetes in 1913. The murder house at No. 4 [now 10] Quadrant Road still stands, although another house has been built in its large side garden. James Peckham's old pub, the Oakfield Tavern, was recently pulled down.

51. The Ramsgate Mystery, 1893

William Noel was born in 1860 and became a journeyman butcher in Whitechapel, before moving on to Southsea. Here he met Miss Sarah Dinah Saunders, a woman of independent means who ran a lodging-house. Although Sarah Dinah was ten years older than the sturdy, bearded young butcher, they began 'walking out', and married in 1878. After some debate whether to stay in Southsea, or perhaps move to London, Noel made use of his wife's money to purchase a butcher's shop at 9 Adelphi Terrace, Grange Road, Ramsgate. The butcher's shop had a large display window to the front, and a smaller window to an alley on the side. Behind the shop was a small sitting room, with a door to the side, and another door to the kitchen and scullery. A small yard separated the house from the stables and workshops where Noel and his assistants butchered various animals, and prepared their meat for sale.

Initially, William Noel's butcher's shop met with difficulties, and he had to borrow £150 from his wife's father to keep it running. A steady, industrious man, Noel worked hard to make his business a success, travelling into the countryside to buy livestock, and employing two journeymen and a lad. The borrowed £150 was soon repaid, and Noel was able to save some money. Mr and Mrs Noel were very respectable people, and pillars of Ramsgate lower-middle-class society. They were strict Wesleyans, and active members of their church community. There was, of course, gossip about this out-of-town childless couple, with the husband being ten years younger than the wife, but although mischievous people were whispering that William Noel was fond of chasing the country lasses when he was out buying livestock, the two Noels appeared to be getting along perfectly well.

On the afternoon of Sunday 14 May 1893, everything seemed perfectly normal in the Noel household. After having had his luncheon, William Noel sat in the downstairs parlour and read through the lessons, since he was a society steward at the St Lawrence Wesleyan Sunday School. The Noels had a servant girl named Nelly Wilson, but she was given Sunday afternoon off. Sarah Dinah Noel counted the morning's collection from church, which amounted to 10s, and went to lock the money away. At around 2.15 p.m., William Noel went off to the Sunday school, leaving his wife behind in the company of the family dog Nip, a large, sturdy

The murder shop, and portraits of the main players in the Ramsgate Mystery, from the *IPN*, 27 May 1893.

THE RAMSGATE MURDER.

Mr and Mrs Noel, the dog, and the murder house at Adelphi Terrace, Grange Road, from the *Illustrated Police Budget*.

black retriever. Nip was something of a disreputable dog, who had savaged a number of smaller dogs, and bitten one or two children as well. His guarding instinct was in good working order, and when a man had tried a retrieve a chair he had deposited in the Noels' backyard, the angry and powerful Nip had kept him out.

At 2.20 p.m., the neighbour Lavinia Squires saw William Noel walking past her house on his way to the Sunday school. He arrived there at 2.25 and took part in the teaching until 3.45 p.m., being observed by many people, and behaving just as he usually did. Some of his pupils accompanied him home; he enjoyed a theological debate with these juvenile Wesleyans on the way. When he knocked at the door at 9 Adelphi Terrace, there was no response, although he could hear the dog barking. Noel went to see some of his neighbours, and with some difficulty, he entered the back yard and forced open the parlour window. Sarah Dinah Noel was lying on the floor in a pool of blood, quite dead and with a bullet wound to the head. The dog Nip was keeping vigil next to the corpse.

The murder house had been ransacked for money, and the cashbox had been broken into and its contents stolen. The murdered woman was wearing five rings and a watch and chain, but these had not been touched. Chief Constable Bush and Inspector Ross were soon at the scene, to take charge of the murder investigation. They found it curious that although

Mrs Noel and the dog Nip, and Noel before the magistrates, from the *Penny Illustrated Paper*, 10 June 1893.

The Ramsgate murder trial, sketched by a *Penny Illustrated Paper* artist.

THE RAMSGATE MURDER

THE FOREMAN OF THE JURY — GIVING THE VERDICT

MR NOEL ARRESTED ON LEAVING COURT

Noel is arrested, from the *IPN*, 10 June 1893.

the dog Nip was considered to be of a ferocious disposition, none of the immediate neighbours had heard any barking from the house. Mrs Noel had been shot at close range, the bullet passing through the head and killing her instantly. When a party of five police constables was detailed to search the murder house, Inspector Ross gave them two bottles of beer from Noel's cellar for them to be in good cheer. At the coroner's inquest on Sarah Dinah Noel, the dog Nip was exhibited in court: he showed no appearance of ferocity, but wagged his tail amiably and made friends with some of the bystanders. Nelly Wilson, the servant girl employed by the Noels, had never heard her master and mistress utter an angry word at each other. On the day of the murder, they had both appeared exactly as usual. The dog Nip was in fact quite timid, she said, and sometimes retreated into the corner of the room on hearing an unusual noise. She had to admit, however, that the dog had once flown at her and bitten her hard. William Noel himself was grilled at length by the coroner and the jury: his wife had been alive and well when he left for the Sunday school; he had never possessed any firearm and did not understand their use; his wife's life had not been insured. An important witness was Mrs Sarah Dyer, the wife of a chemist who lived not far from Noel's shop. At 2.45 p.m. on the afternoon of the murder, she had heard Noel's

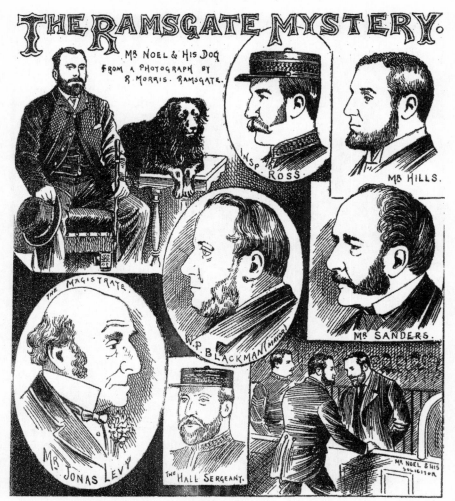

Noel, the dog, Inspector Ross, and other major players in the Ramsgate Mystery, from the *IPN*, 17 June 1893.

dog bark and growl, and then a loud report. The dog ceased barking once the shot had been fired, but recommenced around 4 p.m., when Noel was returning home.

Inspector Ross decided to try a few experiments to investigate whether the dog Nip was gun-shy. The results were wildly divergent: when a blank revolver shot was fired, the dog merely wagged his tail, but when an Alka-seltzer bottle was opened with a pop, the timid canine yelped with fear and ran out into the yard. At the coroner's inquest, Dr Fox testified that the assailant had probably stood just 4 feet away when he shot Mrs Noel; the bullet was a large one, probably emanating from

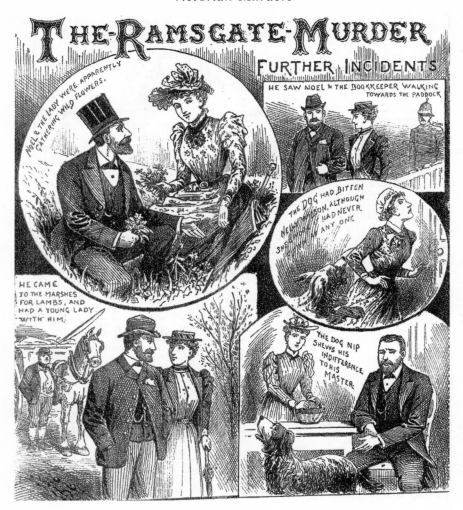

Drawings showing Noel wooing his lady friends, and the haughty dog Nip snubbing his imprisoned master, from the *IPN*, 1 July 1893.

a revolver or pistol of large calibre. Rigor mortis had begun to set in when the body was at the mortuary at 7.30, indicating that she had been murdered five or six hours earlier. A number of witnesses swore to the impressive alibi of William Noel between 2.20 and 4 p.m.: he had been seen by many people walking to the Sunday school, looking quite jolly and contented, and later returning home accompanied by some of his pupils. Miss Martha Saunders, the spinster sister of Mrs Noel, produced a letter, written in the last month, in which the deceased had referred to her husband: 'William, I think, if possible, is more fond of me than ever.' Two days before the murder, when the two sisters had been at Hastings,

The dismal outcome of the Ramsgate Mystery, from the *IPN*, 22 July 1893.

Mrs Noel had expressed herself in a similar strain. There was much newspaper interest in the 'Ramsgate Mystery', which held its own among the celebrated murders of the day, even in the large London newspapers. A worried local, who despaired of the Ramsgate police's ability to solve the crime, appealed to Dr Conan Doyle to come to Ramsgate and make use of his Holmesian powers of deduction, but all he received was a polite reply that Conan Doyle was too busy with his professional duties to have time for any seaside crime-solving excursions.

But Inspector Ross did not agree of this benign picture of William Noel. Since a number of valuables had been left in the murder house, he felt convinced that the robbery had been 'staged' by the murderer. Since Mrs Noel did not seem to have any enemies, and since the dog had not barked much at the time of the murder, he thought William Noel the prime suspect: he had shot his wife just before leaving for the Sunday school, and then successfully played the innocent husband. Inspector Ross lent a willing ear to the Ramsgate gossips who spoke of Noel's immoral activities. The lustful butcher had once employed a young lady bookkeeper named Miss Miller, and an old woman had once seen these two in a compromising position, lying together on the floor. A farm labourer had once met Noel, who was coming to purchase some lambs; he had been accompanied by a young woman, for whom he gathered a bunch of wild flowers. Several other rustic witnesses had also seen Noel chasing the lasses when out in the countryside purchasing livestock. The coroner's inquest returned a verdict of murder against some person or persons unknown, but nevertheless, Inspector Ross decided to act decisively. At the end of the inquest, he arrested Noel and brought him before the Ramsgate Magistrates, charged with murdering his wife.

In long and gruelling examinations, the magistrates put William Noel under considerable pressure. He vehemently denied having murdered his wife, and called the Almighty as a witness as to his innocence. The Ramsgate Wesleyans showed praiseworthy loyalty to Noel, pointing out that he was a very respectable tradesman, who had promised to subscribe £50 for a new chapel at St Lawrence. Noel was allowed to have his meals sent to him in his cell, brought by his niece Alice Simmons; the dog Nip sometimes accompanied her, but this extraordinary dog is said to have shown the utmost indifference to the plight of its master. A number of witnesses told all about the immoral butcher's many young lady friends, and a treacherous Wesleyan testified that Noel had once been accused of indecently interfering with one of his Sunday school pupils, although he had indignantly denied this offence at the time. When cross-examined, Inspector Ross declared himself convinced 'that the alleged robbery was a bogus one, and Noel the author thereof.' Defending William Noel, Mr Hills deplored that: 'The whole country had been scoured to find something against the prisoner's moral character, and it was a monstrous thing that a man should be branded in this way for incidents in his career which had nothing to do with the alleged offence under notice.' There was no motive for Noel to murder his wife, and the police would have been well advised to track down the intruder, and find the murder weapon, instead of listening to malicious gossip about his client. But the outcome of the magisterial inquiry was that Noel was committed to stand trial for murder at the Maidstone Assizes.

When charging the Grand Jury at Maidstone, Mr Justice Grantham paid particular attention to the Noel case. He boldly declared that the evidence against William Noel was wholly inadequate. Indeed, 'In the whole course of his experience he had never met with a case in which there was, on the part of the prosecution, so much incompetence, impropriety, and illegality. During the sixteen days the case was before the Magistrates there was not adduced more evidence than might be compressed into one small piece of paper.' The police had been guilty of vastly exaggerating the case against Noel, and the gullible magistrates had willingly played along. Of course, it remained possible that Noel had committed the crime, but his own task was to evaluate the quality of the evidence against him, and the facts of the case did not at all support the guilt of the Ramsgate butcher. After such an angry juridical tirade from Mr Justice Grantham, the only action open for the Grand Jury was to throw out the bill against William Noel; the butcher was set at liberty, and reunited with his niece Alice Simmons and the dog Nip.

There was dismay in Ramsgate when Mr Justice Grantham and the Grand Jury threw out the bill against William Noel, and the butcher was set free. Over £50 was subscribed to a testimonial to Inspector Ross, who had been so severely criticised by the judge. Local opinion was very much against William Noel, and he never returned to Ramsgate: the butcher's shop was sold, and Noel's name erased from the shop front. The *Maidstone & Kentish Journal* reported a rumour that Noel stayed in the neighbourhood of Maidstone for a while, before going to Shepherd's Bush where he resumed his butchering career under the name of Williams, and married his former bookkeeper in early 1894. This was just a rumour, however, and no person named Noel is recorded to have married in London at the relevant time; thus the career of the Ramsgate murder suspect cannot be traced with certainty. Did Noel change his name to William Jolly, and did he open another butcher's shop in a different part of the country, and marry another wife; on a quiet Sunday afternoon, did he sit contentedly in his parlour, having a swig from his tankard of beer, and giving the dog Nip a nice meaty bone? Or did he become William Furtive, a Ramsgate Ahasverus wandering from town to town pursued by his notoriety, accompanied only by the Black Dog of Guilt; and was he fearful that his silent and sinister canine companion, the sole witness to the murder of Sarah Dinah Noel, would one day become a formidable Dog of Montargis, bent on vengeance for the dead, and devour him?

The evidence against William Noel for murdering his wife largely rests on the persistent local gossip that he was a philanderer who indulged in immoral conduct with various floozies, behind the back of his wife. It may be speculated that he was tired of his much older spouse, and wanted to get rid of her to be able to remarry and have children. Experienced policemen suspected that the burglary was staged, and the dog Nip would not appear to have barked at the murderer, perhaps because it was his own master. And would a burglar have shot the woman dead and allowed the large and powerful dog to live? In defence of William Noel, it must be pointed out that he had a rock-solid alibi from 2.20 p.m., when he was seen walking to the Sunday school, until 3.55 p.m., when he was seen returning to 9 Adelphi Terrace. If the woman Sarah Dyer, who claimed to have heard the dog growling and barking at 2.45 p.m., and then the report of a shot, was telling the truth, then Noel must be innocent. Noel did not have a criminal record, he had no access to firearms, and he was not taken in any lie or contradiction by the police. And what kind of hypocrite would murder his wife in cold blood, before going to the Sunday school to disseminate his unctuous sentiments to the wide-eyed scholars? The evidence against William Noel was clearly not sufficient for him to have been found guilty in a court of law, and Mr Justice Grantham did the right thing when he threw out the bill against him. The forthright judge was also right to criticise the Ramsgate police, who made their minds up that Noel was guilty from an early stage, and failed to investigate alternative suspects; quite inexperienced when it came to investigating mysterious murders, they would have been well advised to have applied for an experienced Scotland Yard detective for assistance.

According to Ramsgate directories from the 1880s, Adelphi Terrace had originally been a terrace of eight Victorian houses in Grange Road, between St Mildred's Road and Edith Road, with shops on the ground floor and two upper stories. Separated from the others by a small alleyway, No. 9 and No. 10 were later additions. The houses were later incorporated into the numbering system for Grange Road, 9 Adelphi Terrace becoming 20 Grange Road. The former butcher's shop is today the 'China City' takeaway, but the building looks virtually unchanged since 1893, except that the side door has been moved to the rear extension. At the bottom of the yard behind the house, William Noel's stables still remain, albeit in a dilapidated condition.

52. The Curse On Amhurst Road, 1893

Hackney originated as a village north-east of London. Until the early nineteenth century, it was still a rural area with many gardens, and considered particularly agreeable for a holiday. But frantic house-building in late Georgian and Victorian times changed this: brick and mortar took over Hackney's rural acres. Parts of Hackney and Shoreditch soon acquired a dubious reputation. Hoxton was a particular trouble-spot, and noted for the 'Hoxton Horror' of 1872, involving the unsolved murders of Mrs Sarah Squires and her daughter Christiana at 46 Hyde Road [the house is long gone]. Amhurst Road, a main artery through late Victorian Hackney, has the well-nigh unique distinction of having two celebrated murders, and two murder houses, in the very

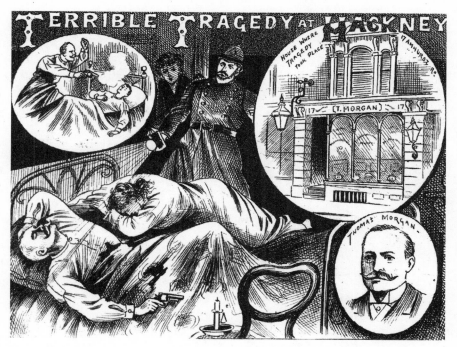

Thomas Morgan goes on a rampage at 17 Amhurst Road, from the *IPN*, 3 June 1893.

same year: No. 17 where Thomas Morgan shot his wife and stepson dead in May 1893, before committing suicide, and No. 53, where the nefarious German nursemaid Emily Newber killed a little baby in December the same year.

Mr Thomas Morgan, a quiet and respectable middle-aged man, kept the coffee house and hotel at 17 Amhurst Road. When he took the coffee house, he was a widower, but in 1889, 52-year-old Thomas Morgan married the 45-year-old widow Emma Jennings, who had several grown-up children and also a ten-year-old son from her previous marriage. They ran Morgan's Coffee House together, with the help of two waitresses, and young Arthur George Jennings the son. Morgan and his wife got on very well, nor was there any indication that he in any way resented his stepson.

All this changed in July 1892, when Thomas Morgan suffered a serious paralytic stroke. Not only was he partially paralysed on the right side of his body, but he had lost much of the capacity for speech as well. He could only utter one or two words at a time, often of an obscene and offensive nature. The stroke had made him a changed man: an angry, grumbling invalid who was often at loggerheads with his long-suffering wife, and very resentful towards his stepson. Once, he had pushed poor

Amhurst Road, N.

C. J. & A. Algar, 180 Stoke Newington Road, N.

Amhurst Road, a postcard stamped and posted in 1905.

THE FEMALE WARDER   EMILY NEWBER

Sketched at the Old Bailey by a "P.I.P." Artist.

Emily Newber in the dock.

Emma down in the kitchen, and made stabbing gestures towards her with a small knife; another time, she had found a mysterious white powder in a cup of coffee he had handed her. When Emma Morgan told her adult sons about these incidents, they thought Thomas belonged in a lunatic asylum, but Emma still cared for her invalid husband, and did not want him to be confined in a madhouse.

On 23 May 1893, Thomas Morgan was at his most obnoxious: he shouted threats and obscenities, and seemed greatly resentful towards his wife. At midnight, the demented invalid, who was still capable of locomotion, went to the room where young Arthur slept, clutching a five-chambered Smith & Wesson revolver. He shot the sleeping lad in the head. Emma was woken up by the gunshot, and when she went to challenge her husband, he shot her in the face. Thomas Morgan then lurched into his own bedroom, and discharged two more bullets into his belly and groin. Groaning with pain, he then seized hold of the bell-rope in his room and pulled it hard to alert the servants.

The two young servant girls employed at the coffee house went to investigate, with the three people lodging on the premises. Finding the carnage upstairs, they called in the police and a doctor. Thomas Morgan was still alive, but his wife and stepson were both dead. The empty revolver was found next to Morgan's bed. While being taken to the German Hospital, Morgan told a police sergeant: 'Yes, I did it!' At the hospital, Dr Hermann Peterson had Morgan taken to the operating room, where it was found that his bowels had been perforated at least four times. He succumbed to his injuries the following day, thus succeeding in his ambition to wipe out his entire family.

At the coroner's inquest on the three casualties, several relations of the murdered woman gave evidence, smugly declaring that she had paid a heavy price for not following their advice to have Morgan put away in a lunatic asylum. Mrs Susan Burham, Thomas Morgan's sister, testified that he had become a changed man after suffering the stroke, and that he had often complained that his wife and stepson treated him unkindly. Frederick James Hillman, son-in-law to Emma Morgan, testified that Morgan had once slapped her face, and that she had told him about an incident when he had threatened to stab her. Hillman had himself seen Morgan in violent paroxysms of rage: he had once seized hold of his own tongue and tried to forcibly tear it out. After the police detectives and the doctor had given evidence about finding the bodies, and the wounds suffered by Morgan himself, the coroner's jury returned a verdict of wilful murder against Thomas Morgan, who had then committed suicide while mentally deranged.

There was a good deal of interest in the 'Hackney Tragedy' from the London newspapers; while most of them reported the double murder and suicide in sombre phrases, the irrepressible *IPN* published a 'thrilling' image of Morgan on a rampage inside the coffee house, with the caption saying 'Terrible Tragedy in Hackney! A Madman's Wild Freaks!' On 2 June 1893, the three victims of the Hackney Tragedy were buried, in three separate graves, in Ilford Cemetery. Many people were present to hear the funeral service and to attend the burial of the deceased. A group of youths held a large cross with the inscription 'Deep Sympathy from Arthur's Young Friends', and there were many wreaths for Mrs Morgan and the boy, but not a single one for the Amhurst Road double murderer.

Although the victims of the Hackney Tragedy had been buried, and the coffee house at No. 17 taken over by new owners, the Curse on Amhurst Road had not been lifted: the roulette wheel of Death was spun once more in December 1893, and this time, Murder would come calling at – No. 53 Amhurst Road.

Mr Solomon Myers was a respectable Hackney solicitor of Jewish origins, who resided at No. 53 with his wife Rosa and their five children. In December 1893, they had three servants: the nursery governess Lottie Bethel, the general servant Beatrice Clark, and the recently employed nursemaid Emily Newber. The last-mentioned was a sturdy, thick-set girl of 15, daughter of the respectable German immigrant Frederick Newber, who was working as a plumber in Holborn. On setting foot in London, he had anglicized his name Friedrich Neuburg to 'Frederick Newber' and his daughter Emilia had followed his example, becoming Emily Newber.

On 8 December 1893, when Emily had been in service with the Myers for just five days, it was noticed that the ten-month-old baby, blessed [or perhaps not] with the unique name Ray Maud Myers, seemed quite unwell. Her lips and eyes were swollen, and there were scratches on her face. When all three domestics were harshly interrogated by Mr Myers, Emily attracted attention through alternately accusing the other two servants, and constantly changing her story. Suspecting that Emily had deliberately injured the baby, the angry Mrs Myers gave her notice, on the spot, something the truculent nursemaid seemed to greatly resent.

The following day, Solomon Myers' young son cried out 'Mummy! Mummy! Baby!' Rosa Myers rushed upstairs to the nursery, where a sheepish-looking Emily Newber was standing by the baby's cot. 'What have you done to this baby again?' the angry Mrs Myers asked. 'Nothing, Ma'am' Emily replied. Mrs Myers saw that little Ray Maud had once more been ill-treated: her lips were swollen and bloody, and she was foaming at the mouth. There was a strong, unpleasant smell of vinegar. When asked which bottles she had been feeding Ray Maud from, Emily fetched an ordinary feeding-bottle, and a glass bottle marked 'Spasmodic

Mixture', but Solomon Myers was not having any of that. He strongly suspected that this sinister German girl had deliberately poisoned his little daughter. All three domestics were again harshly interrogated by the angry solicitor, and now Emily admitted that the day before, she had struck the baby hard in the face, since it had been 'cross' and annoyed her with its squalling. However, s he still stoutly denied poisoning Ray Maud.

In the meantime, the doctor had arrived and the poisoned baby was removed to the German Hospital in Dalston, where the murderous Thomas Morgan had breathed his last half a year earlier. Ray Maud was examined by Dr Zumbusch, who diagnosed that she had been poisoned by some corrosive substance. Since her throat was becoming so swollen she was in danger of suffocation, the dexterous Dr Zumbusch successfully performed a tracheotomy on the little baby. For a while, Ray Maud seemed to recover, but symptoms of pneumonia soon set in, and she died a few days later.

Emily Newber, who had been arrested by the police, was solemnly informed, at the inquest on Ray Maud Myers, that her victim has expired. The autopsy showed that the baby had died from poisoning with acetic acid, leading to burns to the mouth and throat, and pneumonia from the aspiration of corrosive fluids and mucus. It turned out that one of the other domestics had once purchased a bottle of acetic acid, some of which she had used to remove a wart from her face. She had kept this bottle in an open cupboard, from which it had been removed by the poisoner. It was later found in the nursery, with a few drops of acid still remaining inside.

On trial at the Old Bailey, for the wilful murder of Ray Maud Myers, things were not looking good for Emily Newber. She had admitted beating up the baby the day before, and the evidence from the other servants indicated that she was the only person with an opportunity to poison little Ray Maud. There was a good deal in the newspapers about the 'Hackney Poisoning Case'. The journalists found it most unnatural for a young girl to first beat, and then poison, a defenceless little baby. There were ominous rumours that more than once, Emily had previously been dismissed from various nursemaid positions. According to another newspaper story, she very much resented Jews, since she had read a German book about them drinking the blood of Christian children, and plotting to gain world domination. The *Penny Illustrated Paper* was the only periodical to publish Emily Newber's likeness: a coarse-featured, nutcracker-jawed young woman. Her police file in the National Archives contains a letter in a clumsy, childish hand, in which she admits slapping the baby's face since it had been 'cross'.

After the Myers, the other domestics, and the doctors, had given evidence, a Dr Gimblet testified that Emily Newber did not, in his opinion, suffer from 'hysteria'. Instead, he would rather diagnose her as having 'homicidal mania', since she had shown no remorse whatsoever for the murder of the baby. The jury took long to deliberate, before returning a verdict of Guilty of Manslaughter, with a strong recommendation to mercy due to the prisoner's youth. Police Sergeant Nursey then stood up in court and proclaimed that Emily had been discharged from at least two previous positions due to alleged cruelty to children! With remarkable lenience, considering the serious nature of the crime, the bonhomous Judge sentenced Emily Newber to just one week in prison, and five years in a reformatory. Clearly, both judge and jury seem to have disregarded the sordid brutality of the premeditated child murder, on account of the youth of the murderess.

A Victorian reformatory was not a nice place to spend five years, but one has the feeling that the tough, lantern-jawed Emily Newber emerged from its walls in 1898, as mean-spirited as ever. The reader will be relieved that she did not continue her vendetta against defenceless little children. In fact, it would appear that the entire Newber family left Britain very soon after Emily's release from the reformatory, presumably to return to their native land. Did Emily Newber, or rather Emilia Neuburg, become a sturdy, contented German *Frau*, cutting up *wurst* and pouring *bier*? Or did the anti-Semitic child-killer live to fight another day, as a concentration camp matron, after Hitler had made Germany a land fit for scoundrels to live in?

As for the Myers family, they cannot have been very happy with the very light sentence handed down to the Hackney Child Murderess. They remained at No. 53 Amhurst Road for quite a few years to come. No further murderous nursemaids were employed, and the remaining children all reached adulthood. The house at No. 53 does not appear to have been haunted by the ghost of a crying little baby. Like the old shop at No. 17, it has fallen victim to the Developer, and nondescript modern housing occupies the site.

That two unrelated cases of murder occurring in the same terrace of houses, in the very same year, appears to be an unprecedented incident in the annals of the Murder Houses of London. The closest parallel I can find concerns the Curse on Elmhurst Mansions, where two prostitutes were murdered, at No. 203 and No. 8, in 1935 and 1936. Then we have the two unsolved murders at No. 4 and No. 12 Burton Crescent, in 1878 and 1884. Gray's Inn Road had three murder houses, of which two survive; this distinction is shared with Warren Street, which only has one murder house standing today. Doggett Road, Catford, has two murder houses standing, at No. 19 and No. 27; the latter site of the famous murder of Maxwell Confait in 1972. Edward Street, Deptford, also had two murder houses in close vicinity, at No. 172 and No. 180, but both are gone today. Perhaps the most macabre record in the annals of the Murder Houses of London concerns the little terraced house in Roll Gardens, Ilford, where the lunatic Lilian Myra Giles murdered her son in 1958. Released from Broadmoor as early as 1961, she dispatched her husband, through a heavy blow with a chamber pot, in 1968. From Broadmoor, Lilian Myra Giles employed solicitors to claim her husband's estate, since she had been insane when murdering him, but after prolonged legal wrangling, she lost her case, and the estate of Mr Giles, including the double murder house in Roll Gardens, went to his son from an earlier marriage.

So, has the Curse on Amhurst Road eventually been lifted? Some would say it has, since the road remained murder free for many years after 1893; in fact, I have found nothing to suggest that it ever acquired another historical murder house. Hackney was widely 'developed' in the 1950s and 1960s, following wartime damage, and the terrace containing the two murder houses at No. 17 and No. 53 was flattened to allow the construction of a large housing estate. The short terrace of Nos. 1–5 Amhurst Road, not far from Morgan's old coffee house at No. 17, and very much resembling it architecturally, was demolished as late as 2013, as a result of becoming structurally unsound.

But the Amhurst Road Estate itself, and other rough housing estates nearby, have become notorious trouble-spots for gang-related violent crime. The London Fields Boys, the Lords of Stokey, the Smalley Boys, and other dangerous gangs, are infesting these structures, keeping their guns loaded and their knifes sharp and ready for use. In May 2009, 17-year-old Jahmal Mason-Blair was stabbed to death in a fight between two gangs of youths in Amhurst Road; a 14-year-old boy admitted the crime. In September 2009, 29-year-old Edward Thompson was shot dead by two young thugs who had mistaken him for an enemy of theirs. In May 2010, a youth was murdered and two others badly stabbed in an outbreak of gang violence in Amhurst Park, just off Amhurst Road.

The Murder Map of London is constantly changing. The narrow Victorian terraces of Amhurst Road, home to occasional domestic disputes and 'trouble with the servants', have been replaced with vast, sterile housing estates, squalid behemoths of crime, gang culture and religious fanaticism. There is reason to believe that the Curse on Amhurst Road is still alive and well.

53. The Bath Mystery, 1893

In August 1891, the young servant girl Elsie Adeline Luke disappeared from her Bath lodgings. Since she was a somewhat flighty character, fond of chasing the lads, and not much liked by the lasses as a result, it was presumed she had moved away with some bloke, and not much was made of her disappearance. Not long after, two men found some bloodstained cuffs and a gold watch and chain on Hampton Downs. One of them,

The cave where the body of Elsie Adeline Luke was found, from the *IPN*, 7 October 1893.

MURDER WILL OUT!
DISCOVERY OF THE SKELETON OF MURDERED ELSIE WILKIE IN A CAVE NEAR BATH.

The remains of Elsie Adeline Luke are found, from the *Illustrated Police Budget*.

a man named Dill, said he would deliver these items to the police station, but being a dishonest cadger, he kept the watch and chain himself.

More than two years later, in September 1893, the skeleton of a young woman was found in a cave near Hampton Downs. She had clearly

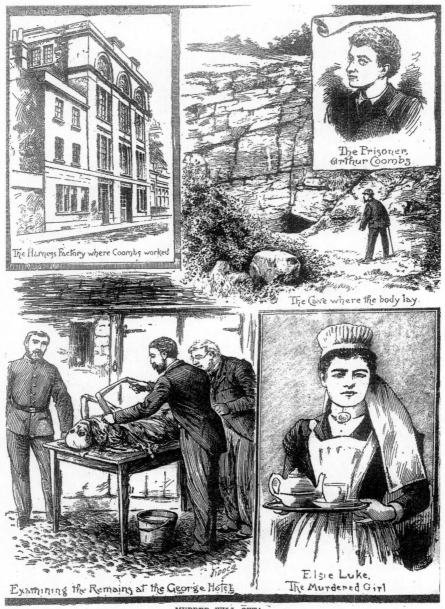

The Harness Factory where Coombs worked

The Prisoner, Arthur Coombs

The Cave where the body lay.

Examining the Remains at the George Hotel

Elsie Luke. The Murdered Girl

MURDER WILL OUT!
FURTHER SKETCHES BY OUR SPECIAL ARTIST OF THE BATH MYSTERY.

Vignettes on the Bath Mystery, from the *Illustrated Police Budget*.

been murdered, since a doctor found that the skull had been bashed in with a blunt instrument. Clearly, many people said, this must be the remains of Elsie Adeline Luke. The skeleton was that of a woman in her twenties, and no other young women had gone missing from this

The prisoner Coombs, Pollie Sheppard, and poor Elsie herself, from the *IPN*, 14 October 1893.

quiet neighbourhood. What clinched the matter was that the skeleton was wrapped in some linen bearing the mark of a certain Mrs Kerry, who had employed Elsie Adeline Luke as cook from March until July 1891. The reason Elsie had been fired after just four months of service was her untruthfulness and dishonesty: not just linen, but other items as well, were discovered to have gone missing after Elsie had left. Thus Elsie's thieving ways had served the purpose of aiding the identification of her remains.

It was well known that Elsie had been 'going out' with local lad Arthur Stevenson Coombs, apprentice to a coachbuilder. After it was discovered that this juvenile Lothario had been 'running' various other lady friends on the side, he became the prime suspect in the investigation of the murder of Elsie Adeline Luke. When Superintendent Rutherford took Coombs into custody, the young apprentice said, 'I did not do it. I kept company with her. After that I am of no use to you.' Still, when Coombs was charged with murdering Elsie Adeline Luke, alias Wilkie, things were not looking good for him. Many people had seen him with Elsie, and he had spoken of her in uncouth and sometimes violent terms, once telling a crony that 'She ought to be dead or killed.' Pollie Sheppard, one of Coombs' other girlfriends, had also made vaguely threatening remarks about her rival. Just after Elsie had disappeared, Coombs had sought medical attention at the Royal United Hospital, for an injured thumb. In the hospital books, the injury was described as being caused by a human bite!

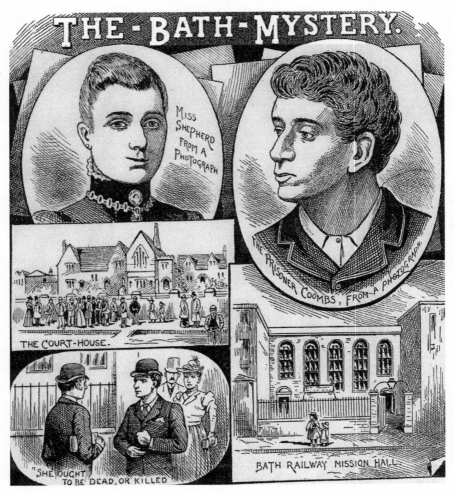

THE·BATH·MYSTERY.

MISS SHEPHERD FROM A PHOTOGRAPH

THE PRISONER COOMBS, FROM A PHOTOGRAPH

THE COURT-HOUSE.

"SHE OUGHT TO BE DEAD, OR KILLED"

BATH RAILWAY MISSION HALL

More vignettes on the Bath Mystery, from the *IPN*, 21 October 1893.

There was a good deal of curiosity about Elsie Adeline Luke, the murder victim. There were rumours that she was of German origin, and that she had once seen better days. Elsie's former employer thought her education and accomplishments superior to those of her fellow domestics. The other servant girls agreed; they had even been annoyed by Elsie's 'airs and graces'. But this newspaper spin to make Elsie a foreign-born mystery woman was short-lived: the hard facts were that she had grown up in London and that her real name was Wilkie. Her parents had kept the coffee shop at the Tidal Basin railway station, Canning Town. In April 1880, Elsie had been arrested for theft, and harshly sentenced to ten days imprisonment and five years detention at the Limpley Stoke reformatory near Bath. She had served all five years, being released in May 1885.

She had kept in touch with the reformatory, and had been seen there as late as 1891, the year she disappeared. A newspaper tracked down Elsie's respectable sister, who was married and living at Tidal Basin. Elsie had not been a particularly good girl, and her family had actually felt quite relieved when she was carted off to the reformatory. The reason she had spent her full term there was probably that her angry, revengeful character had displeased the Matron, with whom Elsie had not been on good terms. After being liberated from this dismal reformatory, Elsie did not want to rejoin her family in London. She remained in the Bath region, doing various menial jobs, and her parents were fearful she led an immoral life. In 1889, she had written to them asking for forgiveness of her past misdemeanours, but the parents, who were much ashamed of her, did not greet this missive with enthusiasm. Nor did Elsie's parents make any exertions to find her after she had disappeared in 1891.

The magisterial examination of Arthur Stevenson Coombs began at Weston on 29 September 1893. The accused, described as a thin, pale young fellow, aged just 20, displayed considerable agitation in court. Several witnesses had seen Arthur and Elsie together; some of them had remarked on the contrast between the feeble-looking, 18-year old swain, and his well-built, 26-year-old lady-friend. Elsie's fellow servant remembered her clandestinely smuggling a young man into the house, and going down into the cellar with him, although she did not identify this dodgy evening caller as Arthur. Elsie had told several people that she was pregnant, and had once made a scene outside the Coombs family residence, accusing Arthur of being responsible for this state of affairs.

When Arthur Stevenson Coombs had been arrested, the Coombs family home had been thoroughly searched by the police. They found a large bag marked A.S.C. containing numerous letters from his various lady friends. Sinisterly, there were none from Elsie Adeline Luke, although witnesses confidently stated that she had more than once written to him. The majority of the letters were from Arthur's present girlfriend, the country lass Pollie Sheppard. Pollie was most indignant about Arthur's dalliances with other women, in particular his affair with Elsie Adeline Luke. She more than once upbraided Arthur for keeping company with such a sluttish person, and made vague threats that something unpleasant might happen to Elsie if the affair went on. When it was Pollie's turn to give evidence, she freely admitted that Elsie had returned her dislike in full. Elsie had been a very uncouth young woman, and she had been fond of shouting abuse at the virtuous Pollie, who was unlikely to have maintained a dignified silence during these shenanigans. Once, these two pugnacious young women had a scrap, which ended with Elsie knocking Pollie down. Pollie admitted her unhappiness about Arthur's conduct, but in spite of his past shortcomings, she testified that she was engaged to Arthur, and that she looked forward to marrying him.

With regard to his injured thumb, Arthur claimed that it had been bitten 'during an altercation at the Liberal fête', but a police constable attending this fête testified that the Liberals had all behaved with decorum, and refrained from fisticuffs and thumb-biting. On an equally ominous note, a lad had told the police that he had once discussed a recent sensational murder with Arthur Stevenson Coombs and some other young fellows. Arthur had suddenly and unexpectedly said 'Oh, I committed a murder once, and it has never been found out!' This remarkable statement was considered a joke at the time.

When the coroner Dr Craddock summed up the case on 6 December, he started with upbraiding various minor witnesses for their drunken and rowdy behaviour in court. The witness Dill, who had stolen what was very likely to have been Elsie Adeline Luke's watch and chain, was named and shamed for failing to communicate his discovery to the police. Being present in court, in a drunken state, Dill vociferously objected to this reprimand. Dr Craddock pointed out that all that was conclusively proven against Arthur Stevenson Coombs was that he had been carrying on an intrigue with Elsie Adeline Luke at the time he had been engaged to marry Pollie Sheppard. Two years had passed since the murder, and all the other evidence was circumstantial. Suspicion might be entertained against a man, but it should not hang him, the coroner pontificated, and the jury took the hint. They returned a verdict that Elsie Adeline Luke had been wilfully murdered by some person unknown, and Coombs was a free man. After being released from custody, Arthur Stevenson Coombs is said to have received hundreds of letters of congratulation and sympathy. The logic behind these effusions is hard to appreciate, since Coombs was, at the very least, a young man of very dubious moral character. But was he also a murderer?

If we accept Elsie's version that she had been carrying his child, which is somewhat hazardous due to her habitual untruthfulness, Coombs had a motive to murder her. He had been seen with her just a few days prior to her disappearance, he had spoken of her in threatening terms, and then there was the very important matter of the bitten thumb, and his attempt to present a false explanation for his injury. In forensic medicine, there are many instances of a woman being choked or throttled inflicting a bite wound on her assailant's hand. The clever hiding of the body speaks in favour of the killer having local knowledge, and perhaps also some degree of premeditation, with Coombs luring Elsie to some desolate spot near the cave, where he had hidden a bludgeon in advance.

An argument that does not appear to have occurred to any person back in 1893 is the *second* significance of Elsie Adeline Luke's body being found *wrapped* in the linen she had once stolen from her employer. Since Elsie was unlikely to have taken the linen with her to some obscure meeting-place, she was probably murdered at her lodgings, where she had hidden her loot of linen. With some degree of premeditation, the murderer had calmly wrapped her body up in the linen and transported it to the (pre-selected?) hiding-place.

On the other hand, would such a short and thin lad as Coombs really have been able to overpower his sturdy mistress, who was eight years older than him, and bash her head in with considerable force, at the cost of only a bitten thumb? And would this rather unimpressive specimen of humanity also have the mental toughness to keep his dreadful deed a secret for two years, apart from one flippant remark? If Pollie Sheppard had knowledge of the crime, or if she had even been Coombs' accomplice, would she really have been able to testify in court with such coolness? Elsie Adeline Luke was not known for her high moral integrity, and it is quite possible that some other swain had come calling at her lodgings; a sturdy, powerful ruffian, he would not take no for an answer, and could have raped and murdered her, before dumping the body in the cave.

Not the least remarkable feature of the Bath Mystery is that the memorial to Elsie Adeline Luke in St Nicholas' Churchyard is still in existence. It has been maintained by a certain Lucy Barlow and her estate, and a replacement stone has recently been erected. It has the inscription 'Here lie the remains of Elsie Adeline Luke, aged 26, who was cruelly murdered on Hampton Down, August 1891.' Since Elsie Adeline Luke had no family living near Bath, the memorial may well have been erected by some person believing Coombs to be the guilty man, to have him shamed until eternity.

54. The Maidenhead Mystery, 1893

In November 1892, the Middlesbrough police made a search of the ship *Lowther Castle*, which had just arrived from Amsterdam. In the cabin of the ship's steward, Dutchman Hendrik de Jong, they found a quantity of cigars of which he could not explain his ownership so he was sentenced to a short prison term for smuggling. Since Hendrik de Jong claimed to be very ill, from an affliction of the throat, he was removed to Middlesbrough Infirmary. The ailing Dutchman soon perked up in the hospital, where he was given nourishing food and attentive nursing. A dapper, moustachioed cove who claimed to be 31 years old, he soon took notice of the pretty, 25-year-old nurse Sarah Ann Juett, a native of Maidenhead. After a brief hospital romance, she agreed to marry him. Her family was far from pleased that Sarah Ann had decided to marry a dodgy foreign sailor who smuggled cigars, but since she was a headstrong young woman, they had to accept her decision.

Hendrik de Jong then returned to his native land, but in April 1893, he wrote to Sarah Ann Juett that it was time they got married. Her Maidenhead parents and brother were far from impressed with the flashy Dutchman, who told them he was a medical man and a hotel proprietor,

Hendrik de Jong and his two wives, from the *IPN*, 7 October 1893.

SARAH ANN JUETT   HENDRIK DE JONG   MARIA SIJBILLA SCHMITZ

DE JONG AND HIS WIVES: A MYSTERY CONCERNING ENGLAND AND HOLLAND.

From Portraits circulated by the Dutch Police.

Portraits of de Jong and his wives, from the *Penny Illustrated Paper*, 30 September 1893.

of considerable wealth. This did not stop him from borrowing money from Mr Juett and various other relatives. And what kind of doctor would serve as a steward on board ship, and then get caught smuggling cigars? But in spite of these doubts, the Juetts accepted Hendrik de Jong as their son-in-law: the marriage was solemnised at the Parish Church of St Luke's, Maidenhead, on 15 June. The marriage certificate lists Hendrik de Jong as a 31-year-old ship's steward, son of the ship's captain William de Jong, deceased. Sarah Ann Juett, a 25-year-old spinster, is described as the daughter of the contractor Daniel Juett; her brother Daniel Jr was one of the witnesses. The creature de Jong borrowed another £30 from his father-in-law and at once set off to Holland with his wife; they would live at the large and fashionable Sluis Hotel in Arnhem, which he had just purchased, he said. In early July, de Jong wrote a letter to Mr Juett, saying that his wife had been taken ill in Arnhem, but that there was no need to worry.

On 19 August 1893, Hendrik de Jong turned up uninvited at Mr Juett's house in Maidenhead. He moaned and cried, saying that Sarah Ann had left him, and that she had gone to New York with a big American she had met in Wiesbaden. When the angry Mr Juett called him a liar, he exclaimed 'Papa, she will come back again!' and handed him a box of cheap Dutch cigars as a present. On the bottom of the box, he wrote 'Great Bat Hotel, Wiesbaden' and 'Mr. W. Wilson, New York' to define the place where the elopement had taken place, and the name of the man responsible. Mr Juett did not believe a word of what de Jong was saying. He went to the police, but by that time, de Jong had returned to his native land.

The Dutch police were informed and it turned out that Hendrik de Jong was well known to them for a life full of crime. As a young man, he had been a hotel waiter, before becoming an attendant at a large lunatic asylum. In Rotterdam, he had married the daughter of a wealthy woman named Kramer, then proceeded to swindle the old woman out of her fortune. After serving two years in prison for this caper, de Jong went abroad, as a trumpeter in a regiment in the Dutch East Indies. He liked to tell people that he was a doctor, but lacked any kind of medical education. Nor had he ever been in a position to own a hotel. He supported himself through various odd jobs, as a mason's labourer, or a house painter, before going to sea as a steward on the Amsterdam ship *Lowther Castle*. He was known as a small-time swindler and smuggler. The Dutch police found evidence that Miss Juett, or Mrs de Jong as she should perhaps be called, had last been sighted at the villages of Heelom and Renkum, with her husband, but then she had completely disappeared.

It also turned out that Hendrik de Jong had been up to further mischief in Holland after his English wife had disappeared. Presenting himself as a military surgeon from the Dutch East Indies, he had married, after a dangerously short acquaintance, a wealthy 40-year-old Dutchwoman named Maria Sybilla Schmitz. In July 1893, he had sold all her furniture and belongings, saying that he would buy her much better things in London. And indeed, when de Jong visited England to tell Mr Juett that his daughter has left him with an American, he had left his second wife behind in London, at Wheeler's Hotel in Devonshire Square. Maria Sybilla Schmitz had visited an Amsterdam music hall with her husband on 28 August. She had last been seen leaving Amsterdam for the village of Bussum, with her husband, but then she had disappeared as well. The Dutch police found this a highly suspicious combination of events: had Hendrik de Jong murdered both of his wives, in quick succession?

The Amsterdam police arrested Hendrik de Jong, but as cool as a cucumber, he denied any involvement in the disappearances of his two wives. There was much interest in his extraordinary career, in both the Dutch and the English newspapers. When three schoolmasters had been returning home near Laren's Camp, outside Amsterdam, they had heard a terrible moaning sound, and a young girl and her father had also heard some person crying out. It was suspected that Maria Sybilla Schmitz had been murdered in this area, and bloodhounds were employed to make a thorough search, but without any human remains being found. An Amsterdam newspaper suggested that de Jong should be hypnotised, to be forced to confess where he had murdered his wives, and where he had buried their bodies. His effigy was exhibited, with considerable success, in an Amsterdam waxworks museum.

As Hendrik de Jong was languishing in the Amsterdam police cells, the Dutch newspapers kept speculating about his murderous career. Here was a Dutchman who was likely to have murdered two women. Now it was well known that the Whitechapel Fiend, Jack the Ripper, had committed a series of murders without parallel in the modern world. Might it be that when his ship arrived in the London Docks, de Jong had repeatedly stalked and murdered women in Whitechapel, before making his escape on the same vessel? The police thought de Jong fully sane, although he had an abnormal liking for women, and was an inveterate customer of street prostitutes. It was said that when de Jong's apartments in Amsterdam were raided by the police, a number of medical textbooks were found, as well as surgical instruments stained with blood. It ought to be investigated whether de Jong's visits to London coincided with the Ripper crimes, the Dutch journalists urged, and his photograph should be shown to a number of Whitechapel prostitutes, to see whether they recognized him.

Both the German and the Scandinavian newspapers enthusiastically took on board the Dutch speculation that the Whitechapel Murderer had been found, but the London papers remained wholly unconvinced. Hendrik de Jong was a common fraudster, who had quite possibly murdered his two wives for profit; Jack the Ripper had been a bloodthirsty maniac on a mission to murder Whitechapel prostitutes. Furthermore, most close students of the Ripper crimes were of the opinion that Jack's career had ended soon after the murder of Mary Kelly in 1888, or possibly after the murder of Alice McKenzie in 1891.

Meanwhile, the Amsterdam police encountered some problems of their own. Hendrik de Jong's story could not be shaken, and in spite of extensive searches, neither Sarah Ann Juett nor Maria Sybilla Schmitz had been found, alive or dead. The story that the young, recently married nurse Sarah Ann Juett would leave her husband and go off with an American seemed particularly unlikely. But although the Amsterdam detectives remained convinced that de Jong was a double murderer, the charge of murder was withdrawn in default of evidence. Instead, Hendrik de Jong was prosecuted for swindling an Amsterdam hotel keeper out of 100 florins, and in April 1894, he was sentenced to three years in prison.

Hendrik de Jong was out of prison in 1897, but in September that year, he was arrested in Arnhem for another swindle, and once more faced prosecution. In January 1899, the skeleton of a woman was found in the Rhine near Renkum, and there was brief newspaper speculation that this was the remains of Sarah Ann Jouett, who had disappeared in that part of Holland back in 1893. In October 1902, a medium at a séance in the Hague claimed to have seen the dead bodies of Sarah Ann Juett and Maria Sybilla Schmitz, but in spite of another brief burst of newspaper enthusiasm, the police took no notice at all.

The facts remain that in June and July 1893, the Dutch con artist Hendrik de Jong married two wives, both of whom disappeared without trace, in quick succession. That the reason for both marriages was swindling appears very likely. Had either wife been alive at the time de Jong was in prison accused of murder, it would have been natural for her to contact the Amsterdam authorities, so it would seem likely that both of them were dead by this time. Since they are unlikely to have died from natural causes, it seems likely that de Jong murdered them, and that he then made use of some cunning plan to dispose of the remains, enabling him to maintain his impressive *sang-froid* while in police custody, since he was certain they would never be found. Dutch researcher Bart Droog, who has spent much time studying the de Jong case, has discovered that after murdering two other women in Belgium in 1898, this very cunning and resourceful criminal fled the country, quite possibly going to the United States. We are preparing an article for *Ripperologist* magazine to chronicle Hendrik de Jong's life and crimes, and to thoroughly assess his Ripperine candidature.

55. The Grafton Street Murder, 1894

The pioneer of London murder house detection was the author, poet and playwright George R. Sims (1847–1922). He was exceedingly popular in his own lifetime, and people likened him to Charles Dickens for his social conscience, and his obvious sympathy for London's poor. When Sims joined the *Referee* newspaper in 1877, he assumed the pen-name 'Dagonet' and wrote a weekly 'Mustard and Cress' column. This column, which would continue for 45 years until Sims died in harness, became enormously popular and did much to keep his name in the public eye. His punning and laborious wit, and frequent 'lapses into poetry', appealed to the literary taste of his contemporaries. Sims also became known for his overblown and ultra-sentimental ballads like *Christmas*

Eve in the Workhouse and *Billy's Rose*, which were fashionable recital pieces in Victorian times. His plays, *The Lights of London* in particular, were equally popular, and provided Sims with a generous income, most of which he spent on gambling and high living. When liver trouble forced the hard-drinking Sims to take to the lemonade bottle, his output of ballads ceased completely, and the remainder of his output also became less sprightly.

George R. Sims sometimes edified his 'Refereaders' about London's history of crime, an area where he was well informed. He was always on the prowl for new items to add to his private crime museum. Sims had a chair from Mrs Pearcey's murder house, among other items of criminal memorabilia. He also managed to buy the hanging beam of old Newgate, a 'Jack the Ripper' letter, and relics of the murderers Percy Lefroy Mapleton, Henry Wainwright, Herbert Bennett and James Canham Read. Sims took an interest in tracking down famous murder houses in London and its vicinity, exclaiming, 'Whenever there is a fine, bright day I say to myself, "Hurrah! Let's have a drive to a place where a murder was committed".' After visiting Camden Place in Chislehurst in 1890, to see the room where Mr and Mrs Bonar had been beaten to death by the footman Nicholson, he promised that 'I have several magnificent murders up my sleeve, and directly we get a few decent days which will allow me to drive down and take notes on the spot, Refereaders will have the benefit

An autographed postcard sent by columnist George R. Sims to one of the admiring readers of the *Referee* newspaper, known as Refereaders.

MARIE HERMANN, THE WOMAN CHARGED WITH THE GRAFTON STREET MURDER.

A portrait of Marie Hermann, from the *Penny Illustrated Paper*, 24 March 1894.

of my investigation. Some of the murders I have unearthed in the country around London are simply enthralling.' In his 1906 book *Mysteries of Modern London*, Sims devoted an entire chapter to notorious murder houses, including the two Huelin houses at 15 Paulton's Square and 24 Wellington Square, Chelsea; Madame Riel's house at 13 Park Lane and the murder shop at 22 Wyndham Road, Camberwell.

Another murder house featured in George R. Sims' *Mysteries of Modern London* was situated just off Tottenham Court Road. A nefarious German woman had moved from this street to another one nearby, bringing with her a very heavy trunk, addressed to 'The Station Master, Berlin – To be Called For'. She was a part-time police informant in London's underworld of brothels and thieves' dens, and when her police 'handler' heard that there were bloodstains on the wall of her old lodgings, he went to see her, suspecting that she had been up to mischief. When the trunk was opened, the corpse of an 18-stone man was found inside, his head split open with a hatchet. The German woman got 12 years in prison for manslaughter, and disappeared into obscurity. Sims went to see the house where she had murdered her burly victim: 'The first floor is to let. Plenty of people have occupied it since Madam gave it up. Some of them have slept night after night in the very room where a man

Marie Hermann advancing on her victim, from the *IPN*, 31 March 1894.

of eighteen stone was done to death, packed up in a trunk, and addressed to the station master at Berlin. Very few of the occupants, I fancy, have had any knowledge of the story of that room ...'

To any person who has a good knowledge of London's annals of murder, it is obvious that George R. Sims is discussing the once-famous Grafton Street Murder of 1894, which is today almost entirely forgotten. Marie Hermann was born in Pillichsdorf, Lower Austria, in 1855, the daughter of the countryman Wenzel Hermann and his wife Anna Marie. She married the innkeeper and publican Johann Geiler, and had four children with him. When Geiler died prematurely, she remarried the farmer Joseph Schramm. Without warning, she left her husband and children in March 1881 and accompanied a wealthy family to London, as the governess of their children. After she had lost her job due to her drunken and immoral habits of life, her only resource was to become a prostitute.

In her early career, Marie's elegant clothes and haughty 'airs and graces' earned her the nickname 'The Duchess' as she patrolled her Piccadilly beat, but a combination of middle age, alcoholism and toothlessness soon reduced her to a wreck of a woman. The only way she could keep starvation from the door, and support herself and her children, was to accept the most elderly, unattractive and perverted clients, with whom the better class of prostitutes were unwilling to consort. Poor Marie Hermann had three children with three different fathers, none of whom cared for their offspring; she also had a pimp who she sometimes called her husband.

On 15 March 1894, Marie Hermann was picked up in Euston Road by a heavily built, elderly man named Charles Anthony Stephens, a retired cab driver. They had some drink at a pub before retiring to Marie's lodgings at 51 Grafton Street, off Tottenham Court Road. In the middle of the night, Marie's neighbours heard a heavy fall, the sound of repeated

Portraits from the coroner's inquest, from the *Penny Illustrated Paper*, March 31 1894.

Marie Hermann at the
Old Bailey, from the
Penny Illustrated Paper,
June 9 1894.

heavy blows, and a groan of 'Murder!' 'I suppose the old people are fighting,' one of them said, but it did not occur to them that maybe it would be a good idea to break up the fight.

The next day, Marie Hermann was seen to use the communal sink; when a suspicious neighbour had a look at it, it had traces of blood. Marie seemed quite jolly, spending much money on drink, whereas she had previously been very hard up. On 17 March, she announced that she was moving out of the lodgings. She paid for her room, packed her belongings, and gave instructions to some removal men to load them onto a van and take them to her new lodgings at 56 Upper Marylebone Street [today New Cavendish Street; the house at No. 56 no longer stands]. The luggage included a large black trunk, which she said was full of books and valuables that she was sending to Berlin. Her vigilant neighbour, who had seen that a the trunk had been so heavy that two strong men could barely lift it, remembered the missing 'customer' of two days earlier and called in the police. When the trunk was opened, it was found to contain the corpse of the 72-year-old former cabbie Charles Anthony Stephens, who had been beaten to death with repeated blows to the head from a blunt instrument.

When asked to explain herself by the police, Marie Hermann made a confused statement that her late-night 'customer' had become angry and truculent. They had struggled on the bed, and Stephens had struck her over the head with a poker. She had taken the poker away from him and dealt him a series of blows in return. Stephens had reeled over to sit in a basket-chair, but it had fallen over and he had measured his length on the floor, hitting his head hard against a fender. This story was not believed, however, the police thought that Marie had deliberately intoxicated her elderly visitor, before bashing his head in and stealing his money. At the coroner's inquest on Stephens, the jury returned a verdict of wilful murder against Marie Hermann.

When the trial began, things looked very bad for her. She was an ugly woman of dissipated habits and a shady reputation. There was no doubt she had beaten Charles Anthony Stephens to death, stolen and spent his money, and tried to conceal the body in the trunk. She was already prejudged in the newspapers, and a drawing in the *IPN* depicted this sinister-looking woman advancing on the helpless Stephens, clutching her lethal poker.

Fortunately for Marie Hermann, she had enough funds to employ the solicitor Arthur Newton, who briefed the brilliant young barrister Edward Marshall Hall to defend her. Marshall Hall realized that the only way to save his client from the gallows was to claim that she had acted in self-defence. She had some bruises on her neck suggesting that at some stage of the fight, Stephens had tried to throttle her. The problem for Marshall Hall was that Stephens's injuries were mostly located on the back of the head. Cleverly, he suggested that after Stephens had overpowered Marie, forced her down on the bed, and seized hold of her neck, the desperate woman had been able to grasp the poker and belabour her attacker's skull with it. Flummoxed by Marshall Hall's oratory, the medical experts had to admit that such a scenario could not be ruled out. Marshall Hall went on to effectively demolish the testimony of the son of Charles Anthony Stephens, whose circumstances in life he had researched: the son had to admit that not only had the drunken old cabbie doubled as the keeper of a brothel, he himself was active in the very same profession.

In his brilliant summing up, Marshall Hall pleaded with the jury to cast aside their prejudice against the unprepossessing Marie Hermann: 'These women are what men make them. Even this woman was once a beautiful and innocent child!' At this remark, the wretched prisoner understandably began to weep. Her theatrical defender pointed at her, exclaiming 'Look at her, gentlemen of the jury! *Look* at her! God never gave her a chance. Won't *you*?' There was applause in court at

Marshall Hall's histrionics. The jury was out for just fifteen minutes before finding Marie Hermann guilty of manslaughter, with a strong recommendation to mercy; in the end, she was sentenced to just six years of penal servitude.

Marie Hermann served her sentence and returned to obscurity; the 1901 Census has her living in London with her blind daughter. Edward Marshall Hall went on to become one of the finest barristers of his generation. Against the odds, the Great Defender, as he was called, saved many a notorious character from the gallows. Marshall Hall successfully defended Robert Wood, accused of the Camden Town murder of 1907, Ronald Light the supposed Green Bicycle murderer of 1919, and Madame Fahmy, who had shot her husband at the Savoy Hotel in London. Once, when his wife asked him how many murderers were walking the streets thanks to his efforts, Marshall Hall rather evasively replied that he was quite certain that all his clients had really been innocent. Madame Fahmy was almost certainly guilty, however, and the case against Ronald Light also looks very strong. Marshall Hall must have had his thoughts also about the case of Marie Hermann: she was a very lucky woman to escape the hangman's noose.

But what about the murder house? The southern terrace in Grafton Street already existed in 1777–8, and the northern terrace was constructed in 1790. An extension to the east, called Grafton Street East and reaching as far as Gower Street, was incorporated with Grafton Street in 1885, and the houses renumbered from east to west: numbers 2–82 in the northern terrace and 1–71 in the southern one. No. 51 was in the southern terrace, the third house to the west from the crossing with Whitfield Street.

By the time of the 194–6 Ordnance Survey, the eastern part of Grafton Street had seen the construction of stores at Nos. 2–46 in the northern terrace, and an extension to the University College Hospital, a bank and a cinema had taken over Nos. 1–31 in the southern terrace. Nos. 33–45, between Tottenham Court Road and Whitfield Street, remained intact, as did Nos. 47–51 just west of Whitfield Street. In the 1921 Ordnance Survey maps, a large modern building occupies the space of the old Nos. 49–66, however, and the murder house is gone. This modern building is likely to be the large block of flats that occupies the space today. The old No. 47 has also fallen to the Developer, although many original houses in the southern terrace survive between Tottenham Court Road and Whitfield Street, showing what the murder house must have looked like.

Grafton Street was renamed Grafton Way in 1937, but the numbering of the houses remained unchanged.

George R. Sims got most of his facts right in his brief account of the Grafton Street Murder, although the original newspaper accounts mention nothing about Marie Hermann ever being a police informant; nor does the file about her in the National Archives. And although she told a neighbour that the trunk was destined for Berlin, there is nothing to suggest that she actually planned to send it to the stationmaster there. Would it not have been rather expensive to send a trunk weighing nearly twenty stone abroad, and would the Teutonic railwaymen not have been able to 'sniff out' that it contained something quite unpleasant? The file in the National Archives shows that Marie Hermann was certainly a native of Austria; her husband, the farmer Joseph Schramm, corresponded with the Scotland Yard detectives, and planned to come to London to see her, not because he wanted her back as his wife, but because he wanted a divorce to be able to marry again. George R. Sims ended his account of the Grafton Street Murder with the words 'The tragedies pass and are forgotten. The houses of tragedy remain and are let to new tenants', but the old murder house at No. 51 no longer frowns upon the passer-by.

56. The Murderous James Canham Read, 1894

James Canham Read, 39, lived at 57 Jamaica Street, Stepney, with his wife Emma and their eight children. He worked as a cashier at the Royal Albert Docks. A handsome, personable man, he fancied himself as a gentleman of means, always on the prowl for young women to seduce. He had enjoyed a long affair with Mrs Bertha Ayriss, the fun-loving wife of a dairyman, and fathered two of her children, but then he met Bertha's attractive younger sister Florence Dennis. It did not take long for this experienced East London Lothario to seduce Florence as well. She knew his real name, but not that he was a married man, and she hoped to marry him one day. In order not to make Bertha jealous, he wrote to Florence under an assumed name, but Bertha found one of his letters and recognized the writing, although she was in no position to take moral high ground and make a scene, being an adulteress herself.

The mustachio-twirling womaniser James Canham Read continued enjoying the favours of Bertha Ayriss and Florence Dennis for some time, but then he met yet another obliging lady friend, the confectioner's

James Canham Read

James Canham Read from *Famous Crimes Past & Present*.

assistant Beatrice Kempton. He introduced himself to her as the commercial traveller Edgar Benson, and set her up at Rose Cottage, Mitcham, where he used to spend the weekends with her. He told

Florence Dennis, from *Famous Crimes Past & Present*.

his wife Emma that he had been diagnosed with some obscure heart condition that forced him to rest all weekend in a country retreat, in order to be able to cope with the strains of his job; being a gullible

THE SOUTHEND MYSTERY.

The discovery of the body of Florence Dennis, from the *IPN*, 7 July 1894.

woman who believed anything she was told, she found nothing wrong with this story. In addition to his eight legitimate children, he was probably the father of two little Ayrisses, and Beatrice gave birth to an infant son in January 1894. Her parents did not like the cad who had seduced their daughter and set her up as his mistress in a country cottage, but he managed to appease them by forging a marriage certificate.

James Canham Read had a younger brother named Harry, an idle wastrel who liked spending his time drinking and smoking. After Harry had lost his job, he became quite depressed and bought a small revolver, which James took away from him to prevent any rash actions on his part. In June 1894, there was trouble when Florence Dennis announced that she was pregnant, and James was the father of her child. She still entertained hopes he would marry her and make her an honest woman, but for obvious reasons, this was not possible. Moreover, the fickle James had begun to tire of both Bertha and Florence, preferring his latest conquest Beatrice Kempton.

The pregnant Florence Dennis lived with her sister Bertha Ayriss in the family home at 24 Wesley Road, Southend. She sent a telegram to James Canham Read, and received one in return, agreeing to meet her to make arrangements for the child. On Sunday 24 June 1894, Florence went out in the evening, and the Ayrisses presumed she was going to see James Canham Read. And indeed, two witnesses saw a young woman resembling Florence walking with a man near Prittlewell outside Southend. This was the last time she was ever seen alive. The next day,

The arrest of Read, Rose Cottage, and other sketches, from the *IPN*, 21 July 1894.

Inspector Baker.

Robert Dowthwaite (the man who identified Read).

Dr. Waters.

Read's Home, Jamaica Street, Stepney.

Read in the Exercise-Cage at Southend.

READ CHARGED WITH THE MURDER OF FLORENCE DENNIS:
SKETCHES IN AND OUT OF COURT AT SOUTHEND; AND PRISONER'S HOUSE IN LONDON.
See " How the World Wags."

Read's house in London, and other sketches, from the *Penny Illustrated Paper*, 4 August 1894.

the Ayrisses missed Florence, and Mr Ayriss sent James Canham Read a telegram asking 'Where is Florrie?' Read, who had hoped she would not be missed, indignantly replied that he had not seen Florence for 18 months. Realising that the search for Florence would soon be on, he stole nearly £160 from his employer and beat a hasty retreat to Rose Cottage in Mitcham. Here, he adopted the identity of 'Edgar Benson' and joined his long-term mistress Beatrice Kempton and their little son

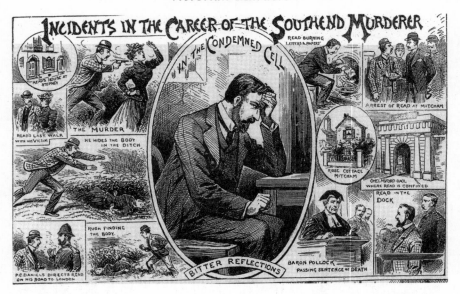

Incidents from the career of James Canham Read, from the *IPN*, 24 November 1894.

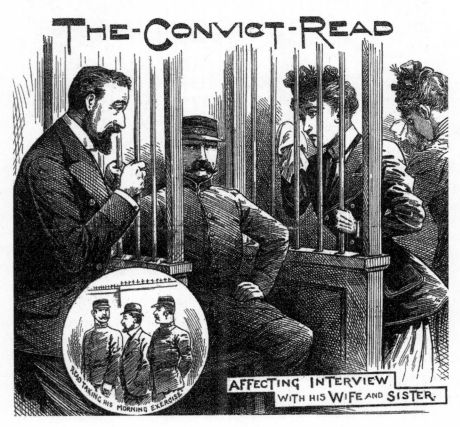

The convict Read, from the *IPN*, 8 December 1894.

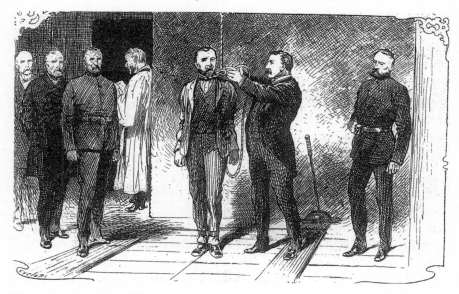

The execution of Read, from *Famous Crimes Past & Present*.

Bertie; he made efforts to disguise himself through growing a beard, and purchasing a new suit of clothes.

On the evening of 25 June, the body of Florence Dennis was found in a ditch near Prittlewell. She had been shot in the head with a revolver, and death had been instantaneous. Bertha Ayriss identified the body, and also told the police all about her sister's troubled relationship with James Canham Read. A number of witnesses had seen a man matching Read's description ask for directions to London. Had the careless murderer missed his train back to the Metropolis, and been forced to tramp all the way as a consequence? A copy of the police 'Wanted' poster, printed with a recent photograph and a good description of James Canham Read, is kept in the police file on the case. When the police came to call at the Read family home at 57 Jamaica Street, poor Emma Read was distraught. She had not seen her husband for several days, she explained. The police kept the house under surveillance, and they noted that after Harry Read the brother had come to visit, Mrs Read had looked a good deal more composed. Did Harry know the whereabouts of his brother the suspected murderer? Having obtained permission to monitor Harry's mail they found that he had written a letter to 'Mr Benson, Rose Cottage, Mitcham', and the detectives soon came to call at this address. The brazen James Canham Read, who had believed himself secure in his disguise, at first denied everything. When searched, he was found to carry a razor, a newspaper report of the murder, and £50 in cash. The pathetic Beatrice Kempton showed the detectives the forged marriage certificate, but they had begun to understand what kind of scoundrel they were dealing with, and were not impressed. Having understood that the man she had cohabited with, the father of her son, was a married man who had 'carried on' with two other women on the side, and a murder suspect as well, poor Beatrice was prostrate with grief, and unable to leave Rose Cottage for several days.

At the Southend police court, a number of witnesses gave some very damning testimony against James Canham Read. One of them had seen him with Florence the day of the murder, and three others picked him out as the man who had asked for directions to London. Bertha Ayriss, who had to confess that she herself had lived with Read as man and wife, told all about his relationship with Florence, and their planned meeting on Sunday 24 June. When Read's desk had been broken open, it was found to contain a dozen of blank forms purporting to be marriage certificates. At least one of these forms had been used by the serial philanderer to forge the marriage certificate between Edgar Benson and Beatrice Kempton, which was also produced in court. Harry Read confessed all about his part in the affair, acting the part of 'Edgar Benson's' friend 'Harry Edwards' to deceive the gullible Beatrice Kempton.

The trial of James Canham Read at the Chelmsford Assizes opened on 12 November, before Baron Pollock. The evidence against him appeared quite solid: he had a motive to want to get rid of Florence and access to the loaded revolver he had once taken away from Brother Harry. He had sent a telegramme agreeing to see Florence on the day of the murder. Although there was no eye-witness to the murder, he had been seen with Florence in Prittlewell before the lethal shot had been fired and also observed by several people making his escape back to London. The defence tried to argue that Read was not the father of Florence's child, and that Bertha Ayriss was lying; the day of the murder, Read had been with another of his mistresses. These arguments were not believed, and James Canham Read was found guilty of murder and sentenced to death. His wife Emma forgave him all his infidelities, and visited him in the condemned cell. No reprieve was forthcoming, and Read was hanged on 4 December 1894.

The people involved in the Canham Read case went on with their lives as well as they could. John and Bertha Ayriss remained married in spite of her infidelities, and they ran a small dairy together.

Mrs Emma Read remarried in 1899, and Beatrice Kempton married a much older man in 1903. The troubled Harry Read did not survive his brother for very long: in May 1895, his body was found in the Regent's Canal. The Read family home at 57 Jamaica Street is long gone, but the house where Florence Dennis lived with her parents at 44 Marine Parade, Sheerness, still stands, as does the Ayriss family home at 24 Wesley Road, Southend. Rose Cottage in Mitcham, which dates back to Georgian times, is today No. 13 Commonside East, and it still resembles the illustrations from back in 1894. It has a reputation for being haunted by a mysterious female figure referred to as 'Lady Jane' and also by a mischievous poltergeist-like entity that causes loud bangs and moves household objects about. Whether either of these suburban spooks have any relation to James Canham Read's residence in the house, however, is unknown. The deformed bullet that had killed Florence Dennis was passed on to the solicitor Mr T. Lamb, of Chancery Lane, who donated it to Scotland Yard's Black Museum in 1927.

Epilogue

This book makes use of a collection press cuttings and illustrations about Victorian murders, of which 56 were researched further to go into this book. Firstly, I wanted no overlap at all with my 2016 book *Rivals of the Ripper*, dealing with fourteen late Victorian unsolved murders of London women. Secondly, I excluded some obviously uninteresting cases, involving botched abortions, child murders by insane women, or wife murders by drunken husbands. Thirdly, I decided to omit a number of high-profile cases, which had already been 'done to death' by other authors, and where I had nothing new to add, like those of Mrs Maybrick, Thomas Neill Cream and Frederick Deeming. Fourthly, there had to be at least one good *IPN* illustration involving the murder case in question, for it to qualify.

Among the original 120 files, the nationality was seriously biased towards English cases, reflecting the xenophobia of the old *IPN*. Just four files dealt with French murder cases, and of these, Troppmann, Barré and Pranzini made it into the book; Madame Clovis Hugues, who gunned down a man named Morin in Paris, did not. Two files dealt with German cases: the prolific family-killer Timm Thode was researched further, a file on beheadings was not. The Swedish murderess Anna Månsdotter was also featured in this book, as the sole Scandinavian representative among the files. There were four Scottish cases, none of which made it into the book: the Arran murder committed by John Watson Laurie, of which much already has been written, a poorly illustrated account of Jessie King, the Stockbridge baby-farmer, and two obscure Caledonian family tragedies. The sole Welsh case was the Llangibby Massacre of 1878. There was not a single Irish murder among the 120 files. Most of the English murder cases are from urban locations and London murders were favoured before provincial ones, although homicides from other large English cities, and from the Home Counties, were also often included. The focus was on murders that were particularly brutal and cunning, especially if perpetrator remained unknown and if there were multiple victims. The *IPN* also favoured gory 'family tragedies'.

Having had, for a good many years, a strong interest in unsolved historical murders, I have taken care to include a number of murder mysteries in this book, as a provincial companion to the wholly London-centered *Rivals of the Ripper*.

The final question must be: did the *IPN* ever accomplish anything worthwhile during its long career in Victorian times. After all, it was a sensationalist, populist, xenophobic and racist newspaper, which offended those of righteous and sanctimonious opinions, with its 'thrilling' illustrations and indecent advertisements. I would argue that to crime historians, the *IPN* is a valuable resource indeed. Its reporting is often dependent on that in other London newspapers, with the occasional scoop thrown in. The great advantage of the *IPN* is the accurate illustrations, which gives faces to some little-known Victorian murderers, victims and suspects. Without the *IPN*, we would not have known what the murderers had once looked like.

The death of Queen Victoria in January 1901 put the *IPN* into deep mourning, and there were features on her long and glorious reign, and drawings of her funeral cortege. After an orgy of jingoistic flag-waving during the Second Boer War, the *IPN* returned to normal, featuring sensational recent crimes, boxers and racehorses, actresses and music hall performers, and a variety of low-quality serialised novels. In February 1914, the newspaper's golden jubilee was briefly and frugally celebrated: a replica of an 1864 cover was reproduced, and readers were invited to collect and submit a series of coupons, to take part in a raffle to win a clock. The outbreak of the Great War was greeted with another orgy of ultra-patriotism, but it soon became clear to the *IPN* editorial staff that this was going to be a lengthy war; with a large proportion of the potential readership in uniform abroad, the newspaper soon hit hard times. Filled with depressing and repetitive war news, its circulation steadily decreased. When the war finally ended, the newspaper was something of an archaic oddity in London's competitive publishing world: in the age of photography, it relied on its draughtsmen just as it had done in the 1860s; nor had its standards of journalism been significantly improved since that time. Still, the *IPN* managed to struggle on throughout the 1920s and early 1930s, and it continued to describe the celebrated murders of the day with gusto. The woeful day of 3 March 1938 saw the publication of the *ultimus* of the *IPN*, the title of which was henceforth permanently changed to *The Sporting Record*. Having degenerated into a newspaper for old men hanging around in bookmakers' shops, it nevertheless survived the Second World War, Clement Attlee, Harold Wilson, and various other calamities: as the *Greyhound and Sporting Record*, it finally perished in the first spring of the Thatcherite renaissance, the last issue ever being published on 2 August 1980. *Requiescat in Pace!*

Sources

Introduction
On the history of the *IPN*, see L. Stratmann, *Cruel Deeds and Dreadful Calamities* (London 2011) and J. Bondeson, *Strange Victoriana* (Stroud 2016), 5–15 and 324–34.

The Murder of Sweet Fanny Adams
IPN Aug 31, Sept 7 and 14, Dec 14 and 28 1867, April 4 1868; *Daily News* Aug 27 1867, *Wrexham Advertiser* Sept 7 1867, *Lloyd's Weekly Newspaper* Sept 8 1867, *Essex Standard* Dec 13 1867, *Famous Crimes Past & Present* 2(23) [1903], 234–6; Anon., *The Alton Murder* (London 1867), *Master Detective* Oct 2000, 16–9, P. Cansfield, *Sweet FA* (Alton 2004).

Mass Murder in Germany
IPN Feb 29 1868; *Hull Packet* Feb 21 1868, *Freeman's Journal* Feb 22 1868. German sources include W. Alexis, *Der Neue Pitaval*, chapter 6, and the scholarly article by M. Fischer (*Lied und populäre Kultur 52* [2007], 119–54).

The Winscombe Murder
IPN March 21 1868; *Standard* March 16 and 17, April 17 1868, *Bristol Mercury* March 21 and April 11 1868, *Lloyd's Weekly Newspaper* March 22 1868, *Glasgow Herald* March 26 1868.

The Murder of a Stationmaster
IPN May 9, Aug 1 and 15 1868; *Standard* May 2 and Aug 14 1868, *Daily News* May 4 and Aug 14 1868.

Murder in Artillery Passage
IPN May 15, June 6, Aug 1 and 29 and Sept 12 1868; *Morning Post* May 9, July 28 and Aug 21 1868, *Daily News* May 9 and 20, Aug 21 1868, *Lloyd's Weekly Newspaper* May 31 and Aug 2 1868, *Times* Aug 21 1868.The trial of Alexander Arthur Mackay is available on the OldBaileyOnline website, and the police file is in NA MEPO 3/85.

The Repentance of William Sheward
IPN Jan 16, Feb 6, April 3 and 24 1869; *Ipswich Journal* Jan 16 1869, *Famous Crimes Past & Present* 3(37) [1903], 252–5; J. Smith-Hughes, *Unfair Comment* (London 1951), 323–60, M. Morson, *Norwich Murders* (Barnsley 2006), 43–66, N.R. Storey, *Norfolk Murders* (Stroud 2009), 35–48.

The Pantin Tragedy
IPN Oct 9 and Dec 4 1869, Jan 8 and 22 1870; *Morning Post* Oct 1, Dec 27 and 30 1869; H.B. Irving, *Studies of French Criminals* (London 1901), 51–70, P. Drachline, *Le Crime de Pantin* (Paris 1984).

The Chelsea Double Murder
IPN May 21 and 28 1870; *Times* May 13, 14, 16, 17, 19 and 21, June 8, 9, 10, 14 and 15 1870, *Famous Crimes Past & Present* 9(114) [1905], 386–92, *Ashburton Guardian* Jan 15 1907; G. Logan, *Masters of Crime* (London 1928), 209–15 and *Dramas of the Dock* (London 1930), 41–68, J. Eddleston, *Foul Deeds in Kensington and Chelsea* (Barnsley 2010), 29–34, A.W. Moss (*Murder Most Foul 62*, 19–21). The trial of Walter Miller is available on the OldBaileyOnline web site, and the police file is in NA MEPO 3/97.

The Denham Massacre
IPN June 4 and 11 1870; *Famous Crimes Past & Present* 3(34) [1904], 177–9 and 10(121) [1905], 79–80; G.B.H. Logan, *Masters of Crime* (London 1928), 53–65, A. Lacey (*Police Journal 66* [1993], 379–82), J. Oates, *Foul Deeds and Suspicious Deaths around Uxbridge* (Barnsley 2008), 77–92 and *Buckinghamshire Murders* (Stroud 2012), 57–70. On the Parry massacre, see J. Bondeson, *Murder Houses of Greater London* (Leicester 2015), 283–7. There is a Metropolitan Police file on the Denham Murders at the National Archives (NA MEPO 3/98), which is quite short because when the detective (Inspector Palmer) arrived, the miscreant was already in custody thanks to the excellent work of the local police.

A Very Strange West Bromwich Murder

IPN July 8 1871; *Birmingham Daily Post* July 1 and 26 1871, *Reynolds's Newspaper* July 30 1871; Aristotle Tump, *Tales of Terror*, Vol. 2 (Stourbridge 1985), 44–9.

The Crime of Christiana Edmunds

IPN Sept 9 and 16 1871, Jan 20 1872; *Penny Illustrated Paper* Jan 20 1872, *Famous Crimes Past & Present* 6(70) [1904], 117–20, *Daily Mail* Sept 27 and 28 1907; T.R. Forbes (*Medical History* 32 [1988], 23–33), J.N. Ainsley (*Canadian Journal of History* 35 [2000], 37–55), S. Jackson, *Death by Chocolate* (London 2012), M. Stevens, *Broadmoor Revealed* (Barnsley 2013), 93–107, K. Jones, *The Case of the Chocolate Cream Killer* (Barnsley 2016).

A Victorian Scholar and Murderer

IPN Oct 21 and 28 1871; *Journal of Mental Science* 18 [1872], 61–115, H. Wyndham, *Famous Trials Re-told* (London 1925), 241–55, R.S. Lambert, *When Justice Faltered* (London 1935), 1–47. There is a file on the case in NA HO 144/2/7940.

The Park Lane Murder

IPN April 20 and 27, May 4 and 11, June 22 1872, Aug 16 1890, Feb 11 1893; *Penny Illustrated Paper* May 20 1872; J. Smith-Hughes, *Unfair Comment* (London 1951), 248–86, *Murder Most Foul* 33, 56–8; the police file on the case is in NA HO 144/3/11984.

The Whitechapel Road Murder

IPN July 26 1890; *Penny Illustrated Paper* Sept 25 1874; H.B. Irving (Ed.), *Trial of the Wainwrights* (Notable British Trials, London 1920), R.D. Altick, *Victorian Studies in Scarlet* (New York 1970), 210–9, B. Marriner (*Murder Most Foul* 49, 50–5), J. Bondeson (*Ripperologist* 136 [2014], 28–33), M. & C. Drinkall, *The Other Whitechapel Murder* (London 2014); the police file on the case is in NA MEPO 3/121.

A Blackburn Sweeney Todd

IPN April 15 and May 6 1876; *Blackburn Standard* April 1 and 8 1876, *Daily News* April 8 1876, *Lloyd's Weekly Newspaper* April 9 1876, *Reynolds's Newspaper* April 16, 23 and 30, July 30 and Aug 20 1876, *Examiner* April 22 1876, *Westport Times* June 23 1876, *Famous Crimes Past & Present* 1(9) [1903], 200–3, *This is Lancashire* March

24 and Dec 27 2001; A. Sewart, *Murder in Lancashire* (London 1988), 135–46, K. Johnson, *Chilling True Tales of Old Preston* (Wigan 1990), 6–10. The website of the National Library of Scotland reproduces a ballad on the murder, with a discussion. On the dog Morgan and his subsequent career, see *Liverpool Mercury* April 18 1876, *Dundee Courier* April 20 1876, *Northern Echo* April 21 1876, *Timaru Herald* July 4 1876, *New York Times* Aug 6 1876, *Aberdeen Weekly Journal* Dec 10 1881 and *North-Eastern Daily Gazette* July 8 1884; also R. & M. Whittington-Egan, *The Bedside Book of Murder* (Newton Abbot 1988), 144–6.

The Great Bravo Mystery
IPN, July 22 1876 and Sept 28 1878; *Penny Illustrated Paper*, August 5 1876. Books on the case include, in chronological order, F.J.P. Veale, *Verdict in Dispute: The Bravo Case* (London 1950), Y. Bridges, *How Charles Bravo Died* (London 1956) [Improved second edition in 1972], J. Williams, *Suddenly at the Priory* (London 1957), E. Jenkins, *Dr Gully* (London 1972), B. Taylor & K. Clarke, *Murder at the Priory* (London 1988) and J. Ruddick, *Death at the Priory* (London 2001); see also *Journal of Psychological Medicine* NS 2 [1876], 341–56, W. Roughead, *Malice Domestic* (Edinburgh 1928), 3–39, W.E. Swinton (*Canadian Medical Association Journal* 123 [1980], 1262–4), R. Whittington-Egan, *Speaking Volumes* (Malvern 2004), 10–13, J. Clark, *Haunted Wandsworth* (Stroud 2009), 9–20. The Bravo police file in NA MEPO 3/123 is not very capacious.

The Pimlico Murder
IPN Dec 30 1876; *Daily News* Dec 16, 18 and 19 1876, Jan 16 and Feb 8 and 9 1877, *Lloyd's Weekly Newspaper* Dec 17 and 24 1876, *Times* Dec 18 and 20 1876, Feb 9 1877, *Morning Post* Dec 30 1876 and Feb 26 1877, *Penny Illustrated Paper* Dec 30 1876; *British Medical Journal* i [1877], 215, 226–8, 243–4, *Lancet* i [1877], 293–5; J.P. Eigen, *Unconscious Crime* (Baltimore 2003), 146–50.

The Macclesfield Murder
IPN April 14 and August 4 1877; *Liverpool Mercury* March 27 1877, *Manchester Times* March 31 1877, *Cheshire Observer* April 14 1877, *York Herald* Aug 13 1877, *Famous Crimes Past & Present* 6(68) [1904], 70–2.

The Wymondham Double Murder
IPN Nov 3 1877; *Middlesborough Daily Gazette* Oct 22 1877, *Bury and Norwich Post* Oct 23 and Nov 13 1877, *Reynolds's Newspaper* Oct 28 1877; M. Morson, *Norwich Murders* (Barnsley 2006), 67–78.

The Halesowen Triple Murder
IPN March 2 1878; *Liverpool Mercury* Feb 14 1878, *Leicester Chronicle* Feb 16 1878, *York Herald* March 18 1878; the only modern accounts of the tragedy are N. Sly, *A Grim Almanac of the Black Country* (Stroud 2013), 26–7 and an article on the BlackCountryMuse homepage.

Horrible Tragedy in Paris
IPN Aug 17 1878; *Morning Post* April 25 1878, *Lloyd's Weekly Newspaper* April 28 1878, *York Herald* July 31 1878, *Reynolds's Newspaper* Aug 4 1878, *Standard* Sept 9 1878 *Timaru Herald* Oct 19 1878; H.B. Irving, *Studies of French Criminals* (London 1901), 73–102; homepage guillotine.cultureforum.net.

The Llangibby Massacre
IPN July 27, Aug 3 and 10, Nov 9 1878; *Western Mail* July 18 and 23 1878, June 24 1879, *Bristol Mercury* July 19, 20, 22, 23 and 27, Oct 31, Nov 18 and 19 1878, *County Observer and Monmouthshire Central Advertiser* July 20 and 27, Aug 3 and 12, Nov 2 and 23 1878, *Monmouthshire Merlin* July 26, Aug 2, Nov 1 and 22 1878, *Famous Crimes Past & Present* 8(101) (1905), 157–9, *South Wales Argus* Aug 11 1977 and June 8 1988, *Western Mail* June 18 2005 and *Pontypool Free Press* July 14 2005; P. Fuller & B. Knapp, *Welsh Murders* (Llandybie 1986), Vol. 1, 68–75, R. Williams, *Their Deadly Trade* (Llandusyl 2004), 3–15, G. Brangham, *Hangings and Hangmen in Usk Prison* (Abertillery 2008), 31–70, and the articles by S. James (*Gwent FHS Journal* 65 [2004], 10–11) and P. Stephenson (*Master Detective* October 2005, 32–6).

The Bradford Murder
IPN Oct 5 and 12 1878; *Leeds Mercury* Oct 2 and 22, Nov 19 1878, Sept 28 1889, *Manchester Times* Oct 5 1878, *Penny Illustrated Paper* Oct 5 1878, *Leicester Chronicle* Feb 8 1879.

The Woodnesborough Murder

IPN Dec 14 and 21 1878; *Pall Mall Gazette* Dec 6, 7 and 24 1878, *Lloyd's Weekly Newspaper* Dec 29 1878 and Jan 19 1879, *Reynolds's Newspaper* Feb 9 1879.

A Richmond Horror Story

IPN May 3 and 17, July 12, Aug 2 and 9 1879; Penny Illustrated Paper July 5 1879; E. O'Donnell, *Trial of Kate Webster* (Notable British Trials, London 1925), C. Kingston, *A Gallery of Rogues* (London 1924), 186–200, R. & M. Whittington-Egan, *The Bedside Book of Murder* (Newton Abbot 1988), 27–38, J. Oates, *Foul Deeds and Suspicious Deaths in Richmond and Kingston* (Barnsley 2010), 53–67, L. Stratmann, *Greater London Murders* (Stroud 2010), 221–30, L. Grex (*Master Detective* April 2011, 14–20); the police file on the case is in NA HO 144/36/82518A.

The Strange Case of Jonathan Geydon

IPN Sept 27 and Nov 1 1879; *Morning Post* June 30 1857, *Essex Standard* Sept 13 and Nov 1 1879;; *New York Times* Nov 7 1879, *Famous Crimes Past & Present* 5(57) [1904], 102–4; C. Kingston, *Dramatic Days at the Old Bailey* (London n.d.), 240–1.

The Widnes Murder

IPN Nov 1 and 8 1879; *Liverpool Mercury* Oct 25, 27, 28, Nov 14 and 21, Dec 5 and 6 1879, Feb 13 and 14 1880, *Lancaster Gazette* Feb 18 1880, *Birmingham Daily Post* March 3 1880, *Lloyd's Weekly Newspaper* March 7 1880.

The Murder of Sarah Jane Roberts

IPN Jan 17 and 24 and Feb 7 and 21 1880; *NZ Truth* Feb 29 1908, *Auckland Star* July 18 1931; G.B.H. Logan, *Dramas of the Dock* (London 1930), 137–153, M. Baggoley, *Murder and Crime in Lancashire* (Stroud 2007), 19–34. On the 'tell-tale eye' delusion and eyeball photography to find the face of the murderer, see J. Bondeson (*Fortean Times* 339 [2016], 36–41).

The Acton Atrocity

IPN Oct 30, Nov 6 and 13, Dec 4 1880; *Pall Mall Gazette* Oct 23 1880, *Standard* Oct 26 and Nov 2 1880, *Lloyd's Weekly Newspaper* Oct 31 and Nov 7 1880, *Reynolds's Newspaper* Oct 31, Nov 28, Dec 5 and 19 1880; J. Oates, *Foul Deeds and Suspicious Deaths in Ealing*, (Barnsley

2007), 77–82; the trial of Pavey is on OldBaileyOnline and the police file is in NA CRIM 1/11/1.

The Chislehurst Double Murder

IPN Nov 6, 13 and 20 1880, Jan 29 1881; *Times* Nov 1, 2 and 3 1880, *Lloyd's Weekly Newspaper* Nov 7 1880; *North West Kent Family History Society Journal* 8(6) [1998–2000], 228–231.

The Murder of Mrs Reville

IPN April 23 and May 7 1881; *Pall Mall Gazette* April 12 1881, *Daily News* April 13, 14, 20, 29 and 30 1881, *Lloyd's Weekly Newspaper* April 17 and 24, May 1 1881; G.B.H. Logan, *Guilty or Not Guilty* (London 1929), 164–80, J. Smith-Hughes, *Nine Verdicts on Violence* (London 1956), 1–22, J. van der Kiste, *Berkshire Murders* (Stroud 2010), 65–71, J. Oates, *Buckinghamshire Murders* (Stroud 2012), 78–88

The Case of Dr Lamson

IPN Dec 17, Dec 24 and Dec 31 1881, March 11 and 18, May 6 1882; *Penny Illustrated Paper* Jan 14, March 11 and 25 1882, *Graphic* March 18 1882, *Aberdeen Weekly Journal* March 25 and May 6 1882, *Standard* March 29 1882, *Famous Crimes Past & Present* 4(49) [1904], 218–222, *New York Daily Tribune* June 1 1907, *Wanganui Chronicle* Aug 21 1919, *Bournemouth Echo* Aug 31 2010; M. Williams, *Leaves of a Life* (London 1890), 294–300, R. Harris (Ed.), *The Reminiscences of Sir Henry Hawkins* (London 1904), Vol. 2, 154–8, H.L. Adam, *The Trial of George Henry Lamson* (Notable British Trials, London 1912), W. Wood, *Survivors' Tales of Famous Crimes* (London 1916), 246–61, H. Eaton, *Famous Poison Trials* (London 1923), 13–53, E. Bowen-Rowlands, *Seventy-two Years at the Bar* (London 1924), 186–9, C. Kingston, *A Gallery of Rogues* (London 1924), 67–9, L.A. Perry, *Some Famous Medical Trials* (New York 1928), 88–103, G. St Aubyn, *Infamous Victorians* (London 1971), 155–236; the police files are in NA CRIM 1/13/3 and HO 144/90/A11385.

The Ramsgate Tragedy

IPN April 22, May 6 and Oct 28 1882; *Lloyd's Weekly Newspaper* April 9 and 16 1882, *Daily News* April 11 and July 24 1882, *Reynolds's Newspaper* April 23 and Oct 22 1882, *Essex Standard* July 21 1883.

The Fulham Tragedy

IPN June 10 and 24, July 1 1882; *Hampshire Telegraph* Aug 22 1866, *Penny Illustrated Paper* June 3 1882, *Lloyd's Weekly Newspaper* Aug 6 1882, *Reynolds's Newspaper* Aug 6 1882, *Bristol Mercury* May 28 1883; L. Stratmann, *Greater London Murders* (Stroud 2010), 111–8; the police file on the case is in NA CRIM 1/14/2.

The Plumstead Poisoner

IPN Oct 28 and Dec 30 1882; *Standard* Oct 28 1882 and Jan 3 1883, *Daily News* Nov 4 and Dec 16 1882, *Lloyd's Weekly Newspaper* Nov 12 and 26 1882, *Berrow's Worcester Journal* Dec 23 1882, *Newcastle Courant* Jan 5 1883, *York Herald* Jan 6 1883; J. Smith-Hughes, *Eight Studies in Justice* (London 1953), 200–28; the police file on the case is in NA CRIM 1/19/7.

The Walthamstow Tragedy

IPN Aug 18 and 25, Sept 22 1883; *Standard* Aug 9, 10, 11, 14, Sept 7, 13, 15 and 28, Oct 11 1883, *Leeds Mercury* Aug 10 1883, *Reynolds's Newspaper* Aug 12 and 19 1883, *Morning Post* Aug 14 1883, *Lloyd's Weekly Newspaper* Aug 19 and Sept 16 1883, *Dundee Courier* Sept 21 and 22 1883, *Chelmsford Chronicle* Jan 25 1935; *Lancet* ii [1883], 520; the trial of William Gouldstone is on OldBaileyOnline and the police file is in NA CRIM 1/19/2.

The Stoke Newington Murder

IPN Jan 12 and 19; *Times* Jan 3, 4, 5, 7 and 8 1884, *Manchester Times* Jan 5 1884, *Pall Mall Gazette* Jan 7 and 8 1884, *Leeds Mercury* Jan 11 and 26 1884, *Penny Illustrated Paper* Jan 12 1884, *Aberdeen Weekly Journal* Jan 16 1884, *Star* March 7 1884, *Standard* Jan 2 and 4 1886, *Hampshire Advertiser* Jan 9 1886, *Lloyd's Weekly Newspaper* Jan 9 1887.

The Man they could not Hang

IPN Nov 22 and 29. Dec 6 and 13 1884, Feb 28 1885; *Penny Illustrated Paper* Nov 22 and 29 1884, *Lloyd's Weekly Newspaper* Nov 23 1884, *Lloyd's Weekly News* Jan 5, 12, 19 and 26 1908; Anon, *Full and Authentic Account of the Babbicombe Tragedy* (Daisy Bank Publications, Manchester n.d.), J. Lee, *The Man they Could Not Hang* (London 1908), F. Keyse, *The Babbacombe Murder* (Babbacombe

1988), M. Holgate, *The Secret of the Babbacombe Murder* (Newton Abbot 2001), M. Holgate & I.D. Waugh, *The Man they Could Not Hang* (Stroud 2005).

The Camden Town Shooting Case
IPN March 28 1885; *Daily News* March 7 1885, *Lloyd's Weekly Newspaper* March 8 and 15 1885, *Standard* March 12 1885; the trial of Rose is on OldBaileyOnline.

Murder in Brecknock Road
IPN June 19 1886; *Times* June 11, 12 and 16, July 1 1886, *Morning Post* June 11 1886, *Standard* June 19 and Aug 5 1886; the police file on the case is in NA CRIM 1/24/2.

The Penzance Triple Murder
IPN Aug 14 1886; *Morning Post* July 29 1886, *Royal Cornwall Gazette* July 30 1886, *Lloyd's Weekly Newspaper* Aug 1 1886; there are internet accounts of the tragedy on the CornishStory and RootsWeb homepages.

The Hoxton Murder
IPN Feb 12 and 26, March 5 and April 2 1887; *Morning Post* Feb 7, 9, 12, 15, 16, 18 and 24, April 14 1887, *Standard* Feb 7, 8, 11, 14 and 17 1887, *Daily News* Feb 8, 9, 12 and 16, March 31, April 1, 2 and 4 1887, *Lloyd's Weekly Newspaper* Feb 13 and 20, March 6, April 3 1887, *Penny Illustrated Paper* Feb 19 and April 23 1887, *Hampshire Telegraph* April 23 1887; the trial of Thomas William Currell is on OldBaileyOnline and the police file on the case is in NA CRIM 1/25/8.

Triple Murder in the Rue de Montaigne
IPN April 23 1887; *Standard* March 23, 24, 25, 26, 28 and 29, April 1, 2, 4, 15, and 22, July 11, 12, 13 and 14, August 22, 26 and 27 1887, *Pall Mall Gazette* March 29 1887, *Penny Illustrated Paper* July 16 1887; H.B. Irving, *Studies of French Criminals* (London 1901), 151–78, G.B.H. Logan, *Rope, Knife and Chair* (London 1930), 11–26 and *Wilful Murder* (London 1935), 211–24, A. Pascal, *Pranzini* (London 1935), P. Lorenz, *L'Affaire Pranzini* (Paris 1971), F. Chauvaud (*Annales de Bretagne et des Pays de l'Ouest* 116(1) [2009], 13–28).

The Bradford Ripper

IPN Jan 5, 12 and 19 1889; *Pall Mall Gazette* Jan 1 1889, *Echo* Jan 2 1889, *Penny Illustrated Paper* Jan 5 and Feb 9 1889, *Lloyd's Weekly Newspaper* Jan 6 and 27 and Feb 3 and 10 1889, *Daily News* Jan 10 and 16 1889, *Sheffield and Rotherham Independent* March 11, 12 and 13 1889.

A Swedish Murderess Beheaded

IPN Aug 23 1890; *Reynolds's Newspaper* Aug 17 1890, 'Brotten som skakade Sverige No. 7' in *Aftonbladet* Dec 25 2008; Y. Lyttkens, *Yngsjömordet* (Stockholm 1951).

The Plumstead Tragedy

IPN Sept 20 and 27, Oct 4 and Nov 1 1890; the trial of Walter James Lyons is on OldBaileyOnline and the police file is in NA CRIM 1/34/3.

The Murderous Mrs Pearcey

IPN Nov 8, 22 and 29, Dec 13, 20 and 27 1890; *Lloyd's Weekly Newspaper* Oct 26 1890, *Star* Dec 13 1890, *Evening Post* Feb 2 1891, *Famous Crimes Past & Present* 1(8) [1903], 180–5; G.B.H. Logan, *Rope, Knife and Chair* (London 1930), 170–88, J. Laurence, *Extraordinary Crimes* (London 1931), 207–20, R. & M. Whittington-Egan, *The Bedside Book of Murder* (London 1988), 39–54, M. Aston, *Foul Deeds and Suspicious Deaths in Hampstead, Holborn and St Pancras*, (Barnsley 2005), 98–106. The trial of Mrs Pearcey is on OldBaileyOnline.

The Murderous 'Gentleman Jim'

IPN July 9 and 16 1892; *Penny Illustrated Paper* July 9 and 16 1892, *Reynolds's Newspaper* July 10 1892; M. Baggoley, *Surrey Executions* (Stroud 2011), 120–2; the trial of James Banbury is on OldBaileyOnline, see also NA COPY 1/409/217.

The Northampton Tragedy

IPN Sept 17 and 24, Dec 31 1892, Jan 14 1893; *Daily News* Sept 10, Nov 18, Dec 23 and 26 1892, *Standard* Sept 12 and Nov 19 1892, *Lloyd's Weekly Newspaper* Oct 23 1892, Jan 8 and 15 1893; G.B.H. Logan, *Dramas of the Dock* (London 1930), 95–115, A. Bruce, *Billington, Victorian Executioner* (Stroud 2009), 65–76.

Murder by a Croydon Publican

IPN Jan 14 and 21 1893; *Times* Jan 4 1893, *Reynolds's Newspaper* Jan 8 1893, *North-Eastern Daily Gazette* March 4 1893, *Leicester Chronicle* Jan 19 1895; C. Maxton, *Foul Deeds and Suspicious Deaths in Croydon* (Barnsley 2006), 145–9.

The Ramsgate Mystery

IPN May 20 and 27, June 10 and 17, July 1, 8 and 22 1893; *Standard* May 15, 26, 27, 30 and 31, June 1, 2, 3, 15, 16, 17, 19, 21, 22, 23, 24, 27, 29 and 30, July 3, 5, 6, 11 and 12 1893, *Dover Express* May 19, June 23 and 30 1893, *Lloyd's Weekly Newspaper* May 21 and 28, June 4, 11 and 18, July 2 and 16 1893, *Morning Post* May 26 and 27, June 2, 3 and 5, July 3, 5, 6 and 15 1893, *Penny Illustrated Paper* June 10 1893, *Illustrated Police Budget* June 17 1893, *Huddersfield Chronicle* July 29 1893, *Maidstone & Kentish Journal* March 22 1894, *Isle of Thanet Gazette* May 10 2013; also J. Bondeson (*Ripperologist* 147 [2015], 45–59).

The Curse on Amhurst Road

On Thomas Morgan, see *Standard* May 24 1893, *IPN* June 3 1893 and *Lloyd's Weekly Newspaper* June 4 1893. On Emily Newber, see NA CRIM 1/40/3 and OldBaileyOnline, also *Standard* Dec 18 and 25 1893, and Feb 9 1894, *Morning Post* Dec 18 and 22 1893, *Lloyd's Weekly Newspaper* Dec 24 1893 and *Penny Illustrated Paper* Feb 17 1894. On both cases, see also J. Bondeson (*Ripperologist* 143 [2015], 41–5).

The Bath Mystery

IPN Oct 7, 14, 21 and 28 1893; *Western Mail* Sept 30 1893, *Standard* Sept 30 1893, *Bristol Mercury* Oct 6, 7 and 26, Nov 25, Dec 7 1893, *Penny Illustrated Paper* Oct 7 1893, *Lloyd's Weekly Newspaper* Oct 8 1893, *Reynolds's Newspaper* Oct 8 1893, *Bath Weekly Chronicle and Herald* Oct 13 1945; K. Elliott, *Foul Deeds and Suspicious Deaths in Bath* (Barnsley 2007), 126–38.

The Maidenhead Mystery

IPN Oct 7, 14 and 21, Nov 4 and 11 1893, May 5 1894; *Penny Illustrated Paper* Sept 30 1893, *Pall Mall Gazette* Oct 2 1893, *Blackburn Weekly Standard* Oct 7 1893, *Huddersfield Daily Chronicle* Oct 11 1893, *Tidningen Kalmar* Oct 13 and 16 1893, *New Zealand Herald*

Nov 11 1893, *Star* Sept 16 1897, *Standard* Jan 27 1899, *North-Eastern Daily Gazette* Jan 27 1899, *Nieuws van de Dag* Oct 25 1902.

The Grafton Street Murder

IPN March 31, April 14 and May 12 1894; *Penny Illustrated Paper* March 24 and 31, and June 9 1894; G.R. Sims, *Mysteries of Modern London* (London 1906), 64–71, E. Marjoribanks, *The Life of Sir Edward Marshall Hall* (London 1930), 87–97; *True Detective* 1985(8), 8–12 and J. Bondeson (*Ripperologist* 139 [2014], 28–32); the police file on the case is in NA HO 144/259/A55866.

The Murderous James Canham Read

IPN July 7, 14 and 21, Sept 1 and 15, Dec 8 1894; *Penny Illustrated Paper* July 7 and 14, and Aug 8 1894, *Famous Crimes Past & Present* 9(111) [1905], 312–9; C. Kingston, *Enemies of Society* (London 1927), 220–31, G.B.H. Logan, *Great Murder Mysteries* (London 1931), 99–115, L. Stratmann, *More Essex Murders* (Stroud 2011), 60–74; the police file on the case is in NA MEPO 3/153.

Index